A BRIDGE OVER TROUBLED WATER

The EFPP Book Series

Editor-in-Chief: Anne-Marie Schloesser

OTHER TITLES IN THE SERIES

Under Chief Editor: John Tsiantis

- *Countertransference in Psychoanalytic Psychotherapy with Children and Adolescents*
- *Supervision and its Vicissitudes*
- *Psychoanalytic Psychotherapy in Institutional Settings*
- *Psychoanalytic Psychotherapy of the Severely Disturbed Adolescent*
- *Work with Parents: Psychoanalytic Psychotherapy with Children and Adolescents*
- *Psychoanalysis and Psychotherapy: The Controversies and the Future*
- *Research on Psychoanalytic Psychotherapy with Adults*

Under Series Editors: Monica Lanyado and Didier Houzel

- *The Therapist at Work: Personal Factors Affecting the Analytic Process*
- *Invisible Boundaries: Psychosis and Autism in Children and Adolescents*
- *The Development of Consciousness: An Integrative Model of Child Development, Neuroscience, and Psychoanalysis*
- *The Analytic Field: A Clinical Concept*
- *Play and Power*
- *Crossing Borders—Integrating Differences: Psychoanalytic Psychotherapy in Transition*
- *Assessing Change in Psychoanalytic Psychotherapy of Children and Adolescents: Today's Challenge*

Under Editor-in-Chief: Anne-Marie Schloesser

- *Bearing Witness: Psychoanalytic Work with People Traumatised by Torture and State Violence*
- *Psychoanalytic Psychotherapy: A Handbook*
- *Families in Transformation: A Psychoanalytic Approach*
- *Siblings: Envy and Rivalry, Coexistence and Concern*

A BRIDGE OVER TROUBLED WATER

Conflicts and Reconciliation in Groups and Society

edited by

Gila Ofer

Routledge
Taylor & Francis Group
LONDON AND NEW YORK

First published 2017 by Karnac Books Ltd.

Published 2018 by Routledge
2 Park Square, Milton Park, Abingdon, Oxon OX14 4RN
711 Third Avenue, New York, NY 10017, USA

Routledge is an imprint of the Taylor & Francis Group, an informa business

British Library Cataloguing in Publication Data

A C.I.P. for this book is available from the British Library

ISBN 9781782205777 (pbk)

Edited, designed and produced by The Studio Publishing Services Ltd
www.publishingservicesuk.co.uk
email: studio@publishingservicesuk.co.uk

CONTENTS

PART II
PROCESSES OF BUILDING AN INTERPERSONAL BRIDGE IN THE GROUP

PART III
THE SOCIAL AND THE GROUP

PART IV
PROCESSES OF RECONCILIATION IN INTER-GROUPS

ACKNOWLEDGMENTS

Thanks are due to the European Federation of Psychoanalytic Psychotherapy (EFPP), an organization that aims to bridge approaches of psychoanalytic psychotherapy in numerous countries, for sponsoring this book, and to the delegates of the group analytic section of the EFPP, whose encouragement and assistance helped to initiate it. I also want to thank Athena Chatjoulis. Under her overall charge, the 2011 conference was held, where some of the papers of this book were presented. Special thanks go to Anne-Marie Schloesser, president of the EFPP and the editor-in-chief of this book series, whose involvement in all stages of this book, and her support, contributed significantly to it. Peter von Tresckow generously provided us with the cover illustration for which we are most grateful. We also thank Rod Tweedy from Karnac. Without his knowledgeable support and patience, this book would not have come out. Last, but not least, to an anonymous donor who financed some of the expenses of the book.

Poems in Chapters Two and Three by Yehuda Amichai, "From the place where we are right", and "The diameter of the bomb was thirty centimeters" are reproduced by kind permission of Chana Amichai.

Chapter Seven features two lyrics.

"I Am A Rock".
Words and music by Paul Simon.

"Bridge Over Troubled Water"
Words and music by Paul Simon.

ABOUT THE EDITOR AND CONTRIBUTORS

Editor

Gila Ofer, PhD, is a training psychoanalyst and group analyst who studied English and French literature at the Hebrew University and then clinical psychology at Tel-Aviv University. She is a founding member and past President of the Tel-Aviv Institute of Contemporary Psychoanalysis, a founding member of the Israeli Institute of Group Analysis. She teaches and supervises in both institutes and in the Program of Psychoanalytic Psychotherapy, Tel-Aviv University. She was on the board of the EFPP for eight years and is currently the coordinator of Eastern European countries EFPP. She is also the editor-in-chief of the *EFPP Psychoanalytic Psychotherapy Review*, and she teaches, lectures, gives workshops, and takes analytic groups in Israel, Europe, and the USA. Among other topics, she writes about theoretical and clinical issues relating to dreams, gender and sexualities, psychoanalysis and literature, and films.

Contributors

Smadar Ben-Asher, PhD, is a specialist psychologist, head of the Kaye Academic College of Education educational counselors program, adjunct lecturer at the Ben-Gurion University of the Negev training programs, and faculty member of the Mandel Leadership Institute in the Negev. She also gives a variety of courses on therapy interview skills, stress situations, and various subjects in the sphere of educational psychology intervention. Her academic specialization is in research of the social representations discourse of groups in Israeli society.

Michael B. Buchholz, PhD, is a training analyst in the German Psychoanalytic Society (DPG), professor of social psychology, and head of the dissertation program at International Psychoanalytic University (IPU), Berlin. Interest in psychotherapy process studies using the method of conversation analysis including prosodic analyses. His most recent publication (in 2014) is "Patterns of empathy as embodied practice in clinical conversation—a musical dimension" (*Frontiers in Psychology*, 5).

Mário David, MD, is Consultant Psychiatrist at Mental Health Community Center (CINTRA) at Centro Hospitalar Psiquiátrico de Lisboa (CHP Lisboa, Portugal). He is also in private practice as an individual psychoanalytic psychotherapist, group analyst, and supervisor. He is a full member of the Sociedade Portuguesa de Grupanálise e Psicoterapia Analítica de Grupo (SPG-PAG), Group Analytic Society International (GASI), and International Society of Neuro-Psychoanalysis (N-PSA) (founding member), and a delegate of the EFPP Group Section.

Robi Friedman, PhD, is a clinical psychologist and group analyst in private practice in Haifa, Israel. He is President of the Group Analytic Society (International), past chair of the Israel Institute for Group Analysis, and Vice President of the International Dialogue Initiative (IDI), which applies psychodynamic concepts on conflict resolution. He conducts experiential dream seminars and writes on the soldiers' matrix and relational disorders.

Uri Levin, MA, is a clinical psychologist, group analyst, and organizational consultant. He is a member of the Israeli Institute of Group

Analysis (IIGA), member of the Group Analytic Society International (GASI), and a board member of the EFPP (European Federation for Psychoanalytic Psychotherapy). He has a private practice in Tel Aviv, and teaches at the Tel Aviv University. His interests include combined therapy, integrating group analysis with psychoanalysis, and the implementation of group analysis in the organizational field.

Isaura Manso Neto, MD, is a senior psychiatrist, training and supervisor member of the Portuguese Society of Group Analysis and Psychoanalytic Group Psychotherapy (Sociedade Portuguesa de Grupanálise e Psicoterapia Analítica de grupo—SPGPAG). She worked in the public sector with severe psychiatric patients and their families for more than thirty-five years and is now in private practice of psychoanalytic psychotherapies—individual and groups. She is a supervisor of individual, group, and teams in the public and the private sectors, a member of GASI management committee from 2006 to 2014, and a delegate to EFPP group section SPGPAG.

Wisam Maree, MA, is a clinical and educational psychologist, Soroka medical center in Beer-Sheva and a PhD candidate at Ben Gurion University, Beer-Sheva, Israel.

Marina Mojović, MD, MSc, is a psychiatrist, individual psychoanalytic psychotherapist, group analyst, and organizational consultant. She is a training group analyst in the Group-Analytic Society-Belgrade, founder of its Psychosocial Section, and of the Serbian-Reflective-Citizens Project with Training, a full member of the International Association for Group Psychotherapy and Group Processes, of the International Society for Psychoanalytic Studies of Organizations, of the Organization for Promoting Understanding of Society (London), and Convener of OPUS Listening Posts. She is also a member of the management committee of the Group Analytic Society-International. Her special interests include large and median groups, social unconscious, social trauma and identity, social–psychic retreats, and social dreaming.

Klimis Navridis, PhD, is Professor of Psychology of Communication in the Psychology Faculty at the University of Athens and a psychoanalyst and group psychotherapist. He is a member of the Hellenic Society of Psychoanalytic Psychotherapy, of the French Association of

Psychoanalytic Group Psychotherapy (SFPPG), and of the Hellenic Society of Psychoanalytic Group Psychotherapy (HSPGP). He has authored several books: *Alice in the Objects-Land. The Child as Advertising Object* (1986), *Clinical Social Psychology* (1994), *Group Psychology. A Clinical Psychodynamic Approach* (2005), and *Groupishness and Mediation* (2011).

John Schlapobersky, MA, is a training analyst, supervisor, and teacher at the Institute of Group Analysis, London, and a research fellow at Birkbeck, University of London. Formerly consultant psychotherapist to the Medical Foundation for Victims of Torture (now Freedom from Torture) and the Traumatic Stress Clinic, University College London, he is in private practice at the Bloomsbury Psychotherapy Practice and works with individuals, couples, and groups. He also teaches internationally and has many publications. His most recent book is *From the Couch to the Circle: Group-analytic Psychotherapy in Practice*.

Vamık D. Volkan, MD, is Professor Emeritus of Psychiatry, University of Virginia, Charlottesville, VA, Senior Erik Erikson Scholar, Erikson Institute for Research and Education of the Austen Riggs Center, Stockbridge, MA, and Training and Supervising Analyst Emeritus, Psychoanalytic Institute, Washington, DC.

Haim Weinberg, PhD, is a clinical psychologist and group analyst in private practice in California. He is Director of the International Program at the professional School of Psychology, Sacramento, former president of the Northern California Group Psychotherapy Society, and the Israeli Association of Group Therapy. He is also a former member of the Board of the International Association of Group Psychotherapy and Group Processes. He co-edits a book series about the social unconscious and has published a book about internet groups.

Shlomit Yadlin-Gadot, PhD, is a clinical psychologist, member of the Tel Aviv Institute of Contemporary Psychoanalysis. Bar-Ilan University doctoral program "Psychoanalysis and Hermeneutics", program of General Studies at Tel-Aviv University. She writes and lectures on the interface of philosophy and psychoanalysis. Her book, *Truth Matters: Theory and Practice in Psychoanalysis* was published by Brill in May 2016.

SERIES EDITOR'S FOREWORD

Anne-Marie Schloesser

Conflicts are constitutive elements of our lives. Their dynamic puts our coping ability to the test when we are concerned with internal confrontations between strong mutually exclusive needs. This kind of conflict, be it latent or manifest, is part of our human condition; we are forced to develop solutions by postponing satisfaction or finding compromises in order to maintain our psychological health. Every psychotherapist is aware of the huge efforts needed by the individual who suffers from severe infantile conflicts, unsolved until today, and exposing themselves by symptoms.

The collection of papers in this book refers to external or interpersonal conflicts in the social area. Societies consist of individuals and groups who stand in a conflictual relationship to each other. This is how social change is triggered. Conflicts in the social field, as pointed out by Robin Celikates (2007), do not represent pathological variations of a normal state. On the contrary, one might understand stable structures of interaction as an exception and only temporarily effective result of solved social conflicts. As a fundamental part of each social relationship they generate discussion and exchange, but can, as another step on the scale of escalation, also lead to terrorism. We see ourselves confronted with ethnic, religious, national, and ideological conflicts. This tension between conflict potential and stability has to be endured by the society as well as by the individual.

Actually, the danger of terror attacks has become a traumatizing part of everyday life, and the series of worldwide attacks challenges us in a way that goes beyond our consulting rooms. What can psychoanalysts contribute to the search for reconciliation that would aim at harmonizing differing positions? Can reconciliation be a stable state, or is it also a necessary process that never ends? The contributors to this book try to find answers to this and other questions.

Reference

Celikates, R. (2007). Nicht versöhnt. Wo bleibt der Kampf im "Kampf um Anerkennung"? In: G. W. Bertram, R. Celikates, C. Landou, & D. Lauer (Eds.), *Socialité et reconnaissance* (pp. 213–228). Paris: L'Harmattan.

FOREWORD

Earl Hopper

This is a vital and important collection of papers. Several of the chapters are based on presentations in the conference "Conflict and Reconciliation in Groups, Couples, Family & Society" in 2012 in Athens. The authors include psychoanalysts and group analysts, who, perhaps coincidentally, have strong ties to Mediterranean countries.

As the title of this collection suggests, its central theme is conflict and reconciliation in groups and societies. However, taken together with its various supporting themes, this book conveys many of the elements and contours of a developing field theory of the vicissitudes of hate, compassion, and forgiveness. The authors recognize that these complementary and dialectical processes are located both in the primal triad and in its contextual concentric circles and spirals. This reflects the importance of transgenerational transmission of chosen traumas, as well as chosen glories.

We find here an appreciation of the conceptual Moebius strip of group analysis, which twists and stretches among the three pillars of psychoanalysis, sociology, and group dynamics, in full appreciation of the systemic relations among these three revolutionary disciplines. Thus, aggressive feelings are thought to arise from envy as well as from frustration. Destructive aggression is understood as inevitable, but, nonetheless, rooted in the interpersonal and societal helplessness of the human condition. Such helplessness can be ameliorated only through political action based on compassionate identification with the other, who cannot be reduced merely to (M)other.

The focus of our discourse is always a matter of what we perceive and what we take as problematic, which are governed by the socially unconscious foundation matrix of contextual societies. Our projects do not and cannot emerge from the magma spontaneously and only by chance. The administration of Freudian desire and Lacanian *jouissance* is saturated by political processes.

The provision of psychoanalytical psychotherapy must be organized; its skills must be taught and transmitted more generally; its practice must be supported and supervised. Our professional organisations are essential to the sensitive regulation of clinical practice and professional development. Such institualization and de-institualization of the sectors and Institutes of our profession can only occur in national and regional contexts with full respect for the conscious and unconscious constraints and restraints of the foundation matrices of the societies involved.

The European Federation of Psychoanalytical Psychotherapy is an umbrella organization that links together the national networks of child, adolescent, and adult psychoanalytical psychotherapists who work with individuals, dyads, groups, and in couples and families. Many members of this organisation work in the public sector. They are devoted to the care and treatment of the people who avail themselves of it. The EFPP sponsors a new E-Journal dedicated to fostering knowledge and encouraging dialog among colleagues who practice within different geographies, traditions, and schools of thought within the field of psychoanalytical psychotherapy in general. Although we speak different languages, we belong to a community that shares a common sensibility and vision of the complex and subtle workings of the personal psyche within the social world.

The dialogue that emerges from these encounters in the book is really an exercise in building bridges. As illustrated in the chapters that comprise the present volume, building bridges fosters relations between people who live on each bank of the metaphorical river, encouraging them to learn each other's languages and to respect their cultural axioms, which structure the range of meanings on which they draw for understanding social psychological processes. This is a profoundly complex and challenging project, almost always involving rivalry over scarce resources, including the river itself. The essential element is the commitment to reach the opposite bank, not in order to control it, but to promote the exchange of ideas and resources with those who reside on the other side. The implicit goal of such exchange is to share the imagination of the other. It is necessary to understand what maturity means to the other, and how they understand time and social psychological space (Hopper, 2009).

This volume of bridge-building chapters will appeal to students and colleagues alike from all sections of the profession of psychoanalytical psychotherapy. The readers will be provoked to ask new questions about the sociality of human nature, and to find new applications of the theories of it to the challenges that continue to beset us. Paradoxically, this is both an eternal and hopeful process.

Reference

Hopper, E. (2009). Building bridges between psychoanalysis and group analysis in theory and clinical practice. *Group Analysis, 42*(4): 406–425.

INTRODUCTION

A bridge over troubled water: conflicts and reconciliation in groups and society

Gila Ofer

I was born in a country that experienced many wars and is in a state of protracted conflict with its neighboring countries. The region surrounding my country is torn by conflicts, wars, and atrocities. In other parts of the world, we witness conflicts that result in great human suffering.

Within my country, there are also many different cultural groups and subgroups: Arabs and Jews, Sephardic Jews and Ashkenazi Jews, immigrants from Europe, Africa, and America, the religious and the secular. There is a continuous tension between these subgroups that sometimes erupts into open hostilities. Living in such an environment, I began searching for processes that could bring about reconciliation and conflict resolution. I also believe that reconciliation, forgiveness, and compassion can lead to renewal, as long as their complex processes are allowed to run their course. As such, they are widening the scope of psychoanalysis and group analysis.

The process of group analysis and group therapy is rife with the tension between the individual and the group, between the psychological and sociological, between private sorrows and public miseries, between the individual search for solutions and the social need for peace.

We are born into relationships and situations that present us with conflicting emotions: love and hate, compassion and carelessness, empathy and cruelty, among others. There are different ways by which conflicts are formed and can be lived through or resolved. For example, the mechanism of projection and introjection, the need to preserve our inner selves as well as the capacity for concern for the other, and the emphatic ability which is part of our humanity. Conflicts are fueled by emotions such as vindictiveness, bitterness, resentment, contempt, and grudge. Because these emotions are difficult to deal with, they trigger powerful defenses. Behind these defenses lies the wish for attachment and rapprochement with one's antagonist, be it a loved or an envied person, group, or country.

How should we, as group analysts, approach the conflicts within us, between us, among us, and around us? How can we, as group analysts, contribute to the reconciliation of conflicts in individuals, in groups, and in society? How can we, as group analysts, build bridges over troubled water?

Attaining resolution for conflict is a difficult task to accomplish and, therefore, it evokes a certain ambivalence. It is my view that, in order to overcome this ambivalence, the following two elements must be part of the path towards reconciliation: the first is self-reflection, which is a prerequisite for reparation; the second is an interpersonal intersubjective relational process. Witnessing and negotiation, referring to the social unconscious and the foundation matrix, mirroring and resonance—all of which are an integral part of group analysis—help facilitate these two essential elements, thus promoting reconciliation.

This book presents a multi-faceted perspective on conflicts and their resolution that is applicable to individuals, groups, and society. Different theories are presented as a framework for conceptualizing and dealing with conflicts, the affects that constitute part of such conflicts, and ways of resolving these conflicts.

The various authors examine a wide range of conflicts: conflicts between countries, nationalities, communities, groups, theories, and people. They offer different approaches to conciliation from several perspectives.

Both Vamık Volkan and John Schlapobersky see the disruption of social relations as located between the psyche and the social world. Volkan emphasizes the importance of identity to individuals and large groups alike, and comments on the formation of this identity. His main focus, however, is on large groups and the concepts of chosen trauma, "depositing" as a form of collective transgenerational transmissions, and the dangers that traumas carry with them, such as entitlement ideologies and the collapse of time. In order to illustrate his ideas, he offers two examples, one on an individual scale and the other on a national scale.

Schlapobersky, in demonstrating his theory, examines four historical conflicts involving war crimes and crimes against humanity, drawing on group-analytic sources to establish a perspective on the intergenerational transmission of trauma, which he investigates between the consulting room and the street—emblematic of the psyche and the social world, respectively.

Three chapters center on conflicts that are characteristic of interpersonal processes. In her chapter, Gila Ofer indicates an important factor in reconciliation: namely, forgiveness. Both sides of every conflict are burdened with hurt, anger, shame and guilt. She describes two stages that are needed for reconciliation to occur, offering examples from literature, cinema, and political conflicts. She then underlines the importance of witnessing and describes how forgiveness can be utilized by individuals in therapeutic groups.

Smadar Ben-Asher and Wissam Maree illuminate and expose the deep significance of the group's work within a traditional Bedouin society, both on the personal level (members) and the collective level (the group). The group members are women who live in a society that is very much at odds with the western society that they meet and are torn between two conflicting value systems. The authors demonstrate how group work can help these women cope with these conflicts.

Isaura Manso Neto and Mario David are looking at therapeutic groups, relating the notion of conflict to affects such as anger, envy, hate, and jealousy that have to be dealt with in groups. They engage the ideas of Cortesau, as well as Foulkes and Bion, in pointing out some paths on the way to reconciliation between people under the influence of these emotions.

In the third part of the book, the authors discuss the impact of the social unconscious (social–cultural–political) on groups. Klimis Navridis argues that groups are potentially destructive, but also have the capacity for survival, creativity, and transformation. His point of view suggests that conflicts within groups are potentially shaped by unconscious transference and countertransfernce in relation to social and political forces. His case study examines the Roma people living in Greece.

Marina Mojović introduces the new concept of "infant gangs". There are positive and protective infant gangs aimed at social progress and negative infant gangs aimed at destruction, decadence, and extremism. In very poetic language, she elaborates on destructive internal and external attacks by "gangs" of organized objects or part objects in the internal world of traumatized persons, stressing the need to distinguish between the two. Her ideas are illustrated by examples and vignettes from poetry, group work, and "citizens reflective" events which she conducts in her country.

In underlining the importance of the social unconscious for understanding conflicts, Weinberg argues for its relevance in individuals, in small groups, in median groups, and in large groups. Discussing the social unconscious from an intersubjective perspective, he illustrates his ideas with clinical vignettes.

The fourth part of this book is devoted to conflicts between groups dominated by fear and subsequent hate, or by the need to draw lines in order to safeguard their identity. In this part, the authors outline possible positive outcomes for conflict, reflecting on growth as a potential outcome of conflict.

Uri Levin argues that the need to establish a clear division between us and them is a basic human process, both on the social and organizational level and on the unconscious psychological level. This is a binary system, in which many groups find themselves trapped, causing severe inter-group conflicts. Consultants need to experience the situation and take part in it, thus acting as the third, acknowledging the otherness which is inherent in our lives. Thus, he hopes, we will be able to reduce the destructive consequences of this fundamental tendency.

Robi Friedman examines dialogue groups in moments when hate and fear dominate the atmosphere. He is mainly concerned with two key issues: the impact of the foundation matrix on the group and the position and attitude of the leader/conductor of the group. His conclusion is that the leader/conductor should attempt to achieve a reflective detachment, while sharing his thoughts and feelings as the container of the process.

In the penultimate chapter, Michael Buchholz observes the professional psychoanalytic community as a large group that is teeming with conflicts between theories and between theoreticians: are conflicts an outcome of drives, inner objects or interpersonal relationships and situations? Buchholz welcomes conflicts in psychoanalysis as stepping-stones toward further growth and depicts four levels of growth. It is with this sense of hope that the book draws to a close.

Shlomit Gadot offers an approach to conflict resolution that emphasizes the crucial elements of self-definition and self-reflection in processes of identity formation on social, groups, and individual levels. Broadly employing the logic of Lacanian thought it underlines the potential dangers of escalating animosity that may ensue from the collapse of intersubjective engagement, and describes the intra-group dynamics that may mitigate and resolve inter-group conflicts in which the group is entrapped.

PART I

BETWEEN THE SOCIAL AND THE PSYCHE

CHAPTER ONE

Large-group trauma at the hands of the "other," transgenerational transmissions, and chosen traumas

Vamık D. Volkan

Massive societal catastrophes can occur for any number of reasons, including natural or man-made disasters, political oppression, economic collapse, or death of a leader, but tragedies, brutalities, and deaths that result from the deliberate actions of other ethnic, national, religious, or ideological groups called "enemies," must be differentiated from other types of massive shared trauma. This is because they involve severe large-group identity issues. When the "other" who possesses a different large-group identity than the victims humiliates and oppresses a large group, the victimized large-group's identity is threatened.

This chapter explores shared transgenerational transmission processes that are put in motion within the victimized large group following a massive trauma at the hands of the "other," processes that nurture the development of "chosen traumas." A chosen trauma refers to the shared mental representation of a traumatic historical event that is a significant large-group identity marker. Under certain circumstances political leaders may reactivate a chosen trauma through propaganda and hate speeches that inflame followers' shared feelings about themselves and their enemy.

Large-group identity

Large-group identity is defined as a subjective feeling of sameness shared among tens, hundreds of thousands, or millions of individuals, most of whom will never meet in their lifetimes. Large-group identities are articulated in terms of commonality such as "we are Bedouins; we are Lithuanian Jews; we are Sunni Muslim; we are communists" and/or "you are Slav; you are French, you are Orthodox Christian; you are capitalists." They are the end-result of myths and realities of common beginnings, historical continuities, geographical realities, and other shared linguistic, societal, religious, and cultural factors. Yet, a simple definition of this abstract concept is not sufficient to explain the power it has to influence political, economic, legal, and military initiatives and to induce seemingly irrational resistances to change (Volkan, 1988, 1997, 2004, 2006).

Think in terms of how we learn to wear two layers, like fabric, from the time we are children. The first layer, the individual layer, fits each of us snugly, like clothing. It is one's core personal identity that provides an inner sense of persistent sameness for the individual (Erikson, 1956). The second layer is like the canvas of a tent, which is loose fitting, but allows us to share a sense of sameness with others under the same large-group tent. Some common threads, such as identifications with intimate others in one's childhood environment, are used in the construction of both layers. Thus, the core individual identity and the core large-group identity, psychologically speaking, are interconnected. While it is the tent pole—the political leader—that holds the tent erect, the tent's canvas psychologically protects both the leader and the large group. From an individual psychology point of view, a person may perceive the pole as a father or the canvas as a nurturing mother. From a large-group psychology point of view the canvas represents the large-group identity that is shared by thousands or millions of people.

In peaceful times, people turn their attention toward their individualized garments and their interactions with their subgroups—families, relatives, clans, neighbors, schools, professional and social organizations, sports clubs, local and national political parties. However, when a large group is humiliated or threatened by "others" who identify with another large group, the attacked population, to a great extent, abandons its routine preoccupations and becomes obsessed with repairing, protecting, and maintaining the canvas of the tent. The attackers who humiliate, maim, and kill in the name of their large-group identity and who live under their own metaphorical tent also wear the canvas of their tent as their shared second garment. Minority dissidents on both sides remain ineffective in the interaction between the enemy groups.

In our routine lives, we are not keenly aware of our large-group identity, the canvas of the tent, just as we are not usually aware of our constant breathing. If we develop pneumonia, or if we are in a burning building, we quickly notice each breath we take. Likewise, if our huge tent's canvas shakes, or parts of it are torn apart by "others," we become preoccupied with the canvas of our huge tent and will do anything to stabilize, repair, maintain, and protect it, and, when we do, we are willing to tolerate extreme sadism or masochism if we think that what we are doing will help to maintain and protect our large-group identity.

Under a huge large-group tent there are subgroups and subgroup identities, such as professional identities. My focus is not on such subgroups. Before going any further, I must explain that here I am speaking of large-group processes shared by the majority of persons under the metaphorical tent, leaving out certain people, such as immigrants, or those who are products of parents from more than one ethnic or religious group. Furthermore, dissenters in a large group do not modify the basic elements of a large-group identity unless they have a huge following and, thus, they start an influential subgroup and become involved in a new large-group identity. History tells us that very seldom does a large group evolve a new large-group identity through the influence of some decades or centuries-long historical events alone.

Each large-group identity includes tribal, ethnic, national, religious, or ideological "identity markers" that belong only to its members. Let us go to the huge tent analogy and look closely at the canvas. Each canvas has its own specific designs. On occasion, a design on a canvas, such as certain religious or linguistic elements, might appear similar to a design on another huge tent's canvas. However, even under these circumstances, we note "minor differences" in such elements (Horowitz, 1985; Volkan, 1997). When conflicts arise between the two large groups, such minor differences become major concerns.

In this chapter, I will describe one special design on the large-group's canvas that is related to transgenerational transmission of ancestors' massive trauma at the hands of the "other." I named this design as a "chosen trauma" (Volkan, 1991). Now, I illustrate a specific type transgenerational transmission, called "depositing," that is used in the evolution of chosen traumas.

Trauma at the hands of the "other" and the concept of "depositing"

Traumas shared by members of a large group are of various types. Some are from natural causes, such as earthquakes. Others are due to famine or economic problems. Some are accidental man-made disasters, like the 1986 Chernobyl accident. Sometimes, the death of a leader, or of a person who functions as a "transference figure" for many members of the society, provokes collective responses (Erlich, 1998; Moses-Hrushovski, 2000; Raviv et al., 2000; Wolfenstein & Kliman, 1965). Other shared experiences of disaster are due to the deliberate actions of an "enemy" large group, as in tribal, ethnic, national, religious, or ideological conflicts. Here, my focus is on this last type of massive trauma and its transmission from one generation to the other. But, first, I describe how transgenerational transmission of trauma appears in an individual.

There are various types of transgenerational transmissions. Here, I describe only a concept that I call "depositing" (Volkan et al., 2002). Memories belonging to one person cannot be transmitted to another person, but an adult can deposit his or her traumatized self- and other images into a child's self-representation and assign tasks to such internal images. Depositing is closely related to the well-known concept of "identification" in childhood.

In identification, the child is the primary active partner in taking in and assimilating object images and related ego and superego functions from another person. In depositing, an adult person more actively pushes his or her specific self- and internalized object images into the developing self-representation of the child. By performing the act of depositing, the depositors externalize their traumatized images into another person in order to become "free" of carrying the troublesome images within themselves and in order to deal with mental conflicts and anxiety associated with such images. On the other hand, the children who are a reservoir are given, metapsychologically speaking, a "psychological gene" that influences their self-representation and, thus, their sense of identity. Depositing can even be considered a version of projective identification (Klein, 1946).

One area where the concept of depositing can be illustrated clearly is the so-called "replacement child phenomenon" (Cain & Cain, 1964; Poznanski, 1972; Volkan & Ast, 1997). A mother has an internalized formed image of her child who has died. She deposits this image into the developing self-representation of her next-born child, usually born after the first child's death. The second child, the replacement child, has no actual experience with the image of the dead sibling. The mother, who has an image of the dead child, treats the second one as the reservoir where the dead child can be kept "alive." Accordingly, the mother gives the second child certain ego tasks, mostly unconsciously, to protect and maintain what is deposited in this child. Obviously, replacement children also develop personal ego functions to deal with what has been pushed into them. For example, replacement children will be preoccupied with the task of integrating the deposited image with the rest of their self-representation. These children might or might not succeed in doing so. Sometimes, the assimilated idealized deposited representation might become a motivation for the individual to excel in certain areas of life experiences. If this task is not successful, replacement children could develop an unintegrated self-representation.

An animal killer

Gregory was an American sailor who worked in a submarine during the Second World War and was in charge of the submarine's torpedoes. He was captured by the Japanese when he was stationed in the Philippines and was in the Bataan Death March in the spring of 1942. The American and Filipino prisoners were forced to march sixty-five miles in the boiling sun, while Japanese guards beat them with whips and rifle butts. Thousands died. After that, he was in a Japanese prison camp until the end of the war where he was exposed to unbelievable cruelty and was very traumatized.

Soon after he returned to the USA, Gregory became friendly with a woman whose husband had left her when their only child, Peter, was three weeks old. Gregory moved in with her, the woman's mother, and Peter, who then was under the age of two, traumatized, overfed, and obese. During Peter's early childhood, Gregory stayed at home while the women went to work, thereby assuming the major parenting role for Peter. In a few years' time, Gregory married Peter's mother and adopted Peter as his son. He, his wife, and his stepson moved to a new house, leaving behind the boy's grandmother, who died before Peter reached puberty.

After he and his family moved to their new house, Gregory built a purple multi-storey martin birdhouse in the garden. For decades this birdhouse remained as a permanent fixture there. Gregory took great pains to paint (and repaint when the old paint faded) numbers on each of the many "apartments" the bird families occupied. Every year it was full of birds. When their eggs hatched, the birds fed their fledglings and helped them to fly to freedom when they were ready. Every year Gregory put a band on one leg of each baby bird after it was hatched. Each band was numbered to correspond with the number on its family's "apartment" in the birdhouse. If a baby bird had an untimely fall from the birdhouse, Gregory would know to which "apartment" it belonged and would then return the baby bird to its proper nest. This was extremely important, because if a baby bird was rescued by a human, but returned to the wrong nest, it would be rejected by the adult birds in that "apartment" and would certainly die.

The purple martin birdhouse symbolically represented Gregory's Japanese prison camp where he suffered a great deal, and was exposed to the deaths of his comrades almost daily. Gregory saw to it that no baby birds would die while occupying his birdhouse. He changed "the function" (Waelder, 1936) of the image of his prison camp; he had created a "camp" where the occupants, the baby birds that were reservoirs of Gregory and his comrades' helpless images, were not allowed to die.

When Peter was in his mid-forties, he sought psychoanalytic treatment primarily for a sadistic narcissistic personality organization. When Peter started his analysis, Gregory was in his seventies and still seemed to have a "normal" life. During his analysis, Peter realized that his stepfather treated his stepson like he treated his baby birds. Adult Peter described how Gregory had been preoccupied with making little Peter strong. While at home with Peter, the stepfather prescribed certain tasks for the boy and taught him how to exercise, lose weight, and develop an athletic body. Gregory introduced young Peter to guns in his early teens and taught him to hunt. Soon, using his contacts, he made sure that Peter enrolled in a military school. After graduation, as a military man, Peter was involved in the war in Vietnam. Later, as a civilian, he worked for the military defense industry and became rich. Adult Peter's hobby was hunting. But he was *not* a sportsman. Whenever he felt anxious, he would kill many animals. Since he had a great deal of money he could afford to hire a helicopter for his hunting trips, and on many occasions he would shoot from the air at a herd of deer below.

Peter and his analyst slowly began to understand that Gregory had deposited his "hunted" self-image (injured, humiliated, and rendered helpless in the Philippines) into the little boy's developing self-representation. Indeed, there was a nice "fit" between Gregory's deposited injured image and little Peter's own obese helpless image in a home dominated by intrusive women. When Gregory gave tasks to his stepson—indeed, acting like his "trainer"—he made him (in fact, his own deposited image as well) a "hunter" instead of the "hunted" one, reversing his helplessness and making the boy feel omnipotently powerful and sadistic.

Peter's understanding of his role as a "reservoir" for his stepfather's injured image became clear when he and his analyst examined the various meanings of one of Peter's major preoccupations as an adult. Gregory had been preoccupied with his birdhouse and its occupants and adult Peter became preoccupied with a special room in his house and its occupants. Peter had built a huge room whose walls were decorated with trophies of his hunts. He unconsciously repeated the "memories" of the prisoner Gregory surrounded by his dead comrades. His hobby also included one of the tasks Gregory had given to him: to resurrect the dead and change the function of the prison camp, as Gregory had done when he protected the lives of baby birds. Thus, Peter took pains to make his trophies look "alive" through skillful taxidermy, spending considerable time and money on taxidermists to achieve this illusion.

Throughout his analysis, Peter had a recurring dream in which he saw himself walking on water like Jesus Christ. Only towards the termination phase of his analysis did he have a new version of this dream. In it, he was not walking on water; he was walking on a submarine which was lying a few inches below the surface of the water. Peter realized that the submarine stood for Gregory, who had worked on a submarine just before he was captured by the Japanese. The new version of his recurring dream gave Peter a firm insight into the fact that his omnipotent self-image was supported by Gregory; in fact, he was an extension of Gregory, the older man's "reservoir." Peter was in the termination phase of his analysis when he had still another version of his repeating dream. In this one the submarine dived, and Peter fell into the water and had to swim to shore as an "average" individual (Volkan, 2006)

Peter's case shows us how an individual's being a "reservoir" of traumatized images becomes connected with identity issues. Now, I illustrate that transgenerationally transmitted traumatized images and associated psychological tasks at a large-group level play a crucial role in shaping future historical and political processes.

Collective transgenerational transmissions

After massive traumas at the hands of the "other," similar transgenerational transmissions shared by tens, or hundreds, or millions of persons can turn some past historical events into significant large-group markers. After a massive trauma at the hands of the "other," members of a large group will face difficult tasks taming and rendering harmless the following psychological features:

1. A sense of victimization and feeling dehumanized.
2. A sense of humiliation due to being helpless.
3. A sense of survival guilt: staying alive while family members, friends, and others die.
4. Difficulty in being assertive without facing humiliation.
5. An increase in externalizations/projections.
6. Exaggeration of "bad" prejudice.
7. An increase in narcissistic investment in large-group identity.
8. Envy toward the victimizer and (defensive) identification with the oppressor.
9. A sense of unending mourning due to significant losses

Attempts to complete unfinished psychological tasks associated with the previous generation's or ancestor's trauma are handed down from generation to generation (shared transgenerational transmissions) (Fromm, 2012; Volkan et al., 2002). Kestenberg's term (1982) "transgenerational transportation" and Faimberg's (1993) description of "the telescoping of generations," I believe, refer to depositing traumatized images.

Depositing in the large-group psychology refers to a process shared by thousands or millions that starts in childhood and becomes like "psychological DNA," creating a sense of belonging. After experiencing a collective catastrophe inflicted by an enemy group, affected individuals are left with self-images similarly (though not identically) traumatized by the shared event. Tens of thousands or millions of individuals deposit such images into their children and give them tasks such as: "Regain my self-esteem for me," "Put my mourning process on the right track," or "Be assertive and take revenge." It is this transgenerational conveyance of long-term "tasks" that perpetuate the cycle of societal trauma. Although each child in the second generation has his or her own individualized personality, all share similar links to the trauma's mental representation and similar unconscious tasks for coping with that representation. If the next generation cannot effectively fulfill their shared tasks—and this is usually the case—they will pass these tasks on to the third generation, and so on. Such conditions create a powerful unseen network among tens of thousands, or millions, of people.

Depending on external conditions, shared tasks might change from generation to generation. For example, in one generation, the shared task might be to grieve for their ancestors' loss and to feel their victimization. In the following generation, the shared task might be to express a sense of revenge for that loss and victimization. But, whatever its expression in a given generation, keeping alive the mental representation of the ancestors' trauma remains the core task. All tasks that are involved in transgenerational transmissions are associated with the shared mental representation of the same event and eventually this mental representation evolves as a most significant large-group identity marker (a chosen trauma).

Similar processes may also be seen in the descendants of victimizers. Among the descendants of perpetrators there is more preoccupation with consequences of shared feelings of shame and guilt than preoccupation with the shared feeling of humiliation and helplessness.

Not all past massive tragedies at the hands of others evolve as chosen traumas. We see the mythologizing of victimized heroes and hear moving stories associated with a trauma popularized in songs and poetry, and we see political leaders of later times create a preoccupation with a past trauma and related events, turning this historic event into a chosen trauma. In April 2010, Polish President Lech Kaczyński, his wife Maria Kaczyńska, and many of Poland's highest military and civilian leaders were killed in an airplane crash on their way to a ceremony during the anniversary of the Katyn Forest massacre of Polish nationals by Russians that occurred in April–May, 1940. I believe that this plane crash will play a role in turning the Katyn massacre into a chosen trauma.

Greeks band together when they share the "memory" of the fall of Constantinople (Istanbul) to the Turks in 1453; Russians recall the "memory" of the Tatar invasion centuries ago; Czechs commemorate the 1620 battle of Bila Hora, which led to their subjugation under the Hapsburg Empire for nearly 300 years; Turks share the "memory" of the defeat of the Ottomans on September 12, 1683 at the gates of Vienna; Scots keep alive the story of the battle of Culloden of 1746 and the failure of Bonnie Prince Charlie to restore a Stuart to the British throne; the Dakota people of the United States recall the anniversary of their decimation at Wounded Knee in 1890; and Crimean Tatars define themselves by the collective suffering of their deportation from Crimea in 1944.

Jews around the globe, including those not personally affected by the Holocaust, all, to some degree, define their large-group identity by direct or indirect reference to the Holocaust. The Holocaust is still too "hot" to be considered a truly established chosen trauma, but it already has become an ethnic marker, even though Orthodox Jews still refer to the 586 BC destruction of the Jewish temple in Jerusalem by Nebuchadnezzar II of Babylonia as the chosen trauma of the Jews.

Some chosen traumas are difficult to detect because they are not simply connected to one well-recognized historical event. For example, the chosen trauma of the Estonians is not related to one specific event, but to the fact that they had lived under almost constant dominance (Swedes, Germans, Russians) for thousands of years.

Entitlement ideologies

Entitlement ideologies refer to a shared sense of entitlement to recover what was lost in reality and fantasy during the collective trauma that evolved as a chosen trauma and during other related shared traumas. Or they refer to the mythologized birth of a large group, a process that later generations idealize. They deny difficulties and losses that had occurred during this process, and imagine their large group as if it was composed of persons belonging to a superior species. Holding on to an entitlement ideology primarily reflects a complication in large-group mourning, an attempt both to deny losses as well as a wish to recover them, a narcissistic reorganization accompanied by "bad" prejudice for the other.

Each large group's entitlement ideology is specific. Some entitlement ideologies are known by specific names in the literature. What Italians call "irredentism" (related to *Italia Irredenta*), what Greeks call "Megali Idea" (Great Idea), what Turks call "Pan-Turanism" (bringing all the Turkic people together from Anatolia to central Asia), what Serbs call "Christoslavism," (Sells, 2002) and what extreme religious Islamists of today call "the return of an Islamic Empire" are examples of entitlement ideologies. The American entitlement ideology, usually called "American exceptionalism," was inflamed after September 11, 2001 (Hollander, 2010).

Time collapse

When representatives of large groups in conflict get together for unofficial diplomatic dialogues, they become spokespersons for their large groups. When one side feels humiliated, they reactivate their chosen traumas (usually contaminated with chosen glories). For example, during a diplomatic dialogue, while discussing current international affairs, Russians might begin to focus on the Tatar invasion, their chosen trauma. When such images of past historical events are reactivated within a large group, a "time collapse" occurs. Shared perceptions, feelings, and thoughts about a past historical image become intertwined with perceptions, feelings, and thoughts about current events. This magnifies the present danger and the large-group's entitlement ideology comes to the surface. Unless a way is found to deal with the time collapse, routine diplomatic efforts will most likely fail.

Today's extreme Muslim religious fundamentalists have reactivated numerous chosen traumas and glories leading to time collapse.

We need to study and understand them in order to develop new and, one hopes, more effective strategies for a peaceful world.

An example of reactivation of a chosen trauma and time collapse

A chosen trauma that I (Volkan, 1997) studied in depth is the Serbian chosen trauma, the shared mental representation of the Battle of Kosovo in 1389, along with the entitlement ideology Christoslavism (Sells, 2002) to which it is linked. I believe that this is critical to understanding the contributions of large-group psychology in the tragedies in Bosnia in 1992 and in Kosovo in 1999. Despite the fact that, in 1389, the leaders of both sides—Ottoman Sultan Murat I and Serbian Prince Lazar—were both killed during the Battle of Kosovo, and despite the fact that Serbia remained autonomous for over seventy years after the battle, the shared representation of the battle evolved as the major Serbian chosen trauma, marking the end of a glorious period of Serbian power and the beginning of their subjugation to the Ottoman Empire. In certain periods, Prince Lazar's image was used to cement a shared sense of victimization and martyrdom under Moslem rule; during others, his image became a symbol of the Serbs' desire to reverse the humiliation of the loss by reconquering Kosovo. As decades passed, Prince Lazar became associated with Jesus Christ, and icons showing Lazar's representation in fact decorated many Serbian churches throughout the six centuries following the battle. Even after Kosovo Province was taken back from the Ottoman Turks in the late nineteenth century, Lazar's "ghost" was still not put to rest. During the communist period, when the government discouraged hero worship, Serbs were able to drink (introject) a popular red wine called Prince Lazar.

After the collapse of communism, mental representations of Lazar and the Battle of Kosovo were resurrected by Slobodan Milošević, along with some members of the Serbian church and some members of the Serbian academic community. As the 600th anniversary of the Battle of Kosovo approached in 1989, with the permission and encouragement of Milošević, Lazar's 600-year-old remains, which had been kept north of Belgrade, were placed in a coffin and taken, over the course of the year, to almost every Serb village and town, where they were received by huge crowds of mourners dressed in black. Again and again during this long journey, Lazar's remains were symbolically buried and reincarnated, until they were buried for good at the original battleground in Kosovo on June 28, 1989. The Serbian people began feeling, without being intellectually aware of it, that the defeat at the Battle of Kosovo had occurred only recently, a development made possible by the fact that the chosen trauma had effectively been kept alive for centuries.

On June 28, 1989, the 600th anniversary of the Battle of Kosovo, a helicopter brought Serbian president Slobodan Milošević to the burial ground where a huge monument made of red stone, symbolizing blood, had been built. In the mythology, Prince Lazar had chosen the Kingdom of Heaven over the Kingdom of Earth. By design, Milošević descended from a helicopter, representing Prince Lazar/Jesus Christ coming to earth to find a new Kingdom, a Greater Serbia. Propaganda prepared an atmosphere that allowed the resurgence of the Serbian entitlement ideology, Christoslavism (Sells, 2002), which gave permission to create a Greater Serbia. Atrocities would eventually be committed against Bosnian and Kosovar Muslims, whom modern Serbs came to perceive as extensions of the Ottoman enemy of distant history. Thus, the Serbian large-group identity was reinforced and reinvigorated by the lasting emotional power of this ancient event—at terrible cost to non-Serbs.

Making a formulation about what exists within a large-group psychology

What I have said above can be summarized in the schema set out in Figure 1.1. Using this schema, we can make a formulation about what exists within a large group's psychology, just as we make a formulation about the internal world of a patient who comes to us for analysis. Making a formulation about a patient's internal world is necessary for good analysis because it gives us direction in terms of what we will be treating. Similarly, making a formulation about what exists in the psychology of a large group can give us directions to help those dealing with the large group and develop helpful strategies.

Massive trauma at the hands of "others"

⇩

Transgenerational transmission

⇩

Change of function

⇩

Chosen trauma: Large-group identity marker
(a psychological gene of the large group)

⇩

Reactivation of chosen trauma

⇩

Enhancement of leader–follower interaction

⇩

Time collapse

⇩

Entitlement for revenge or re-victimization

⇩

Magnification of current large group conflict

⇩

"Irrational" decision-making

⇩

Mobilization of large group activities

Figure 1.1.

Some final words: large-group psychology in its own right

Besides the issues that are originally connected with chosen traumas and their reactivations, other specific psychological processes are present within any large group. These processes, such as circumstances that increase the need to have enemies, shared transference expectations from a political leader, a political leader's utilization of the large-group arena for finding solutions for personal conflicts, also require formulations. Because there are many factors in large-group psychology that stand side by side and complicate the existing realistic situation, any attempt to understand large groups or societies is very difficult and even impossible (Shapiro & Carr, 2006). Still, I have become convinced that, by developing a large-group psychology in its own right, we can make a worthwhile contribution.

Large groups do not have one brain to think with or two eyes to cry. When thousands or millions of members of a large group share a defense mechanism or a psychological journey, what we see are societal, cultural, and political processes that are specific to the large group under study. Large-group psychology in its own right can be examined and theories about it can be developed by finding the shared mental phenomena that initiate such specific societal, cultural, and political processes. Such studies will expand our knowledge in international affairs and help to develop a meaningful link between psychological insights about human nature in large groups and political science.

References

Cain, A. C., & Cain, R. C. (1964). On replacing a child. *Journal of the American Academy of Child Psychiatry*, 3: 443–456.

Erikson, E. H. (1956). The problem of ego identity. *Journal of the American Psychoanalytic Association*, 4: 56–121.

Erlich, H. S. (1998). Adolescents' reactions to Rabin's assassination: a case of patricide? In: A. Esman (Ed.), *Adolescent Psychiatry: Developmental and Clinical Studies* (pp. 189–205). London: Analytic Press.

Faimberg, H. (1993). *The Telescoping of Generations. Listening to the Narcissistic Links Between Generations*. London: Routledge, 2005.

Fromm, M. G. (Ed.) (2012). *Lost in Transmission: Studies of Trauma Across Generations*. London: Karnac.

Hollander, N. (2010). *Uprooted Minds: Surviving the Political Terror in the Americas*. New York: Taylor & Francis.

Horowitz, D. L. (1985). *Ethnic Groups in Conflict*. Berkeley, CA: University of California Press.

Kestenberg, J. S. (1982). A psychological assessment based on analysis of a survivor's child. In: M. S. Bergman & M. E. Jucovy (Eds.), *Generations of the Holocaust* (pp.158–177). New York: Columbia University Press.

Klein, M. (1946). Notes on some schizoid mechanisms. In: J. Riviere (Ed.), *Development of Psychoanalysis* (pp. 292–320). London: Hogarth Press.

Moses-Hrushovski, R. (2000). *Grief and Grievance: The Assassination of Yitzhak Rabin*. London: Minerva Press.

Poznanski, E. O. (1972). The "replacement child": a saga of unresolved parental grief. *Behavioral Pediatrics, 81*: 1190–1193.

Raviv, A., Sadeh, A., Raviv, A., Silberstein, O., & Diver, O. (2000). Young Israelis' reactions to national trauma: the Rabin assassination and terror attacks. *Political Psychology, 21*: 299–322.

Sells, M. A. (2002). The construction of Islam in Serbian religious mythology and its consequences. In: M. Shatzmiller (Ed.), *Islam and Bosnia* (pp. 56–85). Montreal: McGill University Press.

Shapiro, E., & Carr, W. (2006). Those people were some kind of solution: can society in any sense be understood? *Organizational & Social Dynamics, 6*: 241–257.

Volkan, V. D. (1988). *The Need to Have Enemies and Allies: From Clinical Practice to International Relationships*. Northvale, NJ: Jason Aronson.

Volkan, V. D. (1997). *Bloodlines: From Ethnic Pride to Ethnic Terrorism*. New York: Farrar, Straus and Giroux.

Volkan, V. D. (2004). *Blind Trust: Large Groups and Their Leaders in Times of Crises and Terror*. Charlottesville, VA: Pitchstone.

Volkan, V. D. (2006). *Killing in the Name of Identity: A Study of Bloody Conflicts*. Charlottesville, VA: Pitchstone.

Volkan, V. D., & Ast, G. (1997). *Siblings in the Unconscious and Psychopathology*. Madison, CT: International Universities Press.

Volkan, V. D., Ast, G., & Greer, W. (2002). *The Third Reich in the Unconscious: Transgenerational Transmission and its Consequences*. New York: Brunner-Routledge.

Waelder, R. (1936). The principle of multiple function: observations on over-determination. *Psychoanalytic Quarterly, 5*: 45–62.

Wolfenstein, M., & Kliman, G. (Eds.) (1965). *Children and the Death of a President: Multi-disciplinary Studies*. Garden City, NY: Doubleday.

CHAPTER TWO

Group analysis on war and peace

John R. Schlapobersky

Introduction

This chapter applies the principles of group analysis to terror and the dynamics of hatred and polarization that give rise to it. Terrorism seeks to foster these dynamics, building its resources out of hatred. Group analysis is a clinical and theoretical discipline that locates the disturbance of social relations between the psyche and the social world (Brown & Zinkin, 1995). The discipline is used here to guide a survey that takes account of terror following 9/11 and relates this to threats and conflict in Israel during the period of the Second Intifada, 2000–2005. It examines contemporary culture within and outside the country, and four historical conflicts involving war crimes and crimes against humanity. It draws on group analytic sources to provide psychosocial foundations for the applied analysis of historical events to build a perspective on the generational transmission of trauma. This is investigated between the consulting room and the street, each of which serve this paper as emblems for the psyche and the social world.

There are related perspectives in literature that include Tolstoy's *War and Peace* and John Donne's famous lines from *For Whom The Bell*

Tolls, frequently quoted by Foulkes, the founder of group analysis. He believed the identity of a group analyst could best be compared with that of a poet who was sensitive to the spirit of their society through words that could bring to consciousness the problems of their time (Foulkes, 1986[1975], p. 157). Key points of the chapter are illustrated with poetry that became emblematic among the people it was written about. Language that psychotherapy relies on is also found in poetry, where it can provide a symbolic register through which to bring injury to consciousness in order to both articulate and contain it.

The four other historical episodes involving war crimes or crimes against humanity discussed here include the Spanish Civil War, 1937–1939 (850,00 dead, 16.8% of the country's population); the Holocaust (6,000,000 dead, 36% of the world's Jewish population); ethnic cleansing in Bosnia (104,732 dead, 2.5% of the Muslim population of Bosnia); the ongoing conflict between Israel and the Arabs living inside the country and on its borders. The conceptual framework is informed by, and draws on, historical literature and popular culture associated with these periods and it draws on current therapeutic experience with victims of violence and torture. It is attuned to the needs of practitioners in a range of applications who provide health care and rehabilitation for survivors. It also draws on cultural sources in Jewish history that have been integral to survival but which—in doing so—also reinforce polarities. These sources will be considered for the significance they might hold for the future of other threatened peoples.

Although this chapter is rooted in the period it was written, the Second Intifada, it has contemporary relevance in the light of recent terrorist attacks in Boston, USA and Nairobi, Kenya, in the light of continuing and extreme forms of violence in Afghanistan and Iraq, and in the dismemberment of Syria, where polarization between Sunni and Shi'ite Muslims has generated a death toll of more than 200,000 people.

The original presentation was published in *Mikbatz, the Israeli Journal of Group Psychotherapy* (Schlapobersky, 2002). My father's uncles and aunts perished with their families in the killing fields of Lithuania during the Holocaust, but the daughter of one of them survived as a hidden child. Our cousin is named Rivka Strichman (née Schlapobersky), a resident of Haifa and, by strange historical chance, was the engineer responsible for the design of the very hotel in which the conference took place when this presentation was given. This paper is dedicated to her, to her husband Joseph, and to their children and grandchildren. She recounts her own extraordinary story in the chapter of a recent book cited in the References section (Shlapobersky, 2011).

The *Mikbatz* publication applied the principles of depth psychology to the historical determinants of mass murder. This chapter is concerned with terrorism rather than mass murder, but hatred and polarization—at the core of its investigation—are features of both. Events of appalling significance on the world arena always enter the consulting room. They pose challenges for psychotherapy of a whole variety of different kinds. Those of us who specialize in work with trauma knew, while watching broadcasts of catastrophes in the UK involving serious fatalities, that their survivors would, in due course, find their way to us. Their clinical challenges are with us yet and, in some cases, it is heartening to be able to report on therapeutic progress with survivors of unspeakably awful events. The assaults on civic life in the UK in recent years, with traumatic consequences for individuals and society, take in the following: the Kings Cross fire of 1987; the Hillsborough football disaster of 1987; the Lockerbie bombing of Pan Am Flight 103 in 1988; the IRA bombing of mainland Britain that included the Hyde Park and Regents Park bombs in 1982, the Brighton bomb in 1984, the Bishopsgate bomb in 1993, and the Docklands bomb in 1996. Bombing by Islamic fundamentalists included the London underground bombs of 2005 and many subsequent threats that remain the greatest current challenge.

Although the events of September 11, 2001 stand in the context of these other atrocities, they pose a challenge that goes beyond the consulting room. Commentators in the press and elsewhere attribute to the event a "before and after" quality that sets it apart from these other events. For the first time since 1945, people in the West knew something of what people in the Middle East, for example, have been living through, not in the faraway places of the world, but in the homes, offices, and securities of metropolitan life. In the international arena, it was comparable to the bombing of Guernica during the Spanish Civil War, the events that opened the Second World War, including the bombing of Poland, London, and Coventry in the UK, the mass bombing of Dresden and Germany's other cities during the Second World War, the events associated with the nuclear bombs dropped on Hiroshima and Nagasaki that concluded the Second World War, and, finally, the events associated with the Cuban Missile Crisis and the assassination of John Fitzgerald Kennedy.

Terror and the violence of 9/11

In my mother's account of her father bringing the newspaper with its photograph of the first A-bomb cloud and its description of the destruction of Hiroshima into the house in 1945, there was a sense of elemental horror that goes far beyond relief at an enemy vanquished. This sense of horror lasted all her life. "A secret weapon ... a bomb that could destroy an entire city in one explosion ... they sat in appalled silence." As people gazed at the twin towers first engulfed in flame and then crumbling, we witnessed the same elemental horror on the streets of New York. It was then transmitted to London as buildings were evacuated, airports were closed, and some of my patients with responsibilities in the civil service and broadcasting simply disappeared. They reappeared days later to explain that they had been incommunicado in underground shelters, manning emergency facilities against the likelihood of further threat.

We saw terror on the faces of the people covered in dust and scrambling to safety as buildings came down behind them. We heard the terror replayed in phone messages between doomed people on the aeroplanes and their loved ones. Three days later, I was asked to speak to a group of university students from New York, living in London on placement. They wanted to go home immediately: none could study, none could go anywhere, and some had suffered direct losses in these attacks. The dynamics in the room were charged with emotions that I have—until now—only been familiar with among groups of people who have lived through warfare or atrocities during violent conflicts in political turmoil. The horror was in their eyes and the enormity of the event and the shock of its impact was in their inability to describe it. Their desperation to "go home" was the only emotion that had direction in it, conveying a shared quest for familiar security that had now disappeared. The pervasive sense of bewilderment, so familiar in the aftermath of atrocities, enjoyed some sense of resolution when we looked together at the normality of signal anxiety as a physiological reaction to shock, and at the way in which it prepares the body for fight or flight. We found it reassuring to look together at exactly where we had been when each of us got the news, what we first saw on television or heard on the radio, and what our immediate reactions had been. The architects of the attacks in New York and Washington used the immolation of the thousands who died as the vehicle for an assault, through the watching media, on hundreds of millions of others. The deaths that occurred were calculated to inflict terror on millions more. For some hours, and even days, the whole world held its breath, waiting for the next round of attacks. Although this imminent threat has now passed, metropolitan infrastructures will always be seen as inherently fragile. Working with this group of students, we found that in even an elementary excursion into storytelling, the power of narrative to regain a purchase on events that stand outside the normal range of social experience can alleviate panic and reintroduce a sense of psychic order. This immediate impulse seems to stand behind the compulsion to tell their story in most witnesses to horror and is a cornerstone of therapeutic work with trauma.

Violence and terror on the streets of Israel

Let us look now at terror on the streets of Israel. What follows is an extract from the email of a friend, a religious student in Jerusalem, written to us in the UK during the winter of 2000 at the height of the Second Intifada.

> It is less than a week since 3 bombs in the center of town destroyed life and hope and 10 young lives were ripped away. I was feeling high and glowing from one of those heightened Jerusalem Shabbats, the melodies and moods still filling my senses, when I heard the news. Living in Israel at the moment demands radical changes in emotion all the time. BANG! . . . the pain . . . BANG! . . . THE ANGER. I went to Ben Yehuda Street the following day and found clusters of people crying and chanting psalms. The atmosphere has been so tense and dark and Hanukah, the festival of light, looming. Many, many people gathered, some reciting psalms, others sobbing, others praying, lighting candles, laying down flowers, or just standing motionless trying to absorb the tragedy and the deaths of these young people. Down the street, at the site of the second bomb, a group of young people were huddled together, distraught friends of the victims. On a balcony

> above was a group of fanatical religious Jews who gathered menacingly to use the tragedy as a vehicle for their violent politics. One man holding the microphone, a slightly crazed American, was mindfully perverting a chant of the peace movement. "All we are saying, is give WAR a chance!" was his mantra.
>
> But in Mishna Avot, it says:
>
> "Azeh hu gibbor? Hacofesh et yitzro." Who is a warrior? The one who conquers his passions. Avot d'Rabbi Natan, a Midrashic commentary on this Mishna, says, "A true warrior is someone who can turn their enemy into their friend." This warrior however, was telling the crowd that every Jew must go out with a Torah in one hand, a gun in the other and kill every Arab because they are all evil and this land belongs only to the Jews. All this, he said, is "lichvod hamaytim", "for the honour of the dead." The broken young people below, trying to mourn their friends, became hysterical. This man's words were no comfort to them nor to the memory of their friends. (Soloway, 2002)

Terror leads to hatred, hatred to polarization, and polarization to retaliatory acts of violence involving further terror. The cycle of violence is now working between civilian populations on a scale and at a pace that is unprecedented in Israel since the War of Independence. Unlike that war, the situation now is not bringing people together but, on the contrary, threatens social relations in Israeli society. The deep divisions seen on the streets here reflect wider divisive patterns and even those on the same side of the terror divide become threats to one another when their views differ. What contribution can group psychotherapy make when "Havoc has let slip the dogs of war" (Shakespeare, 1991, *Julius Caesar*, Act III, Scene , 268)? Can it contribute to the challenge that this religious student draws from the Talmud? Can we rise above the passions generated in the cycle of violence? Is there any prospect of turning our enemies into friends and, if so, can the self-understanding for which we struggle in the consulting room assist us?

The first of this chapter's poems is by Yehuda Amichai (2013):

The Diameter of the Bomb

> The diameter of the bomb was thirty centimeters
> and the diameter of its effective range about seven meters,
> with four dead and eleven wounded.

> And around these, in a larger circle
> of pain and time, two hospitals are scattered
> and one graveyard. But the young woman
> who was buried in the city she came from,
> at a distance of more than a hundred kilometers,
> enlarges the circle considerably,
> and the solitary man mourning her death
> at the distant shores of a country far across the sea
> includes the entire world in the circle.
> And I won't even mention the howl of orphans
> that reaches up to the throne of God and
> beyond, making
> a circle with no end and no God.

Here, the poet here gives us a picture of horror in concentric circles of injury that emanate from the focal point of the bomb. As the circles extend, we come to understand that they encompass the whole world. The poem takes on an epic quality similar to Donne's famous lines. Foulkes believed that Donne's words gave literary expression to the basic principle of group analysis that "no man is an island".

> Who casts not up his eye to the sun when it rises? but who takes off his eye from a comet when that breaks out? Who bends not his ear to any bell which upon any occasion rings? but who can remove it from that bell which is passing a piece of himself out of this world? No man is an island, entire of itself; every man is a piece of the continent, a part of the main.
>
> If a clod be washed away by the sea, Europe is the less, as well as if a promontory were, as well as if a manor of thy friend's or of thine own were: any man's death diminishes me, because I am involved in mankind, and therefore never send to know for whom the bell tolls; it tolls for thee. (Donne, 1987)

Amichai's poem is another such statement. As it describes a lonely man mourning a distant death, it reminds us that such injury includes "the whole world in the circle"—no one is safe or immune. It sets the experience of horror confined to one locality in the context of terror that punctures the world. What implications does this extended metaphor hold for the practice of group analysis? As practitioners we work in circles, in bounded space that confines injury and localizes its consequences. Therapy can bring reparative process to bear on the transmission of injury through the shared humanity of our work.

Theoretical sources

The oldest attempt to take the fruits of analytic inquiry into the political arena is Freud's *Civilization and Its Discontents* (Freud, 1930a). It was written while he and his family struggled to survive the ascendancy of fascism in Vienna. He questions whether there is an objective measure for human misery and cites what he believes to have been the worst instances of suffering imposed by human beings upon one another: the plight of the galley slaves in the Mediterranean for the 2,000 years that preceded sail, life during the Thirty Years War in Germany, when conflict between Catholics and Protestants laid the country waste; life for Jews in the Spanish Inquisition, and the experience of a Jewish ghetto assaulted by a pogrom. Little did he know, while writing these words, the fate that awaited members of his own immediate family in Dachau, Bergen-Belsen, and Auschwitz. Had he known what the twentieth century had yet to deliver, he would have included death and concentration camps in his list. Furthermore, would he not have extended his list to include the life of people in refugee camps? Is it realistic to expect peace and security when the terms under which we do so deny peace and security to others? Would Freud have been surprised by the savagery of the violence unleashed in recent conflicts in Israel?

There are further sources that establish benchmarks for our inquiry. Foulkes' account of working with war trauma at Northfield in his early writing is relevant. Nitsun's anti-group (1996) and Hopper's concepts of massification and the understanding he brings to encapsulation (2000), all have contributions to make in linking the consulting room with the street. Zinkin's idea of malignant mirroring (1983) and Volkan's (2001) study of chosen trauma provide the other necessary conceptual tools.

Tolstoy on the psyche and the social world

How do we understand the psyche, its social world, and the dialectic between them? Some of the most profound observations come to us not from Freud or Foulkes, but from Tolstoy. *War and Peace* is not only a great novel, but also a profound study of the way the forces of historical destiny shape the individual, and the way the individual struggles with free agency in the course of historical events (Tolstoy, 1982).

The subject of war and the hope for peace are the matters under study in this chapter. Tolstoy's novel gives evidence to the theory set out in its philosophical conclusion where he demonstrates that the closer we are to our subject, the greater the degree of personal freedom we ascribe to individuals who are regarded as free to choose their actions with an agency that allows them to make their own decisions. But the further we are from our subject, the more constrained we see people to be, with their choices really determined by the forces of destiny. The presented quandary, the paradox, is not resolved by the novel, which actually deepens the quandary. We come to its end identified with its characters' biographies and we are overwhelmed by the backdrop of forces against which their sometimes tragic lives are played out. The tension between freedom and determinism is at the core of many philosophical puzzles. The social sciences originated in the nineteenth century around these very questions as they were posed by Kant, Hegel, Saint Simon, Marx, Weber, and Freud.

The question Tolstoy poses for us in the conclusion to his novel is: "What is the force that moves nations?" (Tolstoy, 1982, p. 1404). To focus our attention on this kernel of concern, he gives us a summation of the tide of history as, following their Revolution, the French expanded throughout Europe under Napoleon and then invaded Russia in the early years of the nineteenth century.

> During this period of twenty years, an immense number of fields are left untilled; houses are burned; trade changes its orientation; millions of people grow poor, grow rich, move from place to place; and millions of Christian men professing the law of love for their neighbour murder one another.

And then he comes to pose the following questions that are as real now as they were in his time:

> What does this mean? Why did it happen? What induced these people to burn houses and kill their fellow-creatures? What were the causes of these events? What force compelled men to act in this fashion?

> These are the instinctive, guileless and supremely legitimate questions humanity propounds to itself when it encounters the monuments and traditions of that bygone period of turmoil. (Tolstoy, 1982, pp. 1401–1402)

The dynamics of psychology and history: a conceptual framework for "chosen trauma"

We struggle now with related questions, not with bygone periods but during a time in which death has become a way of life (Grossman, 2003). Civilian casualties in the Second Intifada were utilized daily as points of strategic pressure by which the two main parties to this conflict acted against each other. It is happening today in Afghanistan, Iraq, and in the extreme case of Syria, with much more dire consequences through the conflict between Sunni and Shi'ite. Can group analysis further our understanding of this murderous polarization? The seven principles set out below provide us with a conceptual framework. Although the technical language of its vocabulary is psychoanalytic, the understanding is contained in, and illuminated by, Tolstoy's novel.

1. The traumatic origins of interpersonal violence are often associated with opposition to, or identification with, past aggressors.
2. Unresolved grief and its continuing denial has profound pathogenic potential.
3. Psychic defences can protect against the different forms of psychic pain described in 1 and 2 by preventing the return of the repressed.
4. These defences include:
   (a) splitting;
   (b) dissociation;
   (c) encapsulation;
   (d) displacement.
5. These are all implicated in the generational transmission of traumatically induced injury in the course of seemingly normative family life.
6. These social forms of pathology are found in conflicted relationships which cannot be reduced to individual psychopathology as

victims of one era become perpetrators in the next. Divisions multiply around us between Falangist and Communist, German and Jew, Israeli and Palestinian, Serbian and Bosnian, Sunni and Shi'ite.

7. Cycles of conflict in the social and political arena replicate and rehearse the patterns described in 1–6 above, in which aggression against external threats is driven by bad internal objects.

These repetitive patterns of retaliation in social and political conflicts are amenable to analysis. The patterns repay close scrutiny and it is through their recognition that we can begin to make change. Volkan's concept of the chosen trauma is the most discerning single application of depth psychology to these historical patterns and this framework of seven principles is designed to stand alongside his picture of the chosen trauma and to provide a differentiated set of concepts that can help us see causal agencies at work and get some further purchase on these processes.

From the street to the consulting room

The clinical illustration describes a therapy group at work and compresses the progress of an extended course into two sessions situated many months apart and outlined in a schematic form. It is studied in further detail elsewhere (Schlapobersky, 2016). In this chapter, it is used to provide psychosocial foundations for the applied analysis of historical events that follow.

In the consulting room (1)

Brendan reports a dramatic recent incident. He is an unemployed actor who drives minicabs for income. After dropping a passenger in an empty area of London, he saw two men assaulting a third and, as their victim fell to the ground, they began to kick him where he lay. Before he knew it—he told us—he was out of the car and in the street where he seized a spade from a workman digging a ditch and he attacked them, screaming and brandishing the spade like a sword. They both fled and, when he regained control of himself, he was standing protectively over the bleeding body on the ground. Others quickly came to his assistance and an ambulance picked up the man he had saved. But by the time the police arrived to take a statement from him, he was shaking so much he could hardly speak to them.

As the story unfolded, he began to shake in the group and other members, knowing his history as they did, provided helpful analytic questions that took him back to memories of his childhood in London among other poor Irish families. His father's charm, lovely singing voice, and endearing ways were offset by violent outbursts against the mother when he was drunk. The sight of a defenceless person being beaten in the street took him straight back to forgotten but dreadful pictures of his mother's distraught body under the father's blows. As a boy, he said, he had been too little to protect her but he tells us—with prompting and support from the others—that now, as a big man himself, and armed with a spade, he could have finally brought his father down!

In the group, there are many further associations as people come forward with memories of childhoods blighted by injury, betrayal, and violence. Later, we sit in silence among these memories and associations. Beneath the descriptive content is a dynamic process that allows the return of the repressed. The violence of the external world has ruptured into the containing space of the group and now acts as a catalyst, bringing the range of early injury to the surface. The bad objects of childhood, frequently lost to conscious recollection, emerge in the group's analytic climate. It allows the original injuries and their associated emotions to undergo corrective recapitulation.

The session is nearing its end and I remind them that next week I shall be away. One of the group turns on me with a hostile attack. The ambivalence in her relationship means that I am sometimes the benevolent father she never had and, at other times, the inadequate father at whose hands she suffered. "How can you go away at a time like this? Here we are, talking about all these terrible things, and you just go sailing off." The return of the repressed is now expressed in the transference. She gets angrier still and I interpret the transference suggesting that her rage is perhaps based on a fear that like her father who went to war and came back a changed man three years later, I will come back next week wearing a rough khaki uniform, smelling of cigarettes and drink. She says, half in play, "I could murder you," and she snarls and chuckles at the same time. There is affection towards me evident in the tears in her eyes. "Perhaps you'd like Brendan's spade," I reply, "then you could really bring me down, just as he dreams of doing with his father." She does not say anything but it is clear she is struggling within herself and the struggle shows on her face. It is evident to the others also and is taken up and shared by the group.

Before we conclude, the whole group falls into a discussion in which they share with one another how angry they sometimes get with me. It is important that the anger is shared, discussed, acknowledged, and contained and that I am not provoked into retaliatory behavior. As we prepare to leave, Brendan receives a generous dose of affectionate concern from the others as they make sure that he will be all right driving away.

In the consulting room (2)

One year later, the same group, with a slightly different composition, is meeting, with the room filled with the subject of despondency.

Brendan tells us he is feeling worse and therapy is not helping him. Two women who know him well support each other in disagreeing with him. They say he is like a different person. He is sad about the end of a promising relationship after the breakup with a girlfriend but—unlike the past—he is neither withdrawn nor depressed. The therapist reminds him of an incident he shared with the group last year when he intervened during a street fight and saved someone from being badly beaten. Telling the group about it seemed to mark a turning point and he has been using the group experience in a more open way since. Someone reminds him of another of the violent incidents he has told us about, this one in the street when two men threatened him and he retaliated with such rage they fled. She says, "For a man with your gifts and words to live like a street fighter, what a waste! It's testosterone without intelligence, and yet you're so intelligent."

Another one of the men, a journalist, tells us how he was thrown into a rage by a newspaper that short-changed him on the payment schedule for his writing. It was a relief to have been able to bring these issues to the group over the last few weeks, he reminds us. He thinks back to his days at school when they used to beat up other children. He still has some kind of double-headed monster raging inside him. Looking around, he thinks we all have. It reminds him of the film his own children love to watch, *Shrek*. It is about a monster who is redeemed by love but when he finally meets his princess, the kiss changes her into a monster so she can join him and they live happily ever after.

There is an identification among us that allows each person to own their own hidden anger monsters. It takes place through the bonding, disclosure, mutual acceptance, and humor of the group.

The group's third man tells us more about his history of adoption. We knew he was given up for adoption, but this is the first time we hear his true emotions about this history of abandonment—being "given up"—and about his rescue. For the first six months of his life, he had no one except the care staff in the home. His adoptive mother had him from six months and nourished him throughout his childhood. But he knows that somewhere inside him there are frozen wastes. He has a Siberia somewhere in his heart and knows that this stands behind the history of difficulty in his relationships. That is where the anger monster lives. We are beginning to discover that behind the anger there is desolation—a bleak and empty inner world blighted by neglect and absence.

The uncovering dynamics of the group lead us from depression to numbness. They go back behind the numbness to identify rage; and they then go behind the rage to locate despondency that is seen to have its origins in the earliest experiences of uncertain and insecure attachment. The emotions of early insecurity are encapsulated in defensive character structures that seal off psychic states of despondency and abandonment that are withheld from conscious experience because they are too painful. Their consequences emerge instead as rage. External events act as triggers or targets onto which early affronts are projected and the ensuing rage attacks the early injurious other—whether this be mother or father—who is represented by the person responsible for a current provocation. This is the world inhabited by each of this group's members. In their repetition compulsions, fate neuroses, and ongoing difficulties in life, the originating traumata remain invisible. The group provides a containing resource by which, through mutual acceptance and then identification, we find the anger monsters in all of us. The matrix of experience that conditions the social unconscious of deeply injured people can also provide the vehicle for its repair. Their own anti-group propensities, if harnessed to self-examination, can yield insights that begin to melt the defences represented by Siberian desolation.

From the consulting room to the street

Now, we can extend this examination from the discourse of a small group to the subject matter of history itself. Let us look again at the street scene in Jerusalem and contrast it with the therapy group.

On the street, the injurious experience is an immediate and not a remote one. There is an overwhelming sense of shock. There are dead people to be taken account of and many more injured. The people here are distraught and their emotions cannot be contained. The knowledge that they too—like their dead friends—were intended for annihilation produces countering and retaliatory responses filled with the intention of counter-annihilation. Every other is a threat and every threat must be eliminated. The splitting dynamics are just as complete in the call for war as those internal and group dynamics that directed the perpetrator of this attack to commit his act of murder and self-destruction. Another most alarming consideration is the way in which people's relations with one another take a hysterical form, accentuating panic and fear and producing further internal forms of hatred. In his report to us, the student later gives an account of how he challenged those who wanted war, telling them that they made him ashamed to wear a kippah. "Well then," shouted the man who wanted to give war a chance, "throw your kippah on the ground, you loser." And the crowd turned angrily against the student. The anti-group, organized to defend itself against dangerous external objects has here found a bad internal object and, by rallying itself against this, the crowd finds security in a union of hostility against the single member of the in-group who stands outside the consensus. Difference cannot be lived with and those who carry "otherness" in any form have to be destroyed to maintain a world view based on threatening polarities. The other is an enemy, the enemy is the other, and those from the "in" group who do not see it this way run the risk of becoming enemies themselves. The push toward polarities is primitive and profound. In Israel, it destroyed Yitchak Rabin and in India, many years earlier, it destroyed Mohandas Gandhi. They were both victims of assassination at the hands of their own extremists.

Hopper's idea of aggregation (2000) and Nitsun's of the anti-group (1996) find their place in these constructions. The external attack and the knowledge and expectation of its repetition are one form of terror. The polarization and hatred within the group under attack come to constitute another form of terror. Here, we can see aggregation at work in the breakdown of social relations, splitting of a very primitive kind, scapegoating and a vengeful form of anti-group behavior. Zinkin's concept of malignant mirroring can be called on to help us with the further analysis of polarized dynamics where fear is amplified in circular conflicts that are systemic and self-reinforcing and which allow no perception of the other except as alien and antagonist. His term replaces, with a single process, the experience of two separate projective identifications that have a close, symmetrical, and hostile relationship with one another (Zinkin, 1983).

When whole populations are organized against each other on these terms, each side fears the threat of annihilation at the others' hands. The populace seen to be responsible for the threat is hated and those forms of conduct for which they are hated are visited upon them. Thus, they are subjected to the very violence they are blamed for, which is rationalized as "deterrence", "reprisal", or "revenge". As we are learning at terrible cost, the escalation of violence in order to prevent it has one of only two outcomes: the further escalation of violence or the subjugation of a cowed population from whom only future violence can be expected.

The analysis of hatred and polarization: four historical episodes

In situations where extremists on both sides determine policy for everyone else, we need to look closely at the subject of hatred. Freud saw hatred as the expression of instinctual, homicidal drives that expressed innate aggression. Only civilization, he thought, could lift us above these primitive affects (Freud, 1930a). Klein went on to refine his understanding of the death instinct (Klein, 1964), but Ferenczi, in Hungary (Ferenczi, 1994; Ferenczi & Rank,1986), and his student Balint (Balint, 1951) took issue with both Freud and Klein to formulate a view of hate as a secondary, rather than primary, emotion with its origins in traumatic or otherwise injurious experience. Examination of the large psychoanalytic literature and its controversies on the subject of hatred is beyond the scope of this chapter. These considerations are explored by Nitsun (1996) and de Zulueta (1993). For what follows, I rely on the premises laid out by Ferenczi and Balint that were taken into group theory by Nitsun and de Zulueta. The question I pose belongs as much in the world of culture and history as in the consulting room: What do we do with our hate objects?

I will consider four historical episodes that progress through the twentieth century and see what light they might shed on this question. The first is located in Spain during the Civil War, the second in Eastern Europe during the Holocaust, the third in Yugoslavia in the 1990s, and the fourth in the ongoing conflict between Israel and and its Arab residents and neighbours.

Episode 1: The Spanish Civil War

García Lorca was one of Spain's greatest poets. He was killed by the Nationalists during their Civil War and buried in a *barranco,* a ravine outside Granada. Gerald Brennan gives a moving account of his own return to Spain after the war and his attempt to find Lorca's grave (Brenan, 2010). The locals said his executioners were black and he was red and so he was led out with others to die like animals. They buried them in shallow pits and then pushed the earth over them. When Brennan asked if he might be moved to a cemetery, they replied, "Let them stay where they are. There are bodies buried like this in every barranco in Spain." In García Lorca's *Blood Wedding,* a play written years before his death but strangely prophetic of what was to befall him, the ground is saturated with the blood of loved ones who die with "no graveyard . . . [just] the couch of earth, the bed that shelters them and rocks in the sky" (García Lorca, 2005). Blood and soil run together in the imagery of those who have suffered most as they speak with the voice of those who cry for vengeance from below the ground. This combination of blood and soil is key to what follows in the analysis (Preston, 2012).

Episode 2: The Holocaust

My father's uncle came from Lithuania as a young man to visit his relatives in South Africa where we grew up. He played the mandolin, wore spats, and buffed his fingernails. He came to Johannesburg, considered his prospects there, and returned to his parental home in

Lithuania. His dress and habits made him a curiosity to local boys like my father, but this uncle thought they lived like barbarians in Johannesburg and he was pleased to get back to civilization in the Jewish society of Lithuania. Ten years later, he and his young wife were exterminated, victims of the first systematic killing of the Holocaust in what one SS general called a shooter's paradise (Schlapobersky, 2002). Their only daughter survived as a hidden child and was rescued after the war by an aunt who came out of a concentration camp (Shlapobersky, 2011). These sole survivors of a once numerous family moved to Israel in the 1950s. They left behind killing fields that stand outside every town and village in the Baltic States, Byelorussia, Eastern Poland, and Ukraine. These are the markers of the first stage of the Final Solution when the Einzatzgruppen, led and trained by Heidrich, killed almost half Europe's Jews. This experience formed the basis on which, at the Wansee Conference in Berlin in 1942, for reasons of expediency and economy, they devised gas chambers—industrial rather than military methods—to try and kill the remaining Jews of Europe (Rhodes, 2002).

When it became possible to travel in Eastern Europe, I visited the site where my father's uncles and aunts are buried, guided by the testimony of the only survivor. This survivor describes a pit, three meters wide, three meters deep and ninety meters long, located on the bank of a small river beside a country lane. More than 3,000 Jews are buried here, thrown onto the bodies of the Russian prisoners of war who first dug the pits and whose numbers and identity are even more obscure. This witness was there first as victim and then—after escaping—he returned as a Russian soldier to liberate his country. He was the sole survivor and reports how he stood at the grave of his family with his gun in his hand and heard his mother's voice calling on him from below the ground to take revenge. Who can blame her? Who would judge him? (Rander, quoted in Oshry, 1951, pp. 288–291). His testimony gives no account of the revenge he might or might not have taken. And what of justice? If revenge is the call from below the ground, is justice a call from above it? Did they get either? Joseph Harmatz was one of the few survivors to tell his own story in any detail and has argued that where revenge relates to the past, justice relates to the future (Harmatz, 1998).

The shadows cast by Europe's killing fields continue to haunt us all. In town after town, communities perished in their entirety. In

Keidan, the killing took three days. Here is the testimony provided by this sole survivor:

> I want to tell in a few words of the fate of the town of Keidan. Chaim Rander was the only one of the 3700 Jews who managed to escape from the mass grave (and) he described how the Keidaner Jews were killed. (Among this number, were Jews of the Shat and Jassowa, districts of Keidan.) I quote from one of his letters written to his sister:
>
> "I am the only one who witnessed how our infants, our old people and our women were shot, torn apart and buried half alive. On the 15th of August, 1941, the Jews of the whole town were driven out, and confined in a barn on a farm near Keidan. For thirteen whole days they tortured us. There was the old Rabbi Feinsilber with nineteen Yeshivah students of the Mir Yeshivah, who could not travel with the rest of the Yeshivah because they had not yet received their visas from the Russian Government. Also with them was the Dayan of Keidan, Rabbi Aron Galin, the y'd, the son-in-law of the Keidaner Rov. There were women, children, old weak and ill people. My ears can still hear the groans of the 'gelen shuster' [red-headed cobbler], Yossel Wolpert, who dragged himself, along on the ground, sick and weak. I shall never forget the cries and wails of Sholem Chait, whom they brought, ill, on a garbage wagon when they threw him off onto the ground. I still see Hershel Lubiatkin standing before my eyes. He could not bear the hardship and hanged himself . . . and many more tragedies arise before my eyes. I see how they shot Rabbi Zalman Frank, because he was too old (a very learned man, the son of the Nemeneitzer Rov), Malkele and Motele because they were too young, Gese Rabinowitz's daughter because she was too pretty, Benny Rander, Moshe Zalmenowitz, Feivel Friedland and others—because they were 'responsible for starting the War against the "innocent" Hitler-clique'.
>
> Zadek Schlapobersky died as a hero, taking the German Commandant with him into the grave. He also ripped out the throat of a Lithuanian murderer, one of the police guards.
>
> I went back to Keidan, gun in hand, and I stood at the mass grave in Datnever Street. It is 90 meters long, three meters wide, and three meters deep. It was sown with oats, and through the earth I heard the voice of my old mother and acquaintances calling out to me: 'Chaim, Chaim nem nekomeh! (Chaim, Chaim, take revenge!'). On that spot at their grave-side, I swore that I would take revenge." (Rander, quoted in Oshry, 1951)

I visited the killing fields in Keidan in the autumn of 1992. I was there with my mother, whose own parents had been born in towns nearby and we had a guide–translator and a driver with us who both came from the remnants of the country's surviving Jewish community.

We searched to find the site for some time, guided by Ronder's written testimony. On finding it, we stood in silence in the peace of the willows with the gentle movement of the river below. You could not imagine that a site so peaceful, something like a cricket pitch but longer, wider, and surrounded by trees, could hold so much horror. There was a somber memorial plaque to one side dedicated to the 3,500 buried at this site and, written during the Communist era, they were identified only as victims of "The Hitlerite Fascists and their Lithuanian collaborators". A subsequent inscription on the same plaque, written both in Yiddish—the language they spoke—and in Hebrew, identifies them as Jews. As we stood in strange reverie, we heard a party of children coming up from the river, chatting as they went. We could see their fishing rods as they approached through the vegetation and heard their dogs barking. It was as innocent as anything could be, but our interpreter turned to me with a dismay I could not understand. Then the four children appeared on the path a meter away with the dogs now barking furiously and they all stopped as they saw us, as if transfixed. Then they ran away at a great pace with their fishing rods bouncing and the dogs bounding ahead. The interpreter did her job and explained that she heard one of them say to another, before they saw us, "I wonder what the dogs are barking at—perhaps they're barking at all those dead Jews?" The next moment they saw us and realized why the dogs had been barking. Did they know we were live Jews? Did they think we were ghosts?

These children's grandparents, perhaps those named in the plaque at the massacre site as "the Lithuanian collaborators of the Hitlerite fascists", heard a call "from below the ground", and it called on them to kill. It was explained to me that over that period in Lithuanian history the world had one of two colours. If you were not red, you could only be black. To protect yourself against reds, you had to do what was required of blacks. In this case, the blacks had to kill Jews, who were obviously red. The chilling simplicity of this spurious logic makes polarization a "strategic necessity". But it is not only the children of perpetrators who have to deal with ghosts. They live among us all, and we call this the social unconscious. An Auschwitz survivor I came across by chance in Croatia one summer, a professor of literature with his number across his forearm, said the smoke from those chimneys has contaminated all of us. I discovered what he meant in my own capacity to hate and in the wish to kill.

During a recent visit to Yad Vashem, I found myself going through its familiar displays in the presence of small units of young Israeli soldiers. They were obviously in training and attended fully armed, accompanied by their trainers and officers. Nearing the end of the exhibition—as one comes to a point where there are virtually no Jews left in Europe, only shoes and other artifacts, and the austere landscape of Auschwitz is laid out—one of the young soldiers dropped an ammunition magazine and its bullets scattered on the floor. I helped him pick up some of the bullets and, as I handed them to him, I wanted them back and I wanted to have his weapon too—I wanted to shoot the Nazis. It did not matter where they were. It did not even matter if they no longer existed—a Palestinian would do! In a momentary impulse I knew that I could shoot anyone who looked as if they were once again threatening Jews.

Episode 3: Yugoslavia

We might look into the darker side of terror survived by considering a different people. In Yugoslavia, the failure to acknowledge the enormity of what had befallen large sectors of the population sowed the seeds of another tragedy with blood in the soil. At Jasenovac, the death camp in Croatia, a number close to half a million people perished during the Second World War, Jews, Gypsies, and Serbs, victims of the black Ustasi, the Croatians who worked with the Nazis. In the years of communist administration, shock and numbness gave way to scarcely conscious dreams of vengeance. Denial, dissociation, and displacement at the individual level have generational implications which, when expressed later in political form, lead to primitive talion law, the quest of a life for a life. Retribution is sought against identified hate objects in the delusional belief that mass murder is a form of "cleansing". As the country's fragile federation disintegrated, the Serbian identification of both Croatians and Muslims as hate objects led to a program of mass murder, pillage, and rape blithely referred to as "ethnic cleansing", cultivated and orchestrated by demagogues who used public fear and insecurity to bolster their own positions. Three of the most notorious of these architects of ethnic cleansing have been prosecuted for war crimes and crimes against humanity at the International Criminal Court in The Hague: Milošević, Karadžić, and Mladić. Fear is engendered in circular conflicts of a systemic and self-reinforcing kind that allow no perception of the other except as alien and antagonist. Difference cannot be lived with and those who carry "otherness" in any form have to be destroyed to eliminate threatening polarities. We know too little about the circumstances that lead a voice from below the ground to bury the living with the dead. Those who carry out genocidal programs are the epitome of dead men walking, wanderers in a dream world they occupy with their own forsaken people below the ground, whom they protect by carnage against "the other".

In the summer of 1995, the Muslim residents of Bihac, Gorazde, Srebrenica, and Zepa were hunted and pursued through Bosnia from one threatened enclave to another. A Serbian general Mladić, led the pursuing soldiers. He was finally captured, brought to trial, and the Government of Serbia entered a formal apology for their complicity. It emerged that Mladjić lost many of his own family a generation earlier at Jasenovac. At the time, however, we saw his victims congregate in safe areas in which the United Nations guaranteed their protection. And then we saw them bombed in their houses and finally taken from their homes and places of refuge. Everyone with a television set became a witness to mass murder in which entire towns were stripped of their men, who were shot in batches and buried in remote places. The perpetrators of "ethnic cleansing" were condemned by their own words that revealed their intentions—to destroy another people. Many of the former residents of these "safe areas" lie in mass graves and the most recent of Europe's killing fields is occupied now largely by Muslim victims. What could have been done for the Serb victims of the Second World War to pre-empt this primitive talion law? Their tragic fate was enacted a generation later against another set of victims. And what can now be done for their victims, the Muslims who suffer the voice from below the ground of those who cry for vengeance (Glenny, 1996; Rohde, 2012; Suljagic, 2005)?

Episode 4: Arab–Israeli conflict

Israeli military policy has the notorious event of Qibya early in its history. Martin Gilbert writes that:

> On 13 October 1953 an Israeli mother and her two children . . . were killed by infiltrators from across the Jordan border. On the following night Unit 101, together with a unit of regular paratroopers, carried out a reprisal raid on the Arab village of Qibya, only a few hundred yards from the border. Sharon commanded the raid. In his memoirs he recalled, "The orders were clear. Kibya was to be a lesson. I was to inflict as many casualties as I could on the Arab Home guard and on whatever Jordanian reinforcements showed up. I was also to blow up every major building in the town." The written instructions to the group from army headquarters were to "carry out destruction and maximum killing in order to drive the villagers from their homes". During the raid, 69 Arabs were killed, most of them women and children, and 45 Arab houses blown up.
>
> The world outcry was enormous, and inside Israel there was much heart-searching. A public cover-up attempt was made by Ben-Gurion to present the raid as a spontaneous reprisal by outraged Israeli civilian farmers. Moshe Sharrett called the raid "a serious error". Henceforth, the nature of reprisals changed. Israeli forces were ordered to strike at Arab military targets rather than villages or towns. (Gilbert, 1998, p. 292)

The events of the Sabra and Shatilla Massacre of 1982 during the Israeli invasion of Lebanon, in which Palestinian civilians were killed in their thousands by Christian militia under the watching eyes of the Israeli Defence Force, require no repetition here. But the recognition of its antecedent factors including the Damour Massacre of 1976, when the Christians suffered mass murder at the hands of Lebanese Muslims, only strengthens this analysis. The human cost of violent deterrence creates another cycle of terror visited upon civilians, serving only to make counter-reprisal all the more predictable. The strategic consequences of an escalating cycle of violence confer legitimacy on the further use of military action but, unfortunately, the consequences of this policy only reinforce the cycle.

Where did it begin? Abba Kovner was among the best known survivors of the Partisans of Vilna. His partner, Ruzka Korczak, is quoted at the opening of this chapter and again below. They arrived in Palestine in 1946 and recent publications give a picture of how they established, with others, a group called The Avengers who set out to exact revenge by poisoning the food and water supplies of prison camps in Europe in which the Allies held large numbers of Waffen SS and Gestapo officers. Kovner was thwarted by Ben Gurion and others, who had the British administration place him under arrest. He was released and won away from continuing with his "partisan" action by a plea from Ben Gurion, who is reported to have prevailed upon him with the argument: "We will take our retribution against Germany as a state." States require statesmanship from their leaders. The report of this exchange gives a picture of street fighters being won over to the conduct of statesmen, and Kovner went on to play a distinguished and statesman-like role in foundation work for the State of Israel (Cohen, 2001; Kovner, 1981).

When the learning gained from the study of the small group are applied to this historical pattern, there are simple questions to be posed. To what extent do political and military leaders remain street fighters acting in the service of escalating violence? And to what extent can they become statesmen whose grasp of history can avert its tragic consequences?

Cycles of conflict and the generational transmission of trauma

What can group analysis contribute to understanding the dynamics of these histories and the current murderous crises that rage around us? Can we take these questions and apply them now to the questions posed at the outset of our study? Repetitive patterns in our social and political conflicts are amenable to analysis. The patterns repay close scrutiny and pattern recognition can always allow change. If we take the conduct of Israeli military strategy, has it served to defend the country against its accurately perceived enemies? Or is there some chance that the real and current threats are conflated with those in the country's immediate past? The religious history of the Jews is built on this kind of conflation. The Amalekites, who are described in the Torah harassing the weak and vulnerable during the years that the Israelites wandered in the desert, are found again in the Book of Esther thousands of years and hundreds of kilometers away, where they are described as Hamman's kinsmen responsible for plotting to kill the Jews of Persia. The destruction of the first and second Temples is separated by 650 years. Rabbinic authority has fixed the commemoration of both these events on the same day of mourning—the ninth day of Av. It is hard to believe that Titus's Roman legions knew and chose the date of Nebuchadnezzar's assault on the Temple six centuries earlier for their final attack on the Temple Mount. But we can see the underlying psychology that must have informed the rabbinic intentions in fixing the two occasions on the same commemorative date (Johnson, 1987).

The two attacks are held in the same region of the mind because the threat of annihilation is always the same threat. However, not all enemies merit the same response and not all threats are annihilatory. Those who treat all their adversaries alike discover, to their surprise and, indeed, dismay, that they are treated alike in turn. The bad objects that Brendan seemed to always find in his daily life—in the group described above—changed apparently of their own accord during his time in therapy. Thanks to this hard work, he is no longer at risk of violent enactments when he encounters the aggression of others. But can we say the same of ourselves?

External and current threats need to be differentiated one from another and all of them stand apart from internal and historical threats. Returning to the study of the group, Brendan attacked two people who threatened a third. This was not innate aggression in the service of instinctual drives, the kind of blind hatred that Freud's early arguments directed us towards. This man was in the grip of a precise constellation of object conflicts that led him to conflate hate objects seen in one threat with the prior experience of another. It was fortunate for the threatened individual on the ground that this man came by at the time, but his reactions could have resulted in violence of a very extreme form that could have seen Brendan gravely injured himself or imprisoned for injuring others. External events act as triggers or targets onto which early affronts are projected and the ensuing rage attacks the person responsible for a current provocation. The attack is, however, really intended for the early injurious other. We saw this as the world inhabited by each of this group's members. In their repetition compulsions, fate neuroses, and ongoing difficulties in life, the originating traumata remained invisible.

Is this not the world we inhabit, too? It would be far-fetched to suggest that Israel's position has ever been safe. The armies of five nations mobilized on the declared basis of a combined mission to destroy the country on the day it was born. In the course of the wars that have taken place from then until now, and with the loss of more than 20,000 lives, Israel has proved itself capable of defending its people against external threats. But what now of the Arab populations around and within it, with whom different forms of engagement are imperative? Are the originating traumata associated with the formation of the State of Israel—the experience of near annihilation in the Holocaust and the threats during the War of Independence—going to so distort people's capacity to relate to others as to create a permanent and atavistic paranoia? There is an apocryphal account of an exchange between Henry Kissinger and Golda Meir when she was Prime Minister, in which he charged her—and her associates—with paranoia. "Yes," she is supposed to have said, "We are. But just because we're paranoid it doesn't mean they're not out to get us!" (Burke & Sabbadini, 1993).

Paranoia is most commonly described in psychiatry as a self-fulfilling fear. What modest contribution can psychotherapists make to unraveling the fantasies and the realities? To believe we have no role to play in these difficult times is to underestimate the work done elsewhere in situations just as challenging and difficult. We know that psychotherapists, physicians, and others, played a decisive role in the de-escalation of the Cold War; they did so too in laying the groundwork for the Oslo Accords and in reducing the hostile interface between the Nationalist Government in South Africa and the African National Congress during the last phase of apartheid. During the process that appears to have "taken the gun out of Irish politics", with the Good Friday Agreements and the development of democratic process in the North, mental health professionals played a decisive role, inspired by the work of John Alderdice. The Oxford Research Group in the UK has developed principles for confidential engagement with leaders and decision-makers in situations of acute conflict and, more recently, The International Dialogue Initiative, led by Volkan, Alderdice, and Friedman, has brought together a small group of experts and scholars from diverse disciplines and countries (Austria, Egypt, Germany, India, Iran, Israel, Jordan, Russia, Turkey, the UAE, the UK, and the USA) for a series of meetings to discuss topics and examine processes related to international tensions, especially between the Islamic world and the West.

Conclusion: the gifts of adversity

The fabric of ordinary society carries the potential to lift tensions from the vicious circles of scarcity and conflict and transform them into relations of benevolence and mutual nurture. These are the gifts of adversity. This phrase, the gifts of adversity, is an illuminating one recently coined by Rosenthal (2013), with an ancient history. It captures the essentials of the struggle for regeneration in the aftermath of injury that will have many applications in psychotherapy. The groups we run are designed to set up conditions for this kind of transformation and they stand as one among many of society's regenerative resources. Foulkes, in one of his most influential chapters, "Concerning leadership", describes how

> The spirit in which groups are conducted and the qualities required on the part of the conductor have an essential affinity to education according to the concepts of a democratic way of life and for good world citizenship. (Foulkes, 1964)

Regenerative resources: Example 1

"I will teach you to read and write, and that will be our victory against them."

The first example concerns an Iranian asylum seeker who came to the UK from Teheran, where he had been held by the revolutionary guard in the notorious Evin prison. At the Medical Foundation for Victims of Torture in London, we ran a Group Work Programme since our inception in 1986; this man was one of the first to join.

He had been a teacher before his arrest and in prison, living in a communal cell, he was helped by others to come to terms with the sight of his dead brother's mutilated body. With their help, he regained his physical strength after torture and he became known as the teacher. At one point, he comforted someone who had been brutally beaten by the guards saying, "Old man, we can't strike them back, but whilst we're both here I will teach you to read and to write and that will be our victory against them." He found his own way of fighting back: he called on the coping strategies and natural resilience of his past life as a teacher to survive; he reached out and shared this resilience with the others. He survived by working as a teacher; he taught others to survive and, by helping others, he equipped himself. He was guided by value positions that were not the symmetrical reactions of hatred and vengeance. Their victory against barbarity was the struggle for literacy in the most inclement of conditions.

Example 2

"We are here!"

The second example concerns the survivors of the Holocaust in Lithuania and those words passed down from their ordeal. Hirsch Glick, in a song, *Zog Nit Keinmol,* composed an anthem for those who fought against impossible odds. It spread throughout the ghettos and camps and became a symbol of hope and defiance. It was adopted by Jewish partisans, became known as "Song of the Partisans," and inspired Jews to fight if they could, but if they could not fight, at least to survive. After the war, it was taken up by Jewish communities around the world and continues to be sung as a memorial. It is included by some families in their *Seder* night Passover service.

Mir zeinen do

> Never say you are walking your last road;
> Leaden skies conceal blue days!
> The hour we have longed for with all
> Our longing will yet come–
> Our step will beat out like a drum:
> *We Are Here.*

It includes a verse which asserts that:

> This song (will) go from generation to
> Generation like a password.

Although the authors of the words and music did not survive, their words have provided strength to many since. The heroism and courage that the song both expresses and inspires have formed an integral part of Israel's extraordinary story. Among the generation after the Holocaust, Jews throughout the world would come to their feet when singing this song in honour of both those who perished and those who fought. Our late father searched among his books to find the Yiddish words for the song's different verses as he was dying, and they gave him strength and comfort at the end. During the Second World War, he had been a frontline combatant in the British Eighth Army in Italy where, in 1945–1946, large numbers of Jewish survivors assembled in Displaced Persons Camps prior to embarkation for Palestine. He learned these words from them and, when he died more than fifty years later, we inscribed the phrase "*Mir zeinen do,*" "*We are here,*" on his tombstone.

But it is not only courage and heroism that went like a password from one generation to the next among Jews worldwide. Tragically, there is also something much darker, more problematic, and less visible. Thanks to the work of practitioners in Israel, notably through the writing of Bar On (1989, 1995, 1998), Danieli (1998), Wardi (1992), and others, the term "intergenerational transmission of trauma" has been coined and the set of concepts by which it identifies this process is now in worldwide clinical use.

The state of mind of those having to deal with overwhelming and traumatic loss is best given by Kovner himself. In "The Candle of Anonymity", he says,

> "They stood among heaps of ashes, a flaming stone in their hearts.
> City—how mourn a city whose people are dead
> And whose dead are alive in the heart?"
>
> (Kovner, 1981, p. 50)

Ruzka Korczak, his partner, with whom he spent the remaining years of his life in Israel, had also been one of the leaders of the Partisans of Vilna and one of the few to survive. As she settled in what was then Palestine and gave talks about their life as partisans:

> She asked her audiences to remember a Jewish town from which not a single person survived, a town as lost to us as those ancient civilizations of which we know not even the name. Then she spoke of hate, which she said kept her alive in the War, a thirst for revenge: the desire to kill one more German, blow up one more train. Though the need for revenge, she said, would never go away, she had to come to see, while travelling through Palestine, that the nature of revenge could change: "We can now think of revenge with a plow as we once carried automatic weapons and grenades. Why chase the dead when the living are here to be cared for?" (Korczak, quoted in Cohen, 2001, pp. 187–188)

Example 3

"The truth untold [is] the pity of war, the pity war distilled."

Wilfred Owen's "Strange Meeting" was written months before he was killed in the closing days of the First World War. This poem became an anthem for the lost youth of Britain. Here, he finds words with which to distil the pity of war by focusing on the humanity of his enemy.

Strange Meeting

It seemed that out of battle I escaped
Down some profound dull tunnel, long since scooped
Through granites which titanic wars had groined.

Yet also there encumbered sleepers groaned,
Too fast in thought or death to be bestirred.
Then, as I probed them, one sprang up, and stared
With piteous recognition in fixed eyes,
Lifting distressful hands, as if to bless.
And by his smile, I knew that sullen hall, –
By his dead smile I knew we stood in Hell.
. . .

"Strange friend," I said, here is no cause to mourn."
"None," said that other, "save the undone years,
The hopelessness. Whatever hope is yours,
Was my life also . . .
For by my glee might many men have laughed,
And of my weeping something had been left,
Which must die now. I mean the truth untold,
The pity of war, the pity war distilled".

(Owen, 1994, p. 35)

There are many working across the divisions of society as individuals, groups, and institutions who manifest courage not only in the heroism of war but, equally, by making friends of their enemies.

References

Amichai, Y. (2013). The Diameter of the Bomb was Thirty Centimeters. In: *The Selected Poetry of Yehuda Amichai* (p. 118), C. Bloch & S. Mitchell (Trans.). Berkeley, CA: University of California Press.

Balint, M. (1985/1951). On love and hate. In: *Primary Love and Psychoanalytic Technique* (pp. 141–156). London: Maresfield Library (Karnac).

Bar On, D. (1989). *Legacy of Silence: Encounters with Children of the Third Reich*. Cambridge, MA: Harvard University Press.

Bar On, D. (1995). *Fear and Hope: Three Generations of Holocaust Survivors' Families*. Cambridge, MA: Harvard University Press.

Bar On, D. (1998). *The Indescribable and the Undiscussable: Reconstructing Human Discourse After Trauma*. Plymouth: Central European University Press.

Brenan, G. (2010). *The Face of Spain*. London: Serif.

Brown, D., & Zinkin, L. (1995). *The Psyche and the Social World*. London: Jessica Kingsley, 2000.

Burke, J., & Sabbadini, A. (1993). *Paranoia and Persecution*. London: Routledge.

Cohen, R. (2001). *The Avengers: A Jewish War Story*. London: Vintage.

Danieli, Y. (1998). *International Handbook of Multigenerational Legacies of Trauma*. New York: Plenum Press.

De Zulueta, F. (1993). *From Pain To Violence: The Traumatic Roots of Destructiveness*. London: Whurr.

Donne, J. (1987). Meditation 17 from *Devotions Upon Emergent Occasions*, A. Raspa (Ed.) (pp. 187–188). Oxford: Oxford University Press.

Ferenczi, S. (1994). *Final Contributions to the Problems & Methods of Psycho-Analysis*. London: Karnac.

Ferenczi, S., & Rank, O. (1986). *Development of Psychoanalysis* (Classics in Psychoanalysis, Monograph 4). New York: International Universities Press.

Foulkes, S. H. (1964). *Therapeutic Group Analysis*. London: George Allen and Unwin [reprinted London: Karnac, 1986].

Foulkes, S. H. (1975). *Group Analytic Psychotherapy: Method and Principles*. London: Gordon and Breach [reprinted London: Karnac, 1986].

Freud, S. (1930a). *Civilization and its Discontents*. *S. E., 21*: 59–145. London: Hogarth.

García Lorca, F. (2005). *Blood Wedding*, T. Ronder (Ed.). London: Nick Hern Books.

Gilbert, M. (1998). *Israel: A History*. London: Doubleday.

Glenny, M. (1996). *The Fall of Yugoslavia: The Third Balkan War*. London: Penguin.

Grossman, D. (2003). *Death as a Way of Life: Dispatches from Jerusalem*. London: Bloomsbury.

Harmatz, J. (1998). *From the Wings: A Long Journey 1940–1960*. Lewes, Sussex: The Book Guild.

Hopper, E. (2000). *Traumatic Experience in the Unconscious Life of Groups: A Fourth Basic Assumption.* London: Jessica Kingsley.
Johnson, P. (1987). *A History of The Jews.* London: Weidenfeld and Nicolson.
Klein, M. (1964). *Love, Hate, and Reparation.* New York: W. W. Norton.
Kovner, A. (1981). *Scrolls of Fire.* Jerusalem: Keter.
Nitsun, M. (1996). *The Anti-Group—Destructive Forces in the Group and Their Creative Potential.* London: Routledge.
Oshry, Rabbi Ephraim (1951). *Hurbn Lite: Destruction of the Sacred Communities of Lithuania,* C. Ginsberg (Trans.). New York/Montreal: Jewish Book Committee, pp. 288–291 [reprinted as: *The Annihilation of Lithuanian Jewry.* New York: Judaica Press, 1995].
Owen, W. (1994). Strange Meeting. In: *The Poems of Wilfred Owen* (p. 35), J. Stallworthy (Ed.). London: Chatto and Windus.
Preston, P. (2012). *The Spanish Holocaust: Inquisition and Extermination in Twentieth-Century Spain.* London: Harper Press.
Rhodes, R. (2002). *Masters of Death: The Einzatzgruppen and The Invention of The Holocaust.* New York: Vintage.
Rohde, D. (2012). *Endgame: The Betrayal and Fall of Srebrenica, Europe's Worst Massacre Since World War II.* New York: Farrar, Straus and Giroux.
Rosenthal, N. (2013). *The Gift of Adversity.* New York: Jeremy P. Tarcher/ Penguin.
Schlapobersky, J. (2002). My father's uncle played the mandolin: reflections on the killing fields of Europe. *Mikbatz: The Israeli Journal of Group Psychotherapy, 7*(1): 68–75.
Schlapobersky, J. (2016). *From the Couch to the Circle: Group-Analytic Psychotherapy In Practice.* London: Routledge.
Schlapobersky, R. (2011). From darkness to light. In: S. Abramovich & Y. Zilberg (Eds.), *Smuggled in Potato Sacks: Fifty Storiesof the Hidden Children of the Kovno Ghetto* (pp. 231–240). London: Vallentine Mitchell.
Shakespeare, W. (1991). *Julius Caesar.* New York: Dover Thrift.
Soloway, Rabbi M. (2002). Personal communication by email.
Suljagic, E. (2005). *Postcards From The Grave.* London: Saqi Books.
Tolstoy, L. (1982). *War and Peace,* R. Edmonds (Trans.). London: Penguin Classics.
Volkan, V. D. (2001). Transgenerational transmissions and chosen traumas: an aspect of large-group identity. *Group Analysis, 34*: 79–97.
Wardi, D. (1992). *Memorial Candles: Children of The Holocaust.* London: Routledge.
Zinkin, L. (1983). Malignant mirroring. *Group Analysis, 16*: 113–126.

PART II

PROCESSES OF BUILDING AN INTERPERSONAL BRIDGE IN THE GROUP

CHAPTER THREE

Forgiving and non-forgiving in group analysis

Gila Ofer

From the place where we are right
Flowers will never grow
in the spring.
The place where we are right
is hard and trampled
like a yard.
But doubts and loves
dig up the world
like a mole, a plow.
And a whisper will be heard in the place
where the ruined
House once stood.

(Amichai, 2013, p. 34)

Forgiveness is most important for the continuity of interpersonal relationships, and has an immense impact on the mental, and possibly on the physical, health (Thoresen et al., 2000) of both the victim and the perpetrator, on their creativity, vitality, and other aspects of their life (McCullough & Witvliet, 2002; McCullough et al., 2000). However, the process of forgiving might be difficult to accomplish and, thus, there is an ambivalent attitude towards it. There are two stages in the process of forgiving: the first is reparation and self-reflection; the second is an interpersonal, intersubjective relational process. The structure and culture of group analysis provides a space in which witnessing and vicarious forgiveness contribute to this process.

Forgiving and non-forgiving in group therapy

This chapter addresses the issue of forgiving and not forgiving as both a process and an action which might follow an offense, as some act committed by the offender which has hurt someone.

Forgiveness is a mental, emotional, or spiritual process through which a person stops feeling offended or angry toward another person in relation to an action they considered offensive, controversial, or erroneous. Alternatively, forgiveness is the discontinuation of the demand for punitive or restorative actions. Finally, forgiveness could be seen as a decision to let go of the past, that is, to accept the fact that what's done is done and is now unalterable. Note that these definitions are negative, stating what forgiveness is not and what one has to give up: giving up a grudge, giving up one's due after being offended, putting an end to resentment.

The issue of forgiveness is cardinal to both the viability of interpersonal relationships and to the mental wellbeing of the offended party and, quite often, the offender. Throughout life, one is subjected to offenses, insults, or traumas at the hands of others, and one's taking offense could be either realistic or an overreaction. The ability to deal effectively and adaptively with narcissistic injuries at the hands of other persons is a lifelong human challenge. Even the infant, the child, has to come to terms with the anger and rage that are the outcome of frustrations at the hands of caretakers. Developing a capacity for forgiveness has a considerable influence on interpersonal relationships and even one's creativity, productivity, and health (Horwitz, 2005). Nevertheless, forgiveness entails much difficulty and ambivalence, which are made manifest in our twofold treatment of the subject. Horwitz's (2005) main point is that forgiving is a capacity. This capacity is largely related to the degree to which a person has been able to overcome splitting tendencies and to achieve an integration of self and object representations. It is related more to other relational capacities, such as those for concern, being alone, reparation, and mourning, than to ego capacities such as reality testing, impulse control, and tolerance of anxiety. In this context, Horwitz also classifies mentalization as a relational capacity, since it is defined as the ability to understand how motives and needs influence behavior and as it encourages the individual to empathize with the emotional reactions of others, including perpetrators, providing the infrastructure for the taxing process of forgiving.

In our everyday lives, the expression "I'm sorry" is one of the most often used parts of our vocabulary. Nevertheless, I found that, until recently, the majority of the conceptual material written about forgiveness was mostly restricted to Christian or theological journals such as *Christianity Today*, or *The Scottish Journal of Theology*. Quite surprisingly, psychoanalytic literature has been rather silent on this matter or, as Akhtar says, "Psychoanalysis has had little to say about forgiveness (2002, p. 175). In group analysis, even fewer papers have related to this topic (Urlich et al., 2010; Van Noort, 2003).

Some might argue that forgiveness is irrelevant to psychoanalysis (for possible reasons, see Akhtar, 2002; see also Smith, 2008). Those who do see it as relevant claim that the ability to forgive is related to one's early development, as well as the intersubjective sphere. Therefore, the current theory holds that the inability to forgive is primarily a developmental disorder, related to the fear of retraumatization as the result of further offense and the offended party's shame at letting him or herself be hurt.

The lacuna involving forgiveness in psychoanalytic literature that has existed up to the present day, as well as the renewed endeavor to address the subject, could be explained in several ways.

1. Forgiveness had always been a major element in the various religions, so that it might have been perceived as being "out of bounds" for psychoanalysis. It has been tied up with the bible, religion, and theological disputes. McCullough and colleagues (2000, p. 3) relate this theoretical "neglect" to "traditional links between forgiveness and religious belief, and to social sciences' aversion to religious matters".
2. Asking for forgiveness and being forgiven are sometimes considered insincere or thought to be reaction formations, like turning the other cheek, suppressing anger, or a form of masochism.

3. For most of its existence, psychoanalysis saw itself as a one-person psychology, focusing on intrapsychic processes. Forgiveness was viewed as a behavioral activity, belonging to the interpersonal realm and having nothing to do with one's inner workings. Only recently has the emphasis on relational and intersubjective aspects of experience made room for a two-person psychology.
4. The feuds and bloodshed between and within peoples the world over—Syria, Israel and the Palestinians, England and Ireland, South Africa, the former Soviet Union, Angola—and the longing to achieve peace have brought the possibility of reconciliation to the fore. Most notable in this context are the Truth and Reconciliation Committees founded in South Africa following Nelson Mandela's conciliatory vision. In this context, psychoanalytic theories have been spurred by political events to reconceptualize forgiveness and consider its role in contemporary personal and social life (Volkan, 2001 and this volume).

Generally speaking, the issue of forgiveness evokes a certain emotional ambivalence concerning it. Forgiveness often plays a role in restoring a relationship with a love, or once-loved, object in reclaiming the injured and often dissociated parts of the psyche. The capacity for forgiveness is tremendously important, indicating the existence of ego capabilities and emotional maturity, thus facilitating sounder interpersonal relationships. When the offense was acute, however, the desire for vengeance often hinders or precludes forgiveness. Empirical and other studies have related the ability to forgive to good mental health, demonstrating that people who forgive are happier and healthier than those who withhold forgiveness and cultivate grudges (Thoresen et al., 2000). However, forgiveness could also be a manifestation of pathological constellation. For example, forgiveness could sometimes be considered as an expression of denial or disavowal of internal or external traumatic reality, as if one were saying, "This never happened", or "This really has no significance". Some people even develop a chronic need to accept and forgive as quickly as possible. This is characteristic of placating, masochistic, or destructive personalities, which tend to view the offender as a victim and, thus, engender a false and superficial forgiveness (Akhtar, 2009).

The ambivalence surrounding forgiveness is expressed in the Bible and in both Judaism and Christianity. On the one hand, Judaism obliges the offended party to forgive and reconcile if the offender expressed remorse. Christianity equally considers forgiveness to be a religious duty, imposed on every believer: "as the Lord has forgiven you, so you also must forgive" (Colossians, 3:13). On the other hand, while the Bible acknowledges the value of forgiveness, it holds at least one example of an extremely unforgiving attitude: While the passing of time and generations effaces even the sins and offenses of one's worst enemies, the Torah admonishes against applying this human tendency to the Amalekites:

> Remember what Amalek did unto thee by the way, when ye were come forth out of Egypt; How he met thee by the way, and smote the hindmost of thee, even all that were feeble behind thee, when thou wast faint and weary; . . . Therefore it shall be, when the Lord thy God hath given thee rest from all thine enemies round about, . . . that thou shalt blot out the remembrance of Amalek from under heaven; thou shalt not forget it. (Deuteronomy, 25, 17–19)

Note that this injunction is applicable regardless of time, place, or circumstance. It became so central that the Talmud defines it as one of the three first *mitzvahs* (commandments) to be fulfilled as soon as the people of Israel become a sovereign people. Failure to carry out this mission led to King Saul losing his crown. This indicates how, when the narcissistic injury is most severe—as when Amalek targeted the weak and faltering when the people were tired and weary—no forgiveness is possible.

I would like to suggest that the process of forgiving includes two stages. The first involves intrapersonal reparation: for true forgiveness to take place, reparation must occur as a reflective, internal process. The second stage involves an interpersonal process: a contact between the offended and offending parties, which includes an admission of the wrong that was done.

The internal stage

True forgiveness must entail a meaningful internal process that comes face to face with the depth of the emotions brought about by the offense. Pain and anger must be processed both consciously and unconsciously. If the anger, the need for vengeance, and the sorrow stemming from the offense are not given their proper place, true forgiveness becomes impossible and the grudge might even increase. The most difficult part of the process involves working through the anger and resentment both consciously and unconsciously. It takes time to let go of resentment and other intense negative feelings. In addition, this inner process requires the ability to see the offender in a fuller context, as a complex person, both good and bad, weak and strong. It also involves overcoming defense mechanisms such as the good–bad object split, and developing an integrated view of the other as a whole person (Klein, 1935). The meaning of forgiveness is not replacing hateful feelings with loving ones, but providing a more realistic view of the other in their entirety. Moreover, the complexity of this process prevents us from guaranteeing complete forgiveness on every occasion. We could encounter anything from utter forgiveness to the decision to hold on to the intensity of the accusations and the need for revenge. Finally, the difficulty in bringing this process to completion might be caused by several factors: fear of retraumatization, vengeful wishes, sadism, over-attachment (as hostility makes it impossible to let go of the object), shame, envy, and a sense of power over the offender.

In carrying out healthy reparations, the subject must make peace with deficiencies, narcissistic injuries, mental ruptures, qualities of herself that she dislikes, and imperfect objects. This is a work of mourning: without true internal amendments, no true forgiveness is possible. Reparation is what facilitates action in the external world and, in this case, the act of forgiving.

The interpersonal stage

The second stage is no less important. It is an intersubjective, relational stage, taking place between two people. In order for this to happen, the two must meet, must come in contact with one another: the offender must admit their wrongdoing and there must be true empathy on both sides. Only then can the process of forgiveness be carried out in full. Sometimes, when the meeting between the offender and the offended cannot happen for various reasons, there is the possibility of an occurrence between the offended and another person (e.g., a therapist) through which a vicarious forgiveness might occur.

I now present two examples from popular culture that illustrate the above points: one portraying a true and full process of forgiveness, the other an example of non-forgiving. Showing the kind of forgiveness that follows the internal reparations and interpersonal interaction seen in reality, the film *Invictus* (directed by Clint Eastwood) tells the story of Nelson Mandela, and his desire to forgive as the newly elected president of South Africa. Having spent thirty terrible and painful years in prison, Mandela is freed and later on becomes president. He states, "Throw those knives, those guns, those machetes to the ocean, this is where reconciliation begins". The film relates much of Mandela's inner reparations through his accounts of reading "white" literature, poems, etc. He decides and declares that he will be nothing like those men who have tortured him; he refuses to identify with them, to become one of them. In the film, he decides to support the South African Rugby team, made up solely of white players, except for a single black one. The team is anathema to the black population, for it represents apartheid and the Afrikaaners who subjugated and humiliated them for so many years. Furthermore, they have no understanding of the game itself. Early on in the film, the blacks support a team from another country, cheering against their own national team, which is, indeed, defeated. Against all odds, despite all counsel against it, and forced to confront all the bad blood that remains between whites and blacks, Mandela decides to support the national Rugby team. Within the year, he sees them winning the World Cup. The film shows that he had forgotten nothing of what he had gone through—he even sends the team to visit the prison in which he was incarcerated—but he is still willing to forgive and to look ahead. In his words, "forgiveness sets the soul free. It drives fear away and therefore it is such a powerful weapon".

In this context, it is worth noting the Zulu notion of *Ubuntu*—humanity or compassion. It is an African worldview that considers each person's humanity as derived from the humanity of others. Some say that it is this notion that greatly facilitated the work of the Truth and Reconciliation Committees which followed the collapse of apartheid in the first half of the 1990s.

Another illustration presents an attempt at forgiveness that, nevertheless, yields no true forgiving; it is taken from a letter Kafka wrote to his father. In November 1919, Kafka wrote his father a letter, asking his mother to deliver it to him, in the hope that it might do something to mend their very faulty relationship. The mother failed to deliver the letter to its addressee and, instead, sent it back to its author. In the letter, Kafka tries to delve into the full depths of the gaping abyss that existed between him and his father, in order to study its causes and, possibly, reach some kind of reconciliation or forgiveness.

In my opinion, Kafka is unable to make amends, and not just because the letter failed to reach its destination. Kafka does manage to fathom the roots of the process that took place between him and his father, but he attains no peace, no means of controlling his anger, and his voice is suffused with despair. The process of reparation is incomplete and, naturally, no forgiveness is granted.

Kafka writes thus:

> Dearest Father, you asked me recently why I maintain that I am afraid of you. . . . even in writing, this fear and its consequences hamper me in relation to you . . . To you the matter always seemed very simple, at least in so far as you talked about it in front of me, and indiscriminately in front of many other people. . . . You have not expected any gratitude . . . but have expected at least some sort of obligingness, some sign of sympathy. Instead I have always hidden from you, in my room . . . nor indeed ever shown any family feeling . . . [you] charge me with coldness, estrangements and ingratitude . . .
>
> This, your usual way of representing it, I regard as accurate only in so far as I too believe you are entirely blameless in the matter of our estrangement. But I am equally entirely blameless. If I could get you to acknowledge this, then what would be possible is . . . a kind of peace; no cessation, but still, a diminution of your unceasing reproaches. (Kafka, 2008, p. 115)

Kafka is claiming here that his father is accusing him of ingratitude and conferring upon him the full responsibility for the harshness of their relationship. He is, in fact, both accusing his father and demanding that his father stop accusing him. He adds,

> It is also true that you hardly ever really gave me a beating. But the shouting, the way your face got red, the hasty undoing of the suspenders and laying them ready over the back of the chair, all that was almost worse for me. It is as if someone is going to be hanged. If

> he really is hanged, then he is dead and it is all over. But if he has to go through all the preliminaries to being hanged and he learns of his reprieve only when the noose is dangling before his face, he may suffer from it all his life. (Kafka, 2008, p. 133)

This is a penetrating, score-settling, and touching appeal made by a son who has never received any recognition from his father and was even repeatedly humiliated, and is still willing, not to say eager, to forgive. Nevertheless, he is incapable of this: without admitting it, he clings to his accusations, feeling that his father is the only one who is still making charges. He cannot release himself from the hold his father has on him, a destructive hold that leaves him with a sadistic inner-object. As the offending father does not acknowledge his offense, the son is ensnared with his denied offense. The process of reparation is incomplete as well, but, most of all, what is missing is the level of actual interpersonal interaction, including an admission of guilt or remorse, which could enable the process of forgiveness.

Forgiveness in group analysis

If we consider the capacity to forgive a healthy one (though not at any cost and not in order to placate), it is important to examine the contribution of the therapeutic group to the development of this capacity. Group analysis is an excellent tool that offers multi-faceted opportunities for dealing with the difficult task of forgiveness. Through the matrix of transferences and countertransferences between members and members and conductor, there is a lot of exposure to the different paths of forgiving oneself and others.

I begin with a tri-partite vignette from a group analysis session.

A three-part group forgiveness story

Part I

Eli (fifty-eight years old) and Omer (thirty-two years old) have been in group therapy for several years. The group has eight members. Omer is single and exceedingly fat. He tells the group that even though he would have liked to lose weight for his forthcoming wedding, a year from then, he feels that it is not worth the effort. The members try to explain, each in their own way and with great sensitivity, why weight loss is so important. They also refer to the meaning of being fat. Omer rejects every claim. It is apparent that, in his momentary unwillingness to listen, he is being defensive and is, thus, unapproachable. Eli, quite an obsessive type and still not tuned in to emotional nuance, stubbornly keeps explaining that weight loss is vital. Eventually, he loses his temper and, with a reddening face, he says, "Look at yourself! You have to lose weight! You're not well! Go see a doctor who'll tell you about your high blood pressure! About the heart condition you could have any minute! You have to lose weight!"

Omer, who was already having trouble accepting the groups concerns and interpretations (even though he asked for them), becomes upset and responds with rage: "You can't tell me what to do! Mr. Strict and Spineless!" and other similar statements. The group remains silent for several minutes. Someone then addresses Omer and says, "But he only wants what is best for you, even if he put it the way he did . . ." Omer replies, "I won't have him humiliate me like this, I'm not his puppet. I don't want him thinking he can control me. I had enough of that with my father and I barely talk with him ever since, nothing more than hellos and how do you dos." Eli apologizes to Omer, saying that he might have overreacted but he has nothing but his wellbeing in mind. Omer replies with "Mach nisht kein toives [Yiddish for 'don't do me any favors'], I can understand all that myself". They both relax a bit and their faces return to normal. The group then discusses their interaction. They say to Eli that if he wants to influence someone it has to be through empathy, through understanding where that person is, and not by lecturing. Omer then recounts his father's strict and harsh treatment of him and of how, up until his late adolescence, he never dared to stand up to him. He did get an apology from Eli, though.

Part II

Two weeks later, Eli recounts a difficult fight he had with his son. The son, a twenty-eight-year-old student, took his car without asking, as Eli was asleep at the time. He came back two hours later, with the car slightly dented. Eli says that he ordered his son to get the car fixed at his own expense, even though the cost was several thousand shekels.

He is having second thoughts, as such things rarely happen and his son obviously did not mean for any harm to come to the car. The members are trying to understand and express their different opinions on the matter. Omer is the only one to insist, with much anger, that there is no room for debate and that the son must pay up, no matter what. He repeats this several times and Eli is at a loss for words to answer him. Someone from the group then tells Omer that he is addressing Eli in exactly the same way that Eli spoke to him several weeks ago: "Boy, you two are alike!" The group discusses their notion that Eli and Omer's relationship shares much resemblance to those between Eli and his son and Omer and his father, throughout both these occurrences. Omer is embarrassed, admitting that he really has been acting like his father and that he might suddenly be able to understand him.

Part III

About one month later, Omer shows up and says that he is no longer speaking to his father. He says that he was greatly offended by his father, who asked him for his opinion regarding his new office. When Omer said to him, "You picked out one ugly office," his father replied that he has no intention of minding Omer's unesthetic opinion and that he was being insolent. Some of the members sympathize with Omer's anger, but Itay, another member, calls out, "But you hurt him first!" Omer holds Itay in great reverence and often waits to hear what he has to say. Now, after hearing Itay, he grows silent for a minute and then asks him why he would say such a thing. After Itay explains his point, Omer says that he suddenly understands that he hurts his father too, and that his father still tries to get close to him. At the next meeting, he tells everyone that he and his father are talking again.

This example shows how the group helps Omer to forgive his father for his current offense and for previous ones as well. The process of forgiveness takes place over several stages, through the group process. The first stage has Omer receiving an apology from Eli, enabling him to relax; the offender, even though he meant no harm, asks for forgiveness. In this instance, the group helps Omer mourn the fact that his father is not the one he had wished for, but does nothing to induce him to forgiveness. The second stage has Omer discovering that he shares the very same types of behavior with Eli (and his father). The group helps him perform the inner work necessary, which leads him to stop seeing things in black and white, discovering that no one is either a complete villain or a complete saint, that there are no part-objects but whole objects, which have both good and bad qualities. Here, too, the group is supportive, accepting, and not advocating any forgiveness. The third stage entails a kind of regression, by which Omer again sees his father as a bad object, mindless of the intricacies of their interaction. The group, as an active witness, helps him realize that he, too, gives offense. Nevertheless, he is not sentenced or condemned. This process helps him understand his father. His need to forgive increases and he forgives. In this manner, he is able to implement the interaction that took place in the group in his relationship with his father outside the group.

Vicarious individual forgiveness in intergroup meetings

Here is another vignette from a workshop of Germans and Israelis who have been working together once a year for more than five years:

In this workshop, the German participants, sons and daughters of Nazi parents, worked through many guilt feelings associated to the history of the Holocaust, whereas the Israelis were dealing with their second generation experience of being children to parents victimized by the Nazis. Feelings of enmity between the two subgroups were generally hidden for the sake of friendship, but sometimes came to the surface. In one of the meetings, a German analyst placed in front of the members two thick photo albums. On their covers, the albums had an insignia of a helmet with the Nazi swastika. "I found the albums hidden in the attic of my parent's house", he tells the participants with tears in his eyes.

The group felt frozen and paralyzed; an undisguised horror filled the room. After a long silence, one of the participants suddenly remembered her father's request before she went to Germany. He had told her, "When you meet with the Germans, I would like you to tell them the following story."

Her father was sixteen when the Germans occupied Holland and dismissed all the Jewish teachers. At that point, he made a decision to leave Holland. He got on his bicycle, wanting to go to the unoccupied part of France. On the Belgian border, he was stopped by two German soldiers. One of the soldiers was a young man, about twenty years old, and the other one was around forty-five years old. They asked him to stop and searched his bag. On top of everything in the bag was his stamp collection, and then some clothes. At the bottom of the bag was a little case embroidered with the Star of David. Inside that bag were the talit and tfillin he received on his Bar Mitzvah. Those were, of course, indication of his being a Jew. The young soldier, who immediately realized he was Jewish, quickly packed his things and covered them with the stamps and, instead of detaining him, waved him free.

The psychologist had been asked by her father to tell this story so that the whole group would know that, even in the most horrendous and monstrous times, there were individuals with human conscience, a beacon of light in the darkness that enabled people in the most terrible times to hold on to their belief in the existence of goodness in the world. It gave meaning to life.

The group needed this beacon of light to remind them, at that shocking moment, that the German participant was also a human being full of pain and unbearable guilt; in fact it was a vicarious guilt that requires human echoing.

The spontaneous reaction of an Israeli analyst within the matrix of this particular group enabled the German analyst to experience a human encounter that both acknowledged and recognized his tremendous pain. I believe that through the interpersonal interaction which the group provided, the sharing and empathy that the German analyst received, and through the witnessing of the rest of the group, he was able to attain vicarious forgiveness, and the relationship of the guilty ones *vs.* the righteous ones within the group was changed.

The group provides a transitional space, one that enables play, in its broader sense. This play-space holds two elements which facilitate the process of forgiveness: one is the group's witnessing, which corroborates the offense and the hurt caused by it, and is both active and supportive and a symbol of hope. In self-psychology terms, this witnessing acts as a mirroring, and the group is a self-object. However, witnessing is also an independent therapeutic function that is both non-interpretive and not necessarily a self-object (Ullman, 2006). It is a kind of listening which gives confirmation to suffering while longing to understand its meaning (Poland, 2000). The witness can be thought of as the "live third". The fact that Kafka's mother did not send the letter to his father deprived them of a "live third" who could see both of their perspectives and empathically serve as a witness for both. Mandela and the Truth and Reconciliation Committee had the third in the form the world community that supported their efforts. It might be too much for the dyad to handle its own mutual confessions and forgiveness. The group's listening is by no means a neutral one, but, rather, one that takes a stand in order to enable the development of various forms of self-experience. The group as a witness functions as a live third between the two antagonists. To recapitulate, the group's witnessing:

1. Creates reflexivity for the offended.
2. Induces a positive yet flexible ethics, replacing a strict superego with social flexibility.
3. Creates, for the individual, a receptiveness toward inner parts which have been rejected, denied, or marked as shameful.

The other aspect of the group, perhaps most vital in facilitating forgiveness, is its comprising a number of people who could represent different characters, both past and present, in the offended party's life. This multiplicity makes it possible to use another member as a substitute for the offensive primary object, through which the interpersonal process could be carried out. This forgiveness via a vicarious object could be termed vicarious forgiveness. This element is exclusive to group therapy.

In summary, as I have claimed earlier, the process of forgiveness is composed of two cardinal elements, one being the process of reparation, the other being the interpersonal process. In Nelson Mandela's case, we have seen how his thirty years in prison involved a deep internal process which freed him from anger, making him acknowledge the good and bad in everyone and instilling in him the intense desire not to be like his captors and tormentors. This was followed by an interpersonal and public process, after he was released and given an honorary position: he forgets nothing, sending the white team to visit the place where imprisoned blacks were tortured, and attains a full forgiveness which enables him to change reality. In Kafka's case, the absence of the interpersonal level, which might have brought about remorse, admission of guilt, and a direct address of the offense, precluded a true process of forgiveness.

The example I have cited from a therapeutic group demonstrated that the group was able to facilitate the full fruition of the forgiveness process, on both the concrete and the symbolic levels. Following the group's support and its witnessing function, the process made it possible for Omer to see that the parts which exist in a significant other, the father, or Eli, actually exist in him as well. The things he previously denounced in his father were present in him, too. This was the first step toward complete forgiveness. While the apology was, indeed, not given from the same source as the primary offense, the process of witnessing and the group's transferential qualities permitted Omer to experience the relief it involved and to abandon the need for revenge.

References

Akhtar, S. (2002). Forgiveness: origins, dynamics, psychopathology, and technical relevance. *Psychoanalytic Quarterly, 71*: 175–212.

Akhtar, S. (2009). *Good Feelings*. London: Karnac.

Amichai, Y. (2013). The Place where We are Right. In: *The Selected Poetry of Yehuda Amichai* (p. 34), C. Bloch & S. Mitchell (Trans.). Berkeley, CA: University of California Press.

Eastwood, C. (Director) (2009). *Invictus* (Film). USA: Warner Bros.

Horwitz, L. (2005). The capacity to forgive: intrapsychic and developmental perspectives. *Journal of the American Psychoanalytic Association, 553*: 485–511.

Kafka, F. (2008). Letter to his father. In: *The Sons,* E. Keiser & E. Wilkins (Trans.) (pp. 115–192). New York: Schoken Books.

Klein, M. (1935). A contribution to the psychogenesis of manic-depressive states. *International Journal of Psychoanalysis, 16*: 145–174.

McCullough, M. E., & Witvliet, C. V. (2002). The psychology of forgiveness. *Handbook of Positive Psychology, 2*: 446–455.

McCullough, M. E., Pargament, K., & Thoresen, C. (Eds.) (2000). *Forgiveness: Theory, Research, and Practice*. New York: Guilford Press.

Poland, W. S. (2000). The analyst's witnessing and otherness. *Journal of the American Psychoanalytic Association, 48*: 17–34.

Smith, H. (2008). Leaps of faith: is forgiveness a useful concept? *International Journal of Psychoanalysis, 89*: 919–936.

Thoresen, C. E., Harris, A. H. S., & Luskin, F. (2000). Forgiveness and health: an unanswered question. In: M. E. McCullough, K. Pargament, & C. Thoresen (Eds.), *Forgiveness: Theory, Research, and Practice* (pp. 254–280). New York: Guilford Press.

Ullman, C. (2006). Bearing witness: across the barriers in society and in the clinic. *Psychoanalytic Dialogues, 16*: 181–198.

Urlich, I., Berman, A., & Berger, M. (2010). *Forgiveness, Victimhood and Vengefulness*. New York: Nova Science.

Van Noort, M. (2003). Revenge and forgiveness in group psychotherapy. *Group Analysis, 36*(4): 477–489.

Volkan, V. (2001). Transgenerational transmissions and chosen traumas: an aspect of large group identity. *Group Analysis, 34*(1): 79–97.

CHAPTER FOUR

Conciliation and comfort: group work with Bedouin grandmothers

Smadar Ben-Asher and Wisam Maree

Introduction

Facilitated group work, as opposed to a social discourse that naturally takes place in an encounter between people who share a common background or interest, is accepted and widespread in the West. The ability of a group to contribute to its members has been described in numerous studies (Whitaker, 1985; Yalom & Leszcz, 2005) in the context of providing an experience of shared concerns, social support, expressing anger, sorrow, loss, frustration, failure, a shared yearning for solutions, personal growth, acknowledgment of inner strengths, comfort, and conciliation. Constituting, as it does, a branch of Western psychology, group work is virtually unknown in Arab society in general and Bedouin society in particular. Arab society, which is fundamentally collectivist, sees the individual as part of a family (*hamoula* = clan) without the individual foundations with which the individual comes to the therapy group that is familiar in the West. Consequently, building group work with older women, namely Bedouin grandmothers, most of whom are uneducated, is of particular interest and is the focus of the study described in this chapter.

On the initiative of the social services in the village, a group of grandmothers from the Bedouin sector in Israel met for group work facilitated by an Arab psychologist. In addition to belonging to the same social group and of the same gender, all of the members of the group served as child-minders for the babies and infant children of their sons and daughters-in-law. This task, which is performed with their consent, but not always willingly, raises intergenerational, social, and educational issues, and especially questions concerning their own personal identity. Child-minder grandmothers experience a common fate of intergenerational and intercultural transition in which their past work as "good child-minders" of their own children has lost its potency in the face of a new and alien present and its attendant demands, of which they find it difficult to be a part. While the younger generation leaves the Bedouin village to study or to work in non-traditional workplaces, the grandmothers retain the role they have fulfilled for several decades, but now their experience and socio-cultural knowledge, which is grounded in the culture and traditions of the past, is found to be unsuited to the new world that has come knocking on their doors by means of the younger generation—the parents of their grandchildren. Working in a group enabled these women to share their personal and family experiences, family tensions, secrets from the past, and especially to jointly examine their personal identity within the collective structure that flattens, restricts, and diminishes this identity.

The formation of the group, how it functioned, how it was facilitated, the content that arose within it, the interpersonal and group dynamics, and the group narrative that was woven from the stories of the participants is presented in this chapter in an attempt to illuminate and expose the deep significance of the group's work within a traditional society, both on the personal level of the participants and the collective level of the group. The chapter examines these issues from two perspectives: social representation theory and group facilitation theories.

The I is we: collective social representations in Bedouin society

Social identity is defined as the way in which an individual perceives himself in the context of his relationships with others. It is the combination of the "I" and the "we", expanding the self beyond the individual, and contains within it the other members of the group as well (Smith & Mackie, 1995). An individual's group identity includes broad information that encompasses numerous aspects of life such as history, culture, beliefs, customs, language, place of residence, and occupation, and forms the basis accepted by him/her and the other members of the group regarding how to act within said group. Moreover, membership of the group enables the individual to feel a sense of security and accords meaning to his/her actions and the events that take place in his/her life, which creates a sense that he/she is part of something bigger (Wagner, 1993).

Social representation theory (Moscovici, 1984, 1993, 1994) is based on the premise that any inner discourse that takes place within the individual is a social discourse. Social representations are simultaneously personal and collective, for they provide an organizing structure for communication and constructing the group's shared reality with regard to ideas, values, opinions, actions, action scenarios, norms, and behaviors (Wagner, 1995).

The unique characteristics of a society wherein the family, the community, and religion are more important than the individual should be borne in mind when discussing the discourse that takes place in a group of Bedouin women from the perspective of social representations (Al-Krenawi, 1998). While no longer nomadic, the Bedouin community is still organized on the basis of traditional cultural principles. The kinship group, or tribe, is the most binding framework in the individual's life, and it defines the customs and rules contained within the various domains of social life. The tribe is based on patrilineal descent, and the man is the authoritative figure within it (Halevy, 2002). The adage, "family prestige is expressed in wealth and men", is widely used by Bedouins (Ben-David, 1982). According to traditional perceptions, women are part of the family's wealth, their status is inferior, and their closed community is usually strictly governed by the older women. There is a strict separation between men and women, which is based on the traditional "code of honor and shame". This code ostensibly refers to the honor of the family as a patriarchal unit, but, in fact, refers to the honor of the men in the family. Tradition in Bedouin society preserves the inequality between men and women and perpetuates patriarchal dominance (Karkabi-Sabah, 2009). Maintaining family honor means male dominance, and the women are expected to be traditional housewives. Subordination of women to the man in the traditional Bedouin family is founded on customs and rules supported by the majority of the population (Shapira & Hertz-Lazarowitz, 2009). The separation of women is manifested in the existence of a women's world: the women preserve its boundaries, prefer to spend time in the company of other women, and change their behavior when in the company of men.

Psychosocial intervention in Bedouin women

Pain is a universal, cross-cultural experience. As in general society in Israel, physical pain is treated by means of the country's public health services. Psychological pain in the Bedouin population, however, has been traditionally treated by amulet writers, Quran healers, or fortune-tellers and dervishes, who, according to belief, were ordained by supernatural powers (Al-Krenawi, 2000). Traditional treatments and therapies for women are provided by traditional healers—*fataha, sheikhah, darwisha* or *hajah*—to help them with life's hardships and resolve psychological problems by explaining the supernatural reasons for them or by means of medicinal herbs and amulets (Popper-Givon & Al-Krenawi, 2010). Abu-Rabia-Queder and Weiner-Levy (2010) describe how the sources of power in the community and tradition, on the one hand, and the Israeli space, on the other, are blocked to Arab women in Israel. For this reason, many of them feel that they are at an impasse and do not have the power to contend with the challenges in their life. A popular Bedouin folk proverb states: "It is preferable for pain to remain in the heart than cause shame in public", for, in Arab society, emotional difficulties are perceived as a threat to the family's honor. And the women view their pain as a private one with which they have to contend on their own by living a double life, inner and outer.

Physicians in the Bedouin towns and villages are highly familiar with the phenomenon of women coming to the clinic to get headache pills. When they return home, after chance meetings with other women in the market or in the clinic's waiting room, they wave their prescription to the men to justify their absence from the home (Abu-Rabia, 2009). This illustrates how the women seek out group encounters with other women beyond the closed area of their family dwellings.

The grandmothers' group

Several empowerment and support centers for Bedouin women have opened in recent years, creating a place to meet, learn to read, write, and sew, and promote personal initiative. This group work has gained considerable impetus due to a special National Insurance Institute of Israel program to empower Bedouin women by means of women's clubs (Munk, 2005). Due to the need of these women to meet one another and discuss their difficulties and the traditional social restrictions they face, a social services department in one of the Bedouin villages in the south of Israel decided to form a women's group as well. In the course of identifying the needs of the women in the community, the distinctive "grandmothers" group emerged—women who are employed without pay as part of their familial obligation to take care of their grandchildren.

The formation of the group in a Bedouin village in the Negev, its functioning, and the content of the meetings were all documented by hand by the psychologist/facilitator.

The meetings were held in the mornings at the pre-school center run by the local social services department, and the participants attended with the children in their care. Activities were organized for the children to allow the grandmothers to attend the group sessions that were held in the adjoining room. From time to time, the grandchildren would come into the room where the grandmothers were meeting, and would then be returned to the other room.

The group worked for about six months, and met sixteen times. Initially, eighteen women attended the meetings, and, over time, this number stabilized at twelve participants. The meetings were held once a week, but, from time to time, a meeting was canceled due to a family wedding, a festival, or adverse weather conditions. The documented proceedings of the meetings described the group dynamic processes and the content of the meetings. At the conclusion of the meetings, the center's social worker conducted a summarizing feedback session on the contributions made by the group to its participants. In-depth interviews were conducted with three participants about ten months after the group sessions had ended in order to get an impression of long-term effects. All interaction with the women was conducted in Arabic. Processing and analysis of the documentation of the meetings and the feedback were carried out in Hebrew, employing qualitative research tools.

The review of the meetings addresses both the content and the process. The meanings revealed in this description constitute the basis for the discussion regarding the significance of group work with Bedouin women, the similarities and differences between this unique group and similar groups, and the understandings derived from the described experience.

Description of the meetings

Building a group by means of familiar and new social arrangements

Yalom and Leszcz (2005) describe the importance of the first meeting that begins by receiving and welcoming the participants outside the room. The group of Bedouin women that gathered was welcomed by social workers who waited for the young children in the adjoining room, where they were to keep them occupied during the grandmothers' group meeting. The floor of the room in which the group meetings were held was covered with mattresses arranged around a low table located in the center of the room, thus resembling a traditional seating arrangement. Light refreshments brought by the participants were served at every meeting. The tea was poured and served by the oldest participant, strictly maintaining the hierarchy of respect: First, she served the facilitator, and then each of the participants according to descending age.

Although all the women were from the same family (*hamoula*), they did not all know one another. Initial contact within the group signaled the desire for a different kind of meeting alongside the strong message of strictly observing tradition. This would later emerge as a central *leitmotif* in the group's activities on conscious and unconscious levels alike.

In the first meeting, the participants became acquainted with one another. Each participant told the group about herself and her grandchildren. At this stage, the facilitator was not yet familiar with the intricate relationships between the women. Polygamy, widowhood, and other types of relationships associated with familial obligations emerged in later meetings and included feelings such as anger, conciliation, and comfort. In this meeting, the participants' expectations regarding the content and functioning of the meetings were discussed and unified.

As early as in the first meeting, it clearly emerged that the way this group functioned would be different to the way such groups usually function in Western society, since the "social order" had to be preserved in each and every group activity. Thus, for example, a request to toss a ball of wool from one participant to another to create a "cobweb" was met with refusal from the group members: "How can I pass over my neighbor and throw the ball to someone on the other side of the circle. If I pass over my neighbor I'll offend her . . ." they said, and passed the ball from one to another in order around the circle out of a desire to avoid creating a "different order".

In the first meeting, it also transpired that some of the group members did not know how to read and write. The facilitator decided, with the group's agreement, to avoid writing on the board so as not to create gaps of inferiority and superiority within the group based on differences in education.

As with any group operating in accordance with principles of professional facilitation, the facilitator presented the group members with the basic rules of privilege and confidentiality concerning the content emerging in the group's meetings. Understanding the concept of privilege and confidentiality was also achieved by employing a culturally unique concept that is common in Arab society, namely *amana*. The concept of *amana*, which means "custody", originates from an ancient custom whereby if a Bedouin leaves any of his belongings with another Bedouin during his wanderings, the latter is obliged to look after them until the former returns to reclaim them. A secret, too, is essentially *amana*, and the rules of custody apply to it. This concept also has a religious meaning. In Bedouin tradition, it is customary when endeavoring to keep a secret to say that one is "More loyal than Samuel" and "follow in Prophet Mohammad's footsteps", and the meaning of loyalty is the obligation to keep a secret. Thus, the joint agreement to keep secret anything that was said in the group meetings was based on sources of religious tradition and social culture, and, without a doubt, the fact that the facilitator came from the same culture as the women and was conversant with it helped to make the group's ground rules, which were unfamiliar to the women, more accessible by employing concepts that were familiar to them. On the other hand, building a group also mandated building tools that are inconsistent with accepted tradition and culture. Thus, for example, the facilitator had to contend with the need to set boundaries for the meetings. Unlike the rigid perception of time in modern society, Bedouin society views time as unrestricted and undefined. Traditionally, the boundaries of a Bedouin's tent are open to random visitors at any hour of the day. How can the boundaries of the meeting room and meeting times be delimited? Thus, for example, ten minutes before the end of the first meeting, the call of the muezzin from the mosque was heard. The women stood up, stating it was time for prayer. In their culture and tradition, the time for prayer is the determining time, and not the time on the clock. The facilitator intervened and explained that in the group "other rules" apply, and prayer could wait. The participants accepted the new boundaries and behaved accordingly in the following meetings.

The unique cultural conduct of the group was a condition for its activities. The participants were not addressed by their first names, but in accordance with the family attribution each woman acquired when she gave birth to her eldest son; for example, Umm Ibrahim (mother of Ibrahim). In the course of the meetings, the women in the group preferred to address one another with the honorific "mother of", and only one relatively young woman asked to be addressed by her first name. The women expected, and accorded great importance to, the facilitator remembering their traditional name, and viewed it as an expression of honor and respect. Similarly, they also addressed her by the name of her oldest son, which in their perception accorded her status above and beyond her education or belonging to her husband's family.

Content of the group discourse

A reading of the documented meeting proceedings reveals a variety of subjects that were discussed in the group. The subjects can be divided into three areas:

1. The repressed trauma of entering married life and relocating to the husband's family.

2. The women's role in terms of parenting and family.
3. Threat and hope in their perception of the future, contending with crises, and changes in traditional society.

Entering married life was described by the group members as a vivid and painful memory of their "wedding night". Cautiously, and with profound sadness, the women described their first unprotected night in a strange house (usually their mother-in-law's home) without any mental preparation of any kind. They underwent an experience that was seared into their body like a life-changing trauma. Although this experience took place a generation ago, it was the first subject to be raised in the group. It was their "initiation" into motherhood and the rest of their life. The women's stories can constitute a source for anthropological, sociological, and literary studies, and a different narrative point of departure for viewing women in Bedouin society; however, we have chosen not to expand on them here. We would like to note, however, that from the moment these stories were articulated in the group and received with empathy, support, and containment (at times indistinguishable from identification), they were the subject of most of the first meetings and the foundation on which additional understanding between the group members was built.

Bion (1961) argues that one of the assumptions shared by all members of a group when they gather is that they share a common objective as it was defined by the facilitator before they began, and that this initial assumption is meticulously examined in the first meeting. In the present group, the impression was that there was an innocent, unsophisticated expectation that they would receive pedagogical guidance or counseling from a psychologist about taking care of their grandchildren and their relationships with their sons and daughters-in-law.

The group facilitator, who is knowledgeable and experienced in facilitating groups of educators, describes her apprehensions with regard to the group's unique characteristics. The question arose of whether older women with a social status that is partly expressed in society by describing achievements (primarily in terms of family size) in a language that at times resembles boastfulness, would be able to talk about their difficulties. The initial stages were structured with the aid of exercises, but it quickly became apparent that their need to express themselves, share, and receive comfort, and the respect they gave to each woman as she told her personal story, made it impossible to work according to predefined content or by means of exercises commonly used in facilitated groups. The personal experience was central. The group facilitator flowed with the group to a variety of places, yet, at the same time, felt she was in control of building the group setting, and described the meetings as a fascinating journey the like of which neither the group members nor the facilitator had ever experienced.

The first meeting was unpredictable due to the meaningful content of self-disclosure that was raised in the context of intimate relationships. The disclosure and sharing resembled the eruption of a volcano. A first meeting is usually highly charged with the anxiety and apprehensions of the participants, who endeavor to understand the nature of the meeting beyond its declared title, and consequently tend to protect themselves from over-disclosure (Neri, 1998). Self-disclosure in itself is highly important, since it forms the basis for the group process, the sense of intimacy experienced by its members, and the relationships that develop between them as the process progresses. Rybko (2005) studied self-disclosure in a group's first meeting and its ability to predict the participants' later functioning. In her study, Rybko (2005) shows how self-disclosure in a first meeting constitutes a significant indicator for the group members' level of disclosure later in the process. She found that the group members' ability to overcome the anxiety phase and disclose personal information from the past or present is associated with the experience of security the participants bring with them from the past as part of their individual personality beyond the type of group, the facilitator, and the dynamic that develops within the group. Tschuschke and Dies (1994) argue that self-disclosure leads to further disclosure while creating a positive circle of trust and empathy within the group. The self-disclosure of some group members also constitutes modeling for the opportunity afforded by a group to receive sympathy for what, until then, has been considered non-legitimate pain. Whitaker (1997) claims that a group as a medium for self-help develops unique moods and atmospheres that emerge from the group members and affect the atmosphere and events within it, which, at times, develop gradually and, at other times, occur in the form of an unexpected outburst. We will never know how the group would have developed if not for the profound disclosure of one of the group members who described the grueling experience of her wedding night, thus allowing the dark, difficult secret to emerge from the private domain and be contained by a group offering partnership and sisterhood.

While the literature provides ample descriptions of the content of the first stage as stereotypical and relatively limited to neutral discussion (Yalom & Leszcz, 2005), from the outset the first meeting of the grandmothers' group revealed the profound need of the group members to articulate the suffering in their lives and gain support and empathy within the group. It can be assumed that the need to explore past traumas is linked to the perception of the group being a "different group", protected and safe. It should be borne in mind that the women's whole lives take place within a group of which they are an integral part, without any discrete personal identity, and, at times, the family is experienced as hostile and harsh. Most of the women's stories described the difficult years following their marriage as years of being part of a group in which they were obliged to accept harsh and inferior conditions. Immediately after the wedding, the young bride moves into the home of her husband's family; her mother-in-law runs the extended household with an iron fist, exploits her for hard labor, and emphasizes her inferior status in the family. The women painfully remember those years as a period of loss of freedom, security, and independence. They were required for hard work inside the house and also for shepherding. Their first pregnancies were attended by shame, since their swollen bellies disclosed their sexuality to all and sundry, which was bound up in shame and guilt: the pregnancy attested to the existence of sexual relations, which are considered a sin to which all moral proscriptions apply. They remember their first births as an experience of loneliness and the absence of social support and guidance on the roles of a mother. The rule of the mother-in-law also included the manner of raising children and permitted beatings, discrimination in terms of food and care, and favoring the mother-in-law's children over those of the daughter-in-law: in many cases, the daughter-in-law gave birth at the same time as the mother-in-law, who was still of childbearing age, and the mother-in-law, who controlled the household budget, openly gave preference to her own baby when they had to share the babies' food between them (e.g., infant formula). The young women did not have time to spend with their children, since they were required to look after the herds, bake, and contribute to the household. Means were usually meager, there was no electricity or gas, and water had to be fetched from a considerable distance. Contact with their children was reduced to feeding and protection. It was only when the husband was relatively established in his job, after three or four children had been born, that the woman moved into a home of her own and was able to begin developing intimate relationships within her nuclear family and enjoy parenting the children who were born in her own home. However, financial security also bore a potential for crisis, since it enabled the husband to bring another wife into the home. The decision regarding such changes rests exclusively on the husband, the man of the family.

In the course of the meetings, the women underwent complex processes of anger and jealousy, but also of everyday partnership in maintaining the household and raising their children. The group meetings enabled them, for the first time, to reveal to one another their pain alongside acceptance, conciliation, and comfort.

Stories also emerged about the loss of children who had died, and the grief that was not accorded a legitimate place, making it impossible to process the painful emotions attending it. The grief and anxiety could only be addressed by going to spell-casting sheikhs. Receiving help in traditional ways brought about a need to contend with a new kind of tension due to the expense entailed in purchasing the spells, and the husband's dissatisfaction over these expenses.

The content of the intergenerational encounter in the context of their role as grandmothers taking care of their grandchildren only emerged in the last few meetings. The point of departure for defining personal identity was the number of children each participant had and the number of grandchildren in her care. Difficulties arose due to the situation whereby they were simultaneously grandmothers and mothers raising young children of their own, and jealousy between the two generations. The participants described their multiple roles as women, mothers, grandmothers, and daughters-in-law who were still obligated to their mothers-in-law. Another issue that arose was the desire to give up in the face of difficulties such as diminished strength and health.

The women's request to discuss concrete and practical child rearing methods in the context of their relationships with their children only arose after extensive room was afforded to their personal stories. They expressed a desire to acquire tools for coping with their grandchildren's difficulties, old *vs.* new child-rearing methods, and ways to set boundaries that are not self-evident in the traditional family. The children's parents were presented as demanding child-rearing approaches that were appropriate to the children's ages and needs, which called into question the women's knowledge—something that had been self-evident in the past. The issue of the father's role in the children's education and upbringing, which in the past was perceived to be the exclusive domain and responsibility of the women, was raised as an embarrassing question, and the participants asked the facilitator to help them examine it in accordance with "the new winds and modern times".

The group members shared with one another their concerns about getting old, their fears about the future, and the lack of solutions available for the elderly within their community. One participant summarized the experience of the meetings thus:

> "All day we only work. When we come to the group we forget all about our problems. When we share our stories it eases the burden. I've learnt a lot from the group members. When I first came here I felt as though I was deep down in a well, and today I feel that the group has brought me out of the well . . ."

The traditional analytical approach that places a taboo on the therapist's or facilitator's self-disclosure is countered nowadays by new approaches (Yalom & Leszcz, 2005; Ziv-Beiman, 2010). Therapists or facilitators working under these new paradigms that utilize their personality and are prepared to bring themselves into the interaction in the therapy setting consequently increase the therapeutic power of the group and its joint work. The therapist's self-disclosure, if and when effected in accordance with the needs of the group, is experienced as personal modeling that supports openness and authenticity, and encourages the group members to build a relationship based on trust.

The women in the group, who scrutinized the facilitator, saw a young, educated woman dressed in Western clothes, but wearing the customary, traditional headscarf. From the family perspective as the reference point for examining reality, they sought intimacy with her, expressed interest in her children, and urged her: "When are you going to have another child, another sister for your daughter?" In their status as mature, distinguished women who are well established in their families, their role was to tell the young woman, even though she was the group facilitator, how she should conduct herself and live her life according to their view. The intrusion of the older women into the affairs of the younger ones, their daughters and daughters-in-law, is widely accepted in Bedouin society. These remarks, which were occasionally directed at the group facilitator in social contexts, were experienced as a non-legitimate violation of her privacy. However, as a result of the relationship forged between the facilitator and the women, and their respect for her professionalism, these remarks were received gracefully, as expressions of genuine affection and concern, while maintaining her status as the facilitator.

Laor (2007) describes the reciprocity in the therapy setting as comprising mutual influence, mutual recognition, and mutual regulation between therapist and client. She posits that the setting is constructed and maintained by the two parties to the process: therapist and client. The intersubjective approach holds that reciprocity between therapist and client is legitimate. The facilitator cannot function without becoming involved. The women's painful stories about their wedding night, were jarring and harsh. The empathy she felt toward them when they shared these stories with the group members, as well as stories of loss and grief over children who had died, brought tears to the facilitator's eyes on more than one occasion, which did not pass unnoticed by the women in the group. At times, when one of the women began telling her story, the facilitator stood up, went to sit next to her, and held her hand. At the end of the story, she thanked her for her trust in the group and for sharing her closely guarded secret, her "treasure". The changed setting when the facilitator moved to sit next to the speaker and her intimacy with the women in the group added to the sense of fraternity, unity, and trust without violating the clear boundaries between the facilitator and the group.

In this context, Ziv-Beiman (2010) presents a description of empathic concern as an emotional component of interpersonal communication that involves the ability to be influenced by the emotional states of the other, as well as the ability to conceptualize and name the experienced effect. The facilitator also attests that she could not remain neutral when the women described how they obtained help by means of amulets and spells because she did not question the truth and sincerity of the women's beliefs in their endeavors to remedy the catastrophes that afflicted them. Processes of transference and countertransference, both latent and overt, between the facilitator and the group were clearly evident as a significant element in constructing a meaningful therapy process, which the participants described in their picturesque and metaphoric language as "coming out of the well".

Discussion

Bedouin society in Israel's Negev region is rapidly encountering the social representations of Western culture and modernization, which clash with the social representations of the local culture, and threatens their society as a whole, both as individuals and as a group. Bedouin society is attempting to preserve its extant state and protect its belief system, culture, and religion, yet it cannot stop the forces permeating it. The changes originating in accelerated globalization have an impact on, *inter alia*, the status of women, who, in the past, played an important role in contributing to the family's upkeep (Al-Krenawi, 2001).

Public social services operate under considerably difficult conditions due to a lack of suitable personnel, shortage of posts, and lack of infrastructures. Given this situation, additional frameworks are developed in coordination with the public services, in which services are provided by volunteer organizations or NPOs.

The Bedouin women's group was adapted to the traditional social codes of separation, but, at the same time, it was also revolutionary, since it created a protected and professionally facilitated space that enabled the development of a discourse of empowerment that arose out of support and an experience of sharing: Young motherhood that often lacked support, followed by a more mature motherhood, relationships with adult children, grandmothers, with sons and daughters-in-law, and the desire to provide their adult children with a better child-rearing experience than they themselves had experienced. Unlike work with multicultural groups that are usually organized around a conflict with the majority group, the work of the grandmothers' group did not center on a struggle or conflict with others. In the literature, group processes are described as the individual's narcissistic need to be unique and gain the attention of the group and facilitator, as a power struggle with the facilitator, inciting jealousy, hatred, rivalry, and tension that all originate in unconscious processes within the group. None of these was observed in the grandmothers' group. Clearly evident, by contrast, was the anticipation for creating shared experiences that softened the experience of loneliness and pain they had experienced in the past. The grandmothers' group fits the description presented by Foulkes (1964), who views the group as an entity of positive attachment with the potential for a corrective experience (e.g., Hamenachem & Halevy-Bar-Tendler, 2002).

The level of the group members' self-disclosure was surprising considering the risk this entailed, given that they all belonged to the same family. The expectation that disclosure would cause anxiety among the group members did not materialize, and it seemed that there was a profound need for women, who were encouraged by the safe atmosphere of the group, to raise intimate issues that had weighed on them for many years. The women's discourse in the grandmothers' group reveals both the personal and the collective story. The personal life stories recounted in the group enabled the group members to build their identity, and for the listeners to validate their presence as part of the group. Emerging from the documentation of the group meetings are subjects associated with the personal history of the participants, which, to a large extent, is the collective story of the women in the group. Each of them experienced the traumatic wedding night and the first years of loneliness and humiliation in their husband's family home, the poverty, the hardships of raising children, and the slow process of finding sources of strength and satisfaction in their life.

Classic theories that analyze dynamic processes in a facilitated group depart from the premise of the individual's perception of his personal existence as a member of the group. This perception is challenged when we examine the development of the process that took place in the Bedouin grandmothers' group, and it is doubtful if what took place in the group described in this chapter can be examined by means of the perspective it suggests. We found that social representations theory that engages in the construction of reality by means of social communication is more suited to observing group processes, since this no longer involves the psychology of the individual, but, rather, of the group members as partners. Unlike the social approaches to social identity (e.g., Turner, 1987) that view social components as the self, the social representations approach assumes that the individual has a personal version of the shared representations, and, consequently, the individual's perception of his/her self will always take place in a social context. The accepted norms and social representations of keeping highly violent events secret, which until then regulated the women's behavior outside the group, changed in this encounter when the women in the group created new norms and belief systems. The dynamic of changing social representations is described as a situation wherein emancipated representations that previously existed as personal knowledge become shared social knowledge that the members of the group share with one another (Ben-Asher, 2003; Paryente & Orr, 2010). The nature of emancipated representations is such that when they gain expression and recognition of their legitimacy in a social group, they clash with the conservative hegemonic representations that are accepted in the society. In the Bedouin grandmothers' group the first meeting was the "opening shot" for raising conflictual representations with the traditional male world that had caused them so much suffering and had seemed self-evident to them until then. This was not a shattering or rebellion, but the ability to give expression to harsh feelings and the gradual realization that, despite the process of modernization taking place around them, the patriarchal structures of Arab society remain firm, and they are not part of the change in terms of bettering their lives. In this respect, Karkabi-Sabah (2009) argues that, despite the changes taking place externally in Bedouin society, the situation of women in that society continues to be harsh. Although Arab society is adopting material aspects and external patterns of behavior from the modern world, behind these patterns the rigid patriarchal structure still stands and modernization is merely another way of controlling and supervising women. Thus, for example, cell phones, far from improving or enhancing their life, serve instead as an instrument of male supervision over women, enabling the men to keep track of the women's whereabouts and activities. The discourse that developed in the Bedouin grandmothers' group attested to the women's self-perception, which, even today, is that they are inferior, and their subordination to the man and his family still continues. The representation of inferiority of the woman is a familiar hegemonic one. The hegemonic representations imprinted social proscriptions whose violation brings shame to the family and to the man who has failed to supervise his wife in a manner that preserves the traditional code of family honor. So long as the women were not exposed to the outside world and their activities were restricted to the family dwellings or nearby fields, they did not know any other representations, termed "emancipated representations". However, when the younger women, their daughters or daughters-in-law, continued to study and went out to work (in the main as teachers), and adopted independence strengthening behaviors (e.g., obtaining a driver's license and freely leaving the boundaries of the Bedouin village), emancipated representations that had previously only been in the form of new knowledge began clashing with prior representations.

The women's discourse in the group, which, from the outset, was designed to develop educational and intergenerational skills in a protected space, enabled them to open their personal "Pandora's box". For the first time, they could challenge the absolute control of men, especially concerning the physical experiences of their wedding nights. Even the period of suffering they experienced in the beginning of their marriages, which had been perceived as an unchallengeable decree in the past, emerged in the group for the first time by questioning its legitimacy. Working in a group enabled the women to jointly examine what was familiar to them and share their personal histories from the perspective of the comforting peer group. The participants perceived themselves as good and experienced childminders, and it was evident that they could not be approached from a "knowledgeable" position, but, rather, one that enabled their knowledge and life wisdom to adapt to the new world. In the group work, their shared social representations were manifested, and the group's role was to adapt them to the changing reality. The grandmothers' group built a group identity that enabled acknowledgment of the hardships and pain by alleviating their loneliness. The sense of partnership enabled the group members to observe their lives in the past with appreciation, despite the difficulties, and helped them to change their perception of their role in the family in the present.

Numerous researchers have stressed the importance of empathy in the forgiveness process (Batson et al., 1988), not only toward group members, but also to the wrongdoer himself. The power of forgiveness stems from the inner growth and personal empowerment that occurs in group work; the group members were able to reconstruct their sense of self-worth, the dignity they lost as a result of harsh life events at the start of their married lives, and their parenthood, through group mirroring. Thus, they were able to approach the wrongdoer, who is outside the group and wholly unaware of the process, and return to the painful experience from a place of new strength. Although conciliation begins within the group, it is not confined to the group setting, and continues in the world outside it. Conciliation does not turn back the clock, but it does enable harsh feelings that were associated with a sense of self-blame and diminished self-worth to be softened, and opens a window to acceptance and trust toward the world around them as well as their wounded selves.

In his description of a group, Foulkes (1964) employs the concept of the matrix, which is derived from the Latin word "mater", meaning "mother", "womb". New channels of mental communication can be constructed in a group that go beyond the personal to the group space, wherein past events and harsh thoughts and feelings are re-examined, and which are influenced by human communication, shared experiences, acceptance, and containment (Ezra, 2012; Foulkes, 1990). The vulnerable, wounded individual encounters empathy, and mutual responsibility and the ability to share profound inner pain with members of the group facilitate acceptance and comfort. This is not forgetting, but an experience of forgiveness and conciliation that alleviates painful past events and accords them significance and new meaning.

To a large extent, the subjects raised in the group that touched upon raising children resemble those that arise in other parent groups all over the country: early childhood development, the role of the mother at each stage, setting boundaries, and struggles with adolescent children. However, the existence of the grandmothers' group in the Bedouin sector mandated building group work adapted to the culture and tradition: working in a professionally facilitated group in Arabic, and observing the components of traditional identity within the gathering ritual reduced the dissonance that occurs in the encounter with the new and unfamiliar world, and by grounding in the familiar world and the social support of the women's group, the power for conciliation and comfort emerged and, with it, the sense of empowerment and the ability to jointly cope with the changes to which the participants were exposed.

References

Abu-Rabia, Y. (2009). Lecture by Dr. Yunis Abu-Rabia, Director of the Rahat General Health Services Clinic, at the School for Educational Leadership, Rahat (in Hebrew).

Abu-Rabia-Queder, S., & Weiner-Levy, N. (2010). *Palestinian Women in Israel: Identity, Power Relations and Coping*. Jerusalem: Van-Leer Institute, 14–15 (in Hebrew).

Al-Krenawi, A. (1998). Family therapy with a multiparental/multispousal family. *Family Processes, 37*: 65–81.

Al-Krenawi, A. (2000). *Ethnopsychiatry among the Bedouin-Arab of the Negev*. Tel-Aviv: Hakibbutz Hameuchad (in Hebrew).

Al-Krenawi, A. (2001). Social work practice with the Bedouin-Arab in the Negev: cultural perspective. *Mifgash: Journal of Social-Educational Work, 15*: 37–59 (in Hebrew).

Batson, C. D., Dyck, J. L., Brandt, J. R., Batson, J. G., Powell, A. L., McMaster, M. R., & Griffitt, C. (1988). Five studies testing two new egoistic alternatives to the empathy-altruism hypothesis. *Journal of Personality and Social Psychology, 55*(1): 52–77.

Ben-Asher, S. (2003). Hegemonic, emancipated and polemic social representations: parental dialogue regarding Israeli marine soldiers training in polluted water. *Papers on Social Representations, 12*: 6.1–6.12.

Ben-David, J. (1982). In M. Alatawneh (1993). The linkage between the status of the Bedouin woman (the legal and public), her self-image and psychological well-being. MA Thesis, Ramat Gan: Bar-Ilan University (in Hebrew).

Bion, W. R. (1961). *Experiences in Groups*. London: Karnac.

Ezra, J. (2012). The essence of forgiveness: psychological, social and spiritual introspection. *Mikbatz: The Israel Journal of Group Psychotherapy, 17*(1): 9–20 (in Hebrew).

Foulkes, S. H. (1964). *Therapeutic Group Analysis*. London: Allen and Unwin [reprinted London: Karnac, 1986].

Foulkes, S. H. (1990). *Selected Papers of S. H. Foulkes: Psychoanalysis and Group Analysis*. London: Karnac.

Halevy, R. (2002). Walking the thin line: the multiple struggles of educated Bedouin women in the Negev. MA Thesis. Be'er-Sheva: Ben-Gurion University of the Negev (in Hebrew).

Hamenachem, E., & Halevy-Bar-Tendler, G. (2002). Destructiveness in groups: theoretical aspects and coping. In: L. Kacen & R. Lev-Wiesel (Eds.), *Group Work in a Multicultural Society* (pp. 199–221). Tel Aviv: Cherikover (in Hebrew).

Karkabi-Sabah, M. (2009). The organization of the *Hamoula* and the status of the Arab woman. In: F. Azaiza, C. Abu-Baker, R. Hertz-Lazarowitz, & A. Ghanem (Eds.), *Arab Women in Israel: Current Status and Future Trends* (pp. 47–70). Tel-Aviv: Ramot (in Hebrew).

Laor, I. (2007). The therapist, the patient, and the therapeutic setting: mutual construction of the setting as a therapeutic factor. *Sihot/ Dialogue: Israel Journal of Psychotherapy, 21*(2) (in Hebrew).

Moscovici, S. (1984). The phenomenon of social representations. In: R. M. Farr & S. Moscovici (Eds.), *Social Representations* (pp. 3–69). Cambridge: Cambridge University Press.

Moscovici, S. (1993). *The Invention of Society: Psychological Explanations for Social Phenomena*. Cambridge: Polity Press.

Moscovici, S. (1994). Social representations and pragmatic communication. *Social Science Information, 33*: 163–177.

Munk, M. (2005). *Empowerment Programs for Bedouin Women in the Negev*. Research and Planning Administration, National Insurance Institute of Israel (in Hebrew).

Neri, C. (1998). *Group*. London: Jessica Kingsley.

Paryente, B., & Orr, E. (2010). Hegemonic versus emancipated transmission of values: the case of religiously observant Jews in Israel. *Papers on Social Representations, 19*: 23–36.

Popper-Givon, A., & Al-Krenawi, A. (2010). An encounter of traditional Arab healers and their clients. In: S. Abu-Rabia-Queder & N. Weiner-Levy (Eds.), *Palestinian Women in Israel: Identity, Power Relations and Coping* (pp. 7–24). Jerusalem: Van-Leer Institute (in Hebrew).

Rybko, J. (2005). Attachment style and observed initial self-disclosure as explanatory variables of group functioning. *Mikbatz: The Israel Journal of Group Psychotherapy, 10*(2): 9–32 (in Hebrew).

Shapira, T., & Hertz-Lazarowitz, R. (2009). Blockage and empowerment in the public and private spheres: women in the Arab educational system in Israel. In: F. Azaiza, C. Abu-Baker, R. Hertz-Lazarowitz, & A. Ghanem (Eds.), *Arab Women in Israel: Current Status and Future Trends* (pp. 291–318). Tel-Aviv: Ramot (in Hebrew).

Smith, E. R., & Mackie, D. M. (1995). *Social Psychology*. New York: Worth.

Tschuschke, V., & Dies, R. R. (1994). Intensive analysis of therapeutic factors and outcome in long-term inpatient groups. *International Journal of Group Psychotherapy, 44*: 185–208.

Turner, J. C. (1987). *Rediscovering the Social Group: A Self-categorization Theory*. Oxford: Blackwell.

Wagner, W. (1993). Can representations explain social behavior? A discussion of social representations as rational systems. *Papers on Social Representations, 2*: 236–249.

Wagner, W. (1995). Description, explanation and method in social representation research. *Papers on Social Representations, 4*: 156–176.

Whitaker, D. S. (1985). *Using Groups to Help People*. New York: Routledge & Kegan Paul.

Whitaker, D. S. (1997). The character of the group as a medium for help. In: N. Rosenwasser & L. Natan (Eds.), *Group Facilitation Reader* (pp. 31–47). Jerusalem: Haim Zippori Community Education Center (in Hebrew).

Yalom, I., & Leszcz, M. (2005). *The Theory and Practice of Group Psychotherapy* (5th edn). New York: Basic Books.

Ziv-Beiman, S. (2010). The therapist's self-disclosure: effect on therapy outcomes and perception of the therapist. Doctoral Dissertation, Tel Aviv: Tel Aviv University (in Hebrew).

CHAPTER FIVE

Dealing with conflicts, rage, anger, and aggression in group analysis

Isaura Manso Neto and Mario David

Introduction

Rage, anger, and aggression are ubiquitous phenomena in human beings. Rage is one of the three biologically promoted forms of aggression. The others are predatory aggression and social dominance. They are somehow neurobiologically distinctive among them (Damásio, 1994, 1999; Panksepp, 1998; Siegel, 2005; Panksepp & Biven, 2012). Rage is the only one that seems to rely on a distinct emotional system that is dedicated to a primary-process form of aggression, being a primary-process capacity (Panksepp & Biven, 2012, p. 17). Rage systems exist in all mammalian brains. "Aggression is not always accompanied by anger, and anger does not necessarily lead to aggression, especially in mature humans who can control such base impulses. Aggression is a broader phenomenon than anger itself" (Panksepp, 1998, p. 187).

"Anger and aggression are secondary processes; they are some of the faces of rage" (Panksepp & Biven, 2012, p. 148).

> Jim Averill's (2010) definition states that anger refers to an emotional state that involves both an attribution of blame for some perceived

> wrong and an impulse to correct the wrong or prevent its recurrence; aggression is an attempt to coerce another into taking, or refraining from, some action against his or her will and not for his or her own good. (Panksepp & Biven, 2012, pp. 145–146)

Many stimuli can provoke anger, but the most common are the irritations and frustrations that arise from events that restrict freedom of an action or access to resources, as well as disappointments. Of utmost importance is childhood maltreatment or neglect, which can engender anger that lasts a lifetime (Panksepp, 1998; Panksepp & Biven, 2012).

> A key to recovery from pathological rage is to establish or re-establish a person's capacity to form and sustain warm trusting relationships. Positive emotional experiences in therapeutic contexts can probably help dull edges of many kinds of troublesome memories. Psychotherapy can help patients to rid themselves of issues that would otherwise fester as negativistic and irritating ruminations. (Panksepp & Biven, 2012, p. 173)

Conflicts can be either intrapsychic, interpersonal, or transpersonal, latent, or manifest, and they usually are the cause of some kind of frustration and anger.

Reconciliation refers to the act of re-establishing a friendly relationship after an estrangement; harmonizing positions of conflict, making them compatible (*Concise Oxford Dictionary*, 1995, p. 1148). Thus, we can be reconciled either with our own internal self or partial objects, or with other external objects.

> The Aristotelian emotional wisdom (phronesis) can eventually make anger a balanced tool – allowing us to choose with whom to be angry, with what intensity, and for how long. Understanding and reconciliation may be the best options to aspire for in the long run" (Panksepp & Biven, 2012, p. 150)

"Without the consciousness of aggressiveness and frustration, jealousy and envy, we cannot develop and achieve an analytic transforming process" (Neto, 1993, 2000, 2007). The avoidance of recognizing and mentalizing conflicts and difficult feelings are one of the causes of the crisis in psychoanalysis and group analysis (Neto & Centeno, 2006).

Anger may be either a natural and healthy reaction, based on the reality principle preserving life, or a destructive and unrealistic reaction. Molnos (1986) speaks about "Anger that destroys and anger that heals" (Molnos, 1986). The most important difference between them is the displaced target of the aggression; the anger that destroys is towards a displaced target. Panksepp and Biven (2012, p. 145) quote Aristotle (320 BC): "Anybody can become angry, that is easy; but to be angry with the right person, and to the right degree, and at the right time, and for the right purpose, and in the right way, that is not within everybody's power, that is not easy". Panksepp and Biven also suggest that "the major goal of psychotherapy is to see your emotions clearly and to learn to use them for the betterment of our lives" (Panksepp & Biven, 2012, p. 146).

> I was angry with my friend.
> I told my wrath, my wrath did end.
> I was angry with my foe:
> I told it not, my wrath did grow
>
> (William Blake, 1793, quoted in Panksepp & Biven, 2012, p. 173)

These feelings are more difficult to be mentalized (Fonagy & Target, 2003; Holmes, 2006) and worked through within an individual setting. In the latter kind of relationship, the idealization of the analyst/psychotherapist has a tendency to be too prolonged or even denied by the patient and, even worse, by the analyst. Patients avoid the loss of the idealized object, fear the analyst's anger and consequent abandonment and rejection; analysts may fear the conflict in itself and the departure of the patient. On the other hand, the group setting aids the appearance of interpersonal conflicts that pave the way for a greater consciousness and deeper understanding of internal conflicts.

Our aim is to convey the importance of the group analytic group as a favorable setting for uncovering of conflicts and strong affects, such as love, anger, jealousy, and envy. The spontaneous interaction among the members of the group within the matrix fosters the appearance of these difficult phenomena. Once they are understood, worked through, and overcome, insight and mental growth occurs, bringing about reconciliation. However, conflicts may also be extremely destructive, leading to the breaking of the analytic processes. Overcoming these important situations depends mainly on the group analyst's capacities and creativity. We are referring to the Portuguese concept of group-analytic pattern introduced by Cortesão in 1967 (Cortesão, 1967, 1971b, 2008).

In its beginnings, with the memory of the two World Wars still fresh, group analysis was mostly influenced by the fear of destructive groups and leaders. Moreover, psychoanalysts since Freud have feared groups as settings where free thinking was, in a certain way, forbidden. Therefore, groups have not been considered by psychoanalysis as being a setting that was good enough for therapeutic transformation. Even Foulkes was extremely ambivalent on this issue.

Things began to change during the following decades. In Portugal, Cortesão (1919–1991), who had been trained by Foulkes, introduced group analysis with a very important psychoanalytic framework being used as an important psychoanalytic psychotherapy where unconscious phenomena, transference, and countertransference represent some of the transforming elements in group analysis (Cortesão, 1967, 1971a,b, 1974, 1991, 2008; Dinis, 1997, 2004, 2006). Therefore, working through jealousy, envy, and anger became part of the Portuguese group analytic theory and practice.

In 1991, Nitsun wrote a paper that won the Fernando Arroyave Memorial Prize. He highlighted Foulkes' preconceptions on the importance of destructive forces in every group and their transformative potential, in cases where they are adequately diagnosed, understood, and interpreted. Later on, Nitsun (1996) developed these themes in his book *The Anti-Group: Destructive Forces in the Group and their Creative Potential*, stating,

> The anti-group is not conceived as a monolithic force that inevitably destroys the group. Rather, it is seen in a complementary relationship with creative group processes, but requiring recognition and handling in order that the constructive development of the group can proceed without serious obstruction. The conflict between creative and destructive is itself seen as generative: it heightens and illuminates the paradoxical nature not only of the group but of human life in general and its containment and recognition is strengthening. (1996, p. 45).

In 2009, during his S. H. Foulkes Lecture "Authority and revolt", Nitsun defended the importance of the conductor/conduction—the group analyst—to the transformative potential of group analysis and psychoanalytic group psychotherapy.

This theoretical position had been similarly defended by Cortesão and the Portuguese group analysts, in his concept called the group analytic pattern (Cortesão, 1967, 1971b, 2008). This concept is particularly relevant, as the group analyst will transmit an analytic attitude and culture to the group, which allows for the subsequent development of that therapeutic net, the matrix.

Foulkes always rejected this concept, although he admitted the unique importance of the therapist's personal position in the group.

Cortesão begins with a semantic analysis of the term, setting aside the origins linked with pattern and patronus, because "really, the group analyst should not offer himself as a protector, or a role model, nor should he guide actively or didactically" (Cortesão, 2008, p. 116). In response to an interpretation of the concept offered by Foulkes, Cortesão explains that "it is not really about the imprint which the therapist makes but rather the imprint he conveys" (Cortesão, 1971a, p. 39).

In this sense, the analyst is a conveyor, that is, a transmitter, a catalyst, and is not, in any way, a cause and certainly cannot be a "leader" "to whom someone can identify with, not a 'pattern' for the purpose of adaptation or conformism" (Cortesão, 2008, p. 119, translated for this edition).

The pattern is integrated by the group, stimulating communication and the interpretation promoting regression inside the group analytic matrix. The pattern has three main dimensions.

1. Its nature is related to the group analyst's personality, worked through by his/her own personal GA as well as by his/her continuing theoretical education and training.
2. Its functions, which are related to the set of clinical attitudes and interpretations that arise during the sessions.
3. Its purposes are related to the signification and differentiation of each member's individual self.

The group-analytic pattern consisted of the kind of specific attitudes that the group analyst transmits and sustains in the group-analytic matrix, which have an interpretative function that foments and develops the group-analytic process (Cortesão, 2008, p. 127).

Gans, in his interesting book titled *Difficult Topics in Group Psychotherapy* (2010), defends similar ideas and highlights the importance of leadership in dealing with hostility: "Hostility in group psychotherapy is inevitable and potentially constructive; its understanding and management are crucial to successful group leadership" (Gans, 2010, p. 59).

". . . I also believe that the successful handling of the anti-group represents a turning point in the development of the group" (Nitsun, 1996, p. 44) as well as the development of each member, we would say (Neto, 1999).

In order to write and think about this matter, Neto returned to her handwritten verbatim notes from many of her sessions and appealed to her memory to recall conflicts she had experienced in several groups that she belonged to as a patient, a group analyst, co-therapist, or supervisor, in a variety of settings—mental health institutions, group psychotherapy, private group analytic practice, and teams in general. The authors also organized a scientific meeting with the significant members of group analytic society in order to associate and elaborate on these themes (David, 2012).

Causality and triggers of anger and aggression in groups

We think that conflicts and anger are based upon four main factors:

1. Individual members—the individual psychopathology: primary narcissism, narcissistic injuries (Kohut, 1984), psychotic part of the personality (Bion, 1957), envy, sibling rivalry, Oedipus complex and its correlated conflicts, mental symbiotic relations pattern. Aggression and conflicts may be felt as the only way to achieve separation and autonomy.
2. Group setting—the "Anti-group" (Nitsun, 1991, 1996): in this chapter we do not focus on the hostility based on the contradictory factors contained within group analysis, but mainly on those associated to interpersonal conflicts.
3. The group analyst/group analytic psychotherapist's personality and his/her theoretical and personal training. A "good enough group analyst" who is at ease with conflicts, anger, and aggression is definitely a factor that enhances the transformative poten-

tial of these disturbing human phenomena. We also think that the group analyst must pay attention to, and interpret, each member as well as the group as a whole (Dinis, 2004; Knauss, 2004; Michel, 2004; Zimerman, 2004).

We believe that only dominant interventions targeted towards the group as a whole will lead to frustration and aggression, and will not allow the parties to work through these issues. We consider that the way groups are conducted, that is, the group analyst's pattern is one of the most important tools in the analysis of conflicts and anger.

4. Transference—Conflicts in groups mainly derive from transference. They are especially expressed towards the group analyst directly or displaced towards other members of the group. The "other" becomes the repository of the rejected negative parts of the selves and/or their primary internalized objects. The "other" loses their independence and individuality, becoming the enemy to be destroyed or from whom one must run away. Cortesão (2008) spoke of hostile transference as a resistance mainly based on group members' envy of the power of the analyst or of any "other" envied member of the group. Everyday occurrences, such as the group analysts' absences due to holidays, conferences, and illnesses, are sometimes felt as abandonments and/or rejections, conveying frustration and several rage reactions.

The above relational transference phenomena rooted in past primitive object relationships may be triggered by several causes, more or less determined either by the situation of each member or by the group as a whole. Among these transference phenomena we consider sibling rivalry to be a phenomenon that has not been well conceptualized by psychoanalysts (Mitchell, 2003) and by group analysts who have included it as part of the Oedipus complex.

Sibling rivalry is deeply dependent on the way parents deal with their children as a group as well as with the ubiquitous need of the human baby to be the only son/daughter and be unconditionally loved by the primary care-givers. Therefore, apart from the similarities, there are also differences between Oedipus and sibling rivalries.

Sibling rivalry appears quickly and clearly in groups. "The group analyst is felt either consciously or unconsciously, to be treating one or several group members 'better' than the member who feels jealousy" (Neto & Viera Dinis, 2010).

This kind of conflict might arise between a member of the group and the group analyst alone, or be totally displaced towards the other members. In this case, the rage appears through projections, projective identifications, or several rationalizations.

A new element joining a group triggers conflicts of this kind, which might incite high levels of anger and aggression based mainly on jealousy and envy. These are painful situations that may be analyzed and overcome with healthy consequences for other areas of one's life, familial (husbands, wives, children) and professional. This way, chronic dysfunctional relational patterns may be stopped or, at least, ameliorated. We can say that reconciliation may be achieved.

Envy is also behind conflicts with the group analyst as well as with other members. This is particularly difficult to manage.

We can say that one of the added values of group analysis is the diagnosis, understanding, and potential resolution of misunderstandings, as consequences of transference. Zimerman (2000), a Brazilian psychoanalyst and group analyst, defined psychoanalysis as the science that studies misunderstandings.

The whole set of interactions and relationships established inside a group analytic group includes more or less realistic mirror phenomena. Mirroring can become extremely distorted because of transference and primitive defence mechanisms, leading to a potentially huge destructive force. The concept we are referring to is the one that Zinkin (1983) called malignant mirroring. Malignant mirroring is very frequent among human beings and is responsible for multiple destructive behaviours in many circumstances. It is also a frequent trigger of anger in groups. Every time we need to get rid of parts of ourselves, or parts of our internal objects, we can use splitting and projective identification. Sometimes, these situations are not easily identifiable, which contributes to the difficulty of their management and interpretation and working through. If we are dealing with a group analytic group, it might be possible that this destructiveness can be understood, transformed, and, thus, overcome, making reconciliation possible.

Apart from the above mentioned transference phenomena, we often find the loss of the idealization of the group analyst and last, but not least, real interactive empathic failures are frequent triggers of conflicts and rage, in every type of psychoanalytic psychotherapy, including group analysis.

To conclude this section on causality and triggers, we would like to say that transference and reality are always present in human functioning, in very close interaction. Therefore, it could be difficult to separate transference and reality in a clear way.

Phenomenology: rageful behavior

Hostility and conflicts can be more or less clearly expressed. They might be expressed by anger, violent words, and behavior with strong emotions, or they might be dissimulated and hidden by powerful defences, such as rationalization, reaction formation, and denial.

Rageful behavior can be expressed by verbal and non-verbal communication. Silences, absences, delays, difficulties with payment, actings-out, negative therapeutic reactions, threats of abandoning the group, drop-outs, and scapegoats. The conflicts might be between a group member and the group analyst, or between peers, or as displacements from the group analyst. There is a general agreement on these issues among the majority of the senior members the Portuguese Group Analytic Society (David, 2012).

Working through and interpretation

To begin with, we must identify anger, conflicts, destructive communication and behavior. Most of the time, this is not a simple task. It implies the risk of losing the idealization of the patient as well as that of the group analyst, amplifying rage, unleashing transference and countertransference, fears of breaking the relationship, releasing separation and rejection anxieties. In the case that we avoid identifying destructivity openly, there will be even more risks to the member or members directly involved in the aggressive phenomena as well as to the others and the group as a whole.

After identifying an instance of aggressive communication, group analysts should think about its causes and appeal to the self-analysis of their countertransference. We must try to understand the reasons for this aggression at this particular moment, with that member, in that group, with that group analyst. Therefore, to start with, group analysts must detect their own contribution to the triggering of conflicts and aggression within a therapeutic group, should they be more or less due to transference. In spite of the particular psychopathology of each member, we must never forget our own contribution to aggressive phenomena, which includes the possibility of having not been empathic enough towards the aggressive members as well the possibility of having amplified peer jealousy, which is a major risk in group analysis. Delays, absences, holidays, congresses, etc., are also situations that can frequently provoke frustration and rage. Only after this has been explored are we able to name the aggressive communication, highlight it, and begin the interpretation activity. Most of the time, it is difficult to find an empathic and creative way to point out the aggressive communication.

It takes some time between the process of diagnosis, the time to name it, highlight it, and begin the interpretation activity.

In Neto's experience as a group analyst in small, medium, or large institutional psychotherapeutic groups, as well as in private practice with small groups and operative groups, she has noticed that there are especially difficult aggressive situations to be handled: those based on envy and those based on malignant mirroring, as well as the loss of the idealized group analyst, frequent absences, and chronic delays and difficulties in payment.

Envy is, in her experience, the most difficult affect to deal with within a group. If noticed and named explicitly, it very often leads to drop-outs, even when we try to be empathic and careful. Usually, members who are envious try to avoid the mentalization of such feelings. They feel ashamed and afraid, as it reveals narcissistic vulnerabilities that provoke intense suffering. So, instead, they react more aggressively. The mentalization of envy is the first step in overcoming this kind of narcissistic psychopathology. Only then can we attain and understand the roots of the narcissistic wounds and overcome this terrible personality feature that is so disruptive in other areas of life.

Built upon powerful projections and projective identifications, malignant mirroring, once it has been identified silently, Neto uses to highlight the situation identified. She normally says that it seems that something is happening that she does not fully understand; she asks the group what they all think about what is happening. She normally asks the aggressive member to associate about past life events that are similar to what is happening at that precise moment. Sometimes, the group analyst must be very active while trying to get them to recall repressed memories. This is how the "enemy" is correctly identified. The "current enemy" is gradually recognized as different from the past objects and the transference nature of the frustrating and rageful situation becomes clear enough so that it can be worked through. Progressively, it becomes possible to internalize the projected elements, overcoming the conflict and the aggressive behavior, and paving the way to reconciliation.

Jealousy and loss of idealization, though they can be the cause for intense rage, are easier to deal with, as they are more prone to be accepted and mentalized; this allows for possible interpretation to induce changes and facilitate reconciliation.

Chronic absences, and delays and difficulties in payment are dissimulated forms of aggressive communication that are very difficult to transform. These behavior symptoms are organized in a very rational way. External reality colludes with inner resistances. Neto normally says that she will not discuss the everyday demands of patients' lives; she has no intention of discussing with them what they could do to arrive and pay on time and to be more diligent. Neto avoids discussing rational reasons. She usually says that beyond those reasons, there might be other reasons dictated by unconscious forces. Sometimes, she asks them, and suggests that it would be important to speak about, how they feel about being absent or late. She also asks the group to speak about how they feel about the absences and lateness of "others". She also mentions the members that are missing that session. These behavior symptoms are more frequent in the group setting than in the individual one. What we have often found is that this type of communication is reduced when the members who communicate this way become emotionally convinced that they were missed by the "others".

Never should the group analyst/group psychotherapist and the group give up trying to understand the hidden unconscious.

Conclusions

- Anger and aggression can be natural and healthy reactions based on the life-preserving principle, or destructive and unrealistic.

- If we do not become conscious of conflicts, anger and frustration, jealousy and envy, we cannot develop and achieve an analytic transforming process.
- The group setting facilitates the appearance of anger towards the therapist more than in the individual setting.
- We must take into account that every group contains in itself an aggressive potential that can neither be devaluated nor denied. It will appear spontaneously, reactively to triggers that are more or less predictable.
- Concerning causality, conflicts in groups are mainly of a transference nature. Many of them are the result of peer jealousy and envy, being especially clear and violent upon the entrance of a newcomer. Malignant mirroring is also quite frequently the cause of destructiveness in groups. The loss of the idealization of the psychotherapist is another frequent and necessary cause of frustration and rage.
- Some of the more predictable triggers that occur in every group include interruption of the sessions, mainly due to the group analyst/group psychotherapist, discharges, and drop-outs. Newcomers also feature among this group of triggers. There are other kinds of triggers that are more difficult to anticipate, which are more dependent on the mental organization of each member, including the group analyst. Among these, we highlight empathic injuries and failures that are usually a common and frequent cause of frustrations, anger, and aggression. This aspect will be felt as more violent if the empathic failure is perpetrated by the group analyst/group psychotherapist.
- We must identify the destructive phenomena in a group as soon as they become explicit in a more or less clear way, naming them when possible.
- Afterwards, we must understand the anti-group in the context of the group's evolution, each member's mental organization and life history, transference and countertransference. Then it is the right time to interpret.
- The rageful behaviour must be understood so that it may be transformed, deprived of the displaced transference mechanisms, and converted into more realistic and creative attitudes towards oneself and others. This process was part of what Cortesão called the "aesthetic equilibrium" (Cortesão, 1991).

- The group analyst's pattern (Cortesão, 2008) is one of the most important tools in the analysis of conflicts and anger.
- For "a good enough" finalization of the group analytic process, we believe it is crucial for each group member to have had a reconciliation experience.
- Group analysis/psychoanalytic group psychotherapy is a setting that induces free thinking and a spontaneous interaction among its members, deepening the knowledge of each one of them, thus reducing aggressive feelings and behaviors, conveying reconciliation. "In general there is much less aggression when animals have known each other for a long time than when they are strangers" (Panksepp, 1998, p. 188).

References

Averill, J. (2010). Ten questions about anger that you may never have thought to ask. In: F. Pahlavan (Ed.), *Multiple Facets of Anger: Getting Mad or Restoring Justice?* (pp. 1–25). New York: Nova Science.

Bion, W. R. (1957). Differentiation of the psychotic from the non psychotic personalities. *International Journal of Psychoanalysis, 39*: 144–146 [reprinted in *Second Thoughts*, 1967].

Concise Oxford Dictionary (1995). (9th edn). Oxford: Clarendon Press.

Cortesão, E. L. (1967). Some further thoughts on the concept of group matrix and pattern. *Group Analysis, 1*(1): 35–36.

Cortesão, E. L. (1971a). On interpretation in group analysis. *Group Analysis, 4*(1): 39–53.

Cortesão, E. L. (1971b). Opening remarks. First European Symposium of Group Analysis. *Group Analysis, 4*(1): 2–3.

Cortesão, E. L. (1974). Transference neurosis and the group analytic process. *Group Analysis, 7*(1): 19–22.

Cortesão, E. L. (1991). Group analysis and aesthetic equilibrium. *Group Analysis, 24*(3): 271–277.

Cortesão, E. L. (2008). *Grupanálise—Teoria e Técnica.* Lisbon: Fundação Calouste Gulbenkian.

Damásio, A. (1994). *Descartes' Error: Emotion, Reason, and the Human Body.* New York: Avon Books.

Damásio, A. (1999). *The Feeling of What Happens: Body and Emotion in the Making of Consciousness.* New York: Harcourt Brace.

David, M. (2012). How the Portuguese group-analysts handle conflict and aggressiveness emerging from groups: theoretical conceptualization and technical aspects. *Groupanalysis Revistaonline* (available at: www.grupanalise.pt/grupanaliseonline).

Dinis, C. V. (1997). Begehren und Verlust bei der Gegenübertragung. *Gruppenanlyse, 7*(2): 165–170.

Dinis, C. V. (2004). One among many or primus interpares. Paper presented to the Third EFPP European Conference of Psychoanalytic Group Psychotherapy, "The Individual and the Group—Bridging the Gap", 7–10 October, Lisbon, Portugal. In: *Book of Abstracts* (pp. 3–14).

Dinis, C. V. (2006). Le temps et le changement. *Temps et Psychothérapie, Collection Explorations Psychoanalytiques*, 27–37.

Fonagy, P., & Target, M. (2003). *Psychoanalytic Theories. Perspective from Developmental Psychopathology*. London: Whurr.

Gans, J. S. (2010). Hostility. In: *Difficult Topics in Group Psychotherapy* (pp. 41–61). London: Karnac.

Holmes, J. (2006). Mentalizing from a psychoanalytic perspective: what's new? In: J. G. Allen & P. Fonagy (Eds.), *Handbook of Mentalization-Based Treatment* (pp. 31–49). London: Wiley.

Knauss, W. (2004). The group in the unconscious—a bridge between the group and the society. Paper presented to the Third EFPP European Conference of Psychoanalytic Group Psychotherapy, "The Individual and the Group—Bridging the Gap", 7–10 October, Lisbon, Portugal. In: *Book of Abstracts* (pp. 56–69).

Kohut, H. (1984). *How Does Analysis Cure*? Chicago, IL: Chicago University Press.

Michel, L. (2004). The pleasure in group. Paper presented to the Third EFPP European Conference of Psychoanalytic Group Psychotherapy, "The Individual and the Group—Bridging the Gap", 7–10 October, Lisbon, Portugal. In: *Book of Abstracts* (pp. 39–54).

Mitchell, J. (2003). *Siblings. Sex and Violence*. New York: Polity Press.

Molnos, A. (1986). Anger that destroys and anger that heals: handling hostility in group-analysis and in dynamic brief psychotherapy. *Group Analysis, 19*(3): 207–221.

Neto, I. M. (1993). Agressividade e Narcisismo. Paper presented to the 2nd Encontro Luso-Brasileiro de Grupanálise e Psicoterapia Analítica de Grupo, Lisbon, Portugal.

Neto, I. M. (1999). The freedom and the capacity to say NO and its healing potential. Paper presented to EFPP—Second European Conference on Group Analytic Psychotherapy, 28–30 May, Barcelona, Spain.

Neto, I. M. (2000). Agressividade—da Destrutividade à Elaboração. Paper presented to the 2nd Encontro de Saúde Mental do Concelho de Cascais—Departamento de Psiquiatria e Saúde Mental do Hospital S. Francisco Xavier, 23 November, Lisbon, Portugal.

Neto, I. M. (2007). *Violência e Terrorismo: Maldade, Fundamentalismo, Fanatismo e Insight Social*. Paper presented to the Eleventh Congress of Nacional da Sociedade Portuguesa de Grupanálise, Hospital Miguel Bombarda, 19–20 October, Lisbon, Portugal.

Neto, I. M., & Centeno, M. J. (2006). Is there a crisis in psychoanalysis and group analysis? Essence and preconception. Presented to the 34th GAS Winter Workshop "Group Analysis Today: Concepts and Preconceptions", 12–15 January, Lisbon, Portugal.

Neto, I. M., & Vieira Dinis, F. (2010). Evil, evilness, violence and terrorism. *Revista Portuguesa de Grupanálise*, 87–101 (see electronic edition: www.grupanalise.pt/grupanaliseonline).

Nitsun, M. (1991). The anti-group: destructive forces in the group and their therapeutic potential. *Group Analysis, 24*(1): 7–20.

Nitsun, M. (1996). *The Anti-Group: Destructive Forces in the Group and their Creative Potential*. London: Routledge.

Panksepp, J. (1998). *Affective Neuroscience*. New York: Oxford University Press.

Panksepp, J., & Biven, L. (2012). *The Archaelogy of Mind: Neuro-evolutionary Origins of Human Emotions*. New York: W. W. Norton.

Siegel, A. (2005). *The Neurobiology of Aggression and Rage*. Boca Raton, FL: CRC Press.

Zimerman, D. E. (2000). *Fundamentos Básicos das Grupoterapias* (2nd edn). Porto Alegre, Brasil: Artes Médicas Sul.

Zimerman, D. E. (2004). Transformation in my personal way of practicing group analysis throughout an experience of over 40 years. Paper presented to the Third EFPP European Conference of Psychoanalytic Group Psychotherapy, "The Individual and the Group—Bridging the Gap", 7–10 October, Lisbon, Portugal. In: *Book of Abstracts* (pp. 15–38).

Zinkin, L. (1983). Malignant mirroring. *Group Analysis, 16*(2): 113–126.

PART III

THE SOCIAL AND THE GROUP

CHAPTER SIX

Conflicts and social transference in groups

Klimis Navridis

The psychoanalytical experience of groups, at its very core, is explosive. The group frequently brings psychoanalytical clinical thinking face to face with the complexity of social and cultural influences, which are easily set aside and "tamed" in the classic one-on-one setting of private practice. This happens because, de facto, the clinical space of freestanding private practice in its dualistic psychoanalytical configuration, in my opinion, operates with a relative lack of freedom. Things are placed beyond limits on the pretext of legitimate psychologization (Castel, 1973); many manifestations of social conflicts, cultural differences, and distinctiveness that could potentially, or actually, be conveyed by patients undergoing analysis are censored.

On the other hand, group clinical work is carried out in a variety of very different settings: from the protected milieu of the private practice to the very open community setting, encompassing the hospital or the broader institutional setting, schools, universities, as well as education or training in the context of psychoanalytic group psychotherapy and Societies for group analysis.

Very diverse populations may participate: psychiatric patients, adults, children or adolescents, adults and very young children (toddler groups) (Navridi et al., 2012), teachers, parents, families, mental health professionals, business executives, members of various social groups, refugees, unemployed, Roma, drug addicts, HIV positive individuals, etc.

It is suitable for persons with different needs, who might, therefore, have diverse objectives: therapy, analysis, education or training, provision of psychosocial assistance with respect to problems causing "social pain" (de Gaulejac et al., 2007), or for the purposes of action research (Barus-Michel et al., 2002); consequently, it requires (or takes place in) very diverse settings: institutional or freestanding, public or private, small, medium, or large groups, closed, evolving or open, and so forth. It also uses various methods and techniques: verbal communication and expression groups, back-to-back (*dos-à-dos*[1]) groups, psychodrama, gestalt therapy, socio-drama, or other types of group therapy through art, mediation groups, etc.

Professionals working within groups, not only in the capacity of therapist or analyst, but also as teachers, trainers, or moderators, are called upon to deal with situations they are unable to explain, and neither can they perceive how they arose, nor why they are evolving in a specific manner.

Therapists themselves could be beset by emotions that are not only hard to experience, but also to accept, since they give rise to feelings of guilt and professional incompetence; emotions such as boredom, loneliness, and neglect, jealousy, envy, apprehension, fear that the group will suddenly break up, or that something excessively violent will occur, rage and vengefulness, or even hatred towards the group or certain participants.

There are several cases where, during group work in a therapeutic, educational, or psychosocial setting, professionals might catch themselves making a serious mistake that is extremely rare for them. For example, they might end the session before time is up, or they might neglect to notify certain participants who happened to be absent on one session that one of the forthcoming sessions has been postponed. They might even note that during a specific session or particular phase, contrary to their customary habits, and for reasons they cannot explain to themselves, they remain silent for long periods of time, might become distracted, overly talkative, have a tendency to explain too much and be "didactic", become aggressive or protective, or might even have the tendency to self-censorship.

Such situations are known to be related to countertransference and are due to the fact that, within the group, the professional is constantly being exposed to projections and diffracted transference[2] (Kaës, 2007) of the participants, who unconsciously and, therefore, without the therapist becoming aware of it, invoke certain fantasies and repressed representations that make him or her succumb to and participate in phenomena of projected identification, triggering various emotional reactions and might sometimes result in uncontrolled enactments.

In other words, specialists, as the subject of the unconscious, unwittingly act out the unconscious of the group, just like all the participants. It is, therefore, imperative for specialists to possess the most solid, experiential psychoanalytical education possible. This is precisely what will permit them, through introspection, to understand and satisfactorily handle the various difficult situations of transference they will be called upon to face, and to survive with the fewest possible losses.

On the other hand, another well-known fact is that outside the protection of the private practice, the group setting is, *de facto*, greatly exposed and permeable from within, in other words unconsciously, *vis-à-vis* extremely strong social, institutional, and cultural factors (Ofer & Hadar, 2001). Consequently, professionals working with groups must remain open to identifying and attempting to comprehend these factors, instead of persistently remaining within the dogmatically strict psychoanalytical process of observation and listening (Foulkes, 1964; Hopper, 2007).

Group transferences in the broader social space, are not only defined by their psychic and inter-subjective group components (Kaës, 1976). They also refer to what we would term the social real,[3] to social pain, to a social symbolic and a social imaginary. For example, students with their teachers, or teachers among themselves, do not interact within the school environment simply as subjects of the unconscious, but also as social subjects. The same thing occurs with the executives within a private or state organization within the relevant workplace frameworks (Giust-Desprairies & de Gaulejac, 2009).

Furthermore, phenomena have been described in clinical-type psychocultural or sociological studies inspired by psychoanalysis which indicate that, not only users of social care or health services, but also "welcoming" staff of the institutions offering such services, reciprocally transfer or countertransfer unconscious social representations that have to do with relationships to a threatening otherness, such as the "stranger", the "sick", or the "marginalised" (de Gaulejac et al., 1996).

In other words, transferences, as we observe and experience them unfold within the group milieu in the public space, outside private practice, always bear the imprint of what we might term a social transference. It is precisely this social aspect of transference and countertransference that we, as professionals, should not ignore and, more importantly, should not deny.

Several years ago, I was invited to conduct a twelve-hour experiential verbal communication seminar in the center of Athens, within the context of a broader training program for gypsies. The program had been organized by a non-governmental organization (NGO) responsible for matters of local government. The participants, about fifteen, if I remember correctly, were Roma gypsies who had recently been housed in residences built specially for them in an extremely run-down, working-class area on the outskirts of the capital. Besides my own seminar, the program included several other courses: history, civics, social behavior, home economics, etc. The aim was to provide interested parties with some basic knowledge and skills that would supposedly facilitate their passage from a primarily nomadic way of life to a more permanent domestic settlement in a community context that would not consist solely of Roma.

This specific program took place in the training centre of the NGO, located in a rather modern building in the centre of Athens, with smart offices and training rooms. Outside the room provided for the group sessions was a long table with coffee, soft drinks, small sandwiches, and biscuits. The premises, furniture, and the entire atmosphere were perhaps more fitting for a training seminar addressed to top-level executives of a multi-national organization and seemed to be rather too luxurious for our workshop.

The gypsies, three or four women and about ten men, aged between 20–25 and 35–40 years old, found it virtually impossible to adapt to the setting: before the first session began and after each break, they would literally remain "glued" around the table with the snacks and refreshments and it was impossible to "unglue" them, resulting in the session invariably starting with a 10–15-minute delay. Moreover, during a session, two or three of them, not always the same persons, would get up, leaving the room abruptly to use the washroom, returning shortly afterwards with a sandwich or coffee in hand.

All of this gave rise to an internal irritation in me, as well as the unpleasant feeling that these people, who were somehow insulting me, were attracted more by the refreshments in the room outside rather than by anything I had to offer them.

Nevertheless, from the very outset, I had been impressed by their excessive politeness and the respect they showed me when they addressed me or looked at me, and how well dressed they were. This was particularly true for one of them, who had slicked back his hair and wore a completely grotesque white suit with broad red stripes, and a patterned tie with vivid colours, looking more like someone who was about to perform on stage, rather than participating in a life-long-learning workshop.

However, when addressing each other, they were quite aggressive and frequently sarcastic, using expressions like "Get lost, you *gyftos* [gypsy]",[4] "You're acting like a *gyftos*", or "Don't try to 'gyp' us like that". Suddenly, halfway through the first session of the second meeting—out of a total of four meetings of three sixty-minute sessions each—one of the participants said something in their language to the man in the striped suit and flashy tie, and called him a *gyftos*. The latter, beside himself with rage, sprang up and leaped over the tables, screaming his head off, in an attempt to wring the other's neck.

Two or three participants tried to separate them, shouting and gesticulating agitatedly, while I was still unable to grasp a word of what they were saying. The women screeched and the others simply looked on with condescending concern, like spectators at a bullfight, and I was terrified that something dreadful was about to take place right before my eyes and that I would be utterly unable to avert it. At the same time, I thought that it was as though I was the one excluded from the group, and that I was the one left to observe this strange bullfight from the stands, where this wild, untamed beast condemned to death appeared to be none other than myself.

I was also wondering what else, besides myself and my extreme (and possibly terribly worrying) difference compared to them, this bizarre person might represent to the imaginary of the group. The person stood out "like a sore thumb" and seemed to incarnate with his appearance a ridiculous caricature of bourgeois respectability. This tremendous tension lasted several minutes and then ended as suddenly as it had started. Silence reigned, and then I said, "It looks as though when you feel that others look at you as something so undesirable and bad it is an insult, and it can, at times, make you feel as though you are in real danger . . ."

They looked at me, startled that I was still present amongst them in spite of everything, and, after a couple of minutes of silence, they started quite unexpectedly to talk about their dietary habits.

They described how they remove the prickles from hedgehogs and how they cook them, as well as how much they enjoyed eating thistles. They told me how they say "hedgehog" and "thistle" in their own language. They also said that although priests think it is a sin to eat hedgehogs, they had once met a priest who loved their meat.

This animated discussion on recipes for thistles and hedgehogs had really stirred my interest and I listened attentively as I enjoyed learning various things of which I knew absolutely nothing. It occurred to me that, for a moment, the learning relationship appeared to be reversed: they had now become my teachers.

The atmosphere seemed to have changed as if by magic. Stress and resistance seemed to gradually subside; this allowed participants to transfer the source for satisfaction of their oral emotional needs from the catering's material goods to the intersubjective space of the team. At the same time, the group was brought to a state more open to thought and learning through experience (Bion, 1962).

I believe that the change effected was enabled by the metaphorization and consequent symbolic/verbal and emotional processing within the group of an internalized social conflict and a shared, prolonged, and repeated social trauma[5] (Hopper, 2003).

Initially, this happened through the transposition of the transference conflict from the group onto a pair of participants and the subsequent enactment: my imaginary representative and the group member who attacked him by calling him a "gyftos", undertook, probably unwittingly, to dramatize and then to enact on behalf of the group,[6] something that the others were possibly experiencing in relation to me, that is, the disparagement, scorn, and rejection that cause rage and hatred.

My intervention followed the outbreak of the enactment, after which the group was able to "use" the topic of food as a mediating object. From the "prim and proper" and, to them, unfamiliar food of the catering—which, at the level of social imaginary condensed, among others, my own presence together with the "spiritual sustenance" I had brought to offer them—with all its derogatory connotations of looking down on them, we moved on to thistles and hedgehogs, that is, foods that, on the one hand, were familiar to them and, on the other, carried all that symbolic weight which helped to verbalize our relationship through a game of metaphors, that is, the social border which separates us with its "prickles". However, once these are removed and what remains is suitably "cooked", it becomes something that is not only edible, but also something we are able to share.

In other words, a transitional space was created, which permitted the transition, at a purely symbolic level, of the transference conflict and the processing of negativity reintegrated through its ambivalence, precisely through the imaginary "use" of foods and their preparation as objects and procedures of mediation (Navridis, 2006; Vacheret, 2002). At the same time, the ability to create ties within the group was restored while paving the way for the group to be able to "feed" not only on foods that "hurt", but also to enjoy these without fear. Thistles and hedgehogs might be prickly, but they are extremely tasty. These gypsy treats may be sinful and forbidden, yet secretly delight some priests ("fathers"?), nevertheless.

The above example clearly illustrates the double reference that transference and countertransference may have in similar cases: on the one hand, they refer to what initially defined them, that is, the primary relationships with objects of early childhood, and, on the other, relationships with social and political objects (Giust-Desprairies, 2003). In cases like the aforementioned, that is, cases in which social and cultural differences stand out dramatically with respect to the imaginary difference between parent and child—which in any case is subjected and fostered within the same context—the group analyst, the group moderator, the trainer, or the teacher might unconsciously be experienced as the transference representative of parental objects, as well as the representative of political and ideological power (de Gaulejac et al., 2007; Hopper, 2007). This other aspect of transference corresponds to what we might call social transference.

However, what is interesting about our example is the manner in which the Roma taking part in this program were treated: on the one hand, by the State, which, with the hypocritical enticement of a supposedly better life, was attempting to immobilize them geographically (ignoring and violating the main cultural element characterizing them as a social group, i.e., the nomadic way of life) and integrate them socially, possibly in order to control them better, and, on the other hand, the NGO organizing the training, which was receiving them with a covert symbolic aggressiveness and arrogance, as if willfully denying their cultural identity by treating them not as Roma, but as executives in a multi-national company. In this case, too, we also come across, as we might say, a type of social and institutional countertransference—and a particularly violent one at that (de Gaulejac et al., 1996).

Of course, the same hypocrisy characterized the beneficiaries: the Roma acted as though they wished to be trained, whereas what actually seemed to interest them mainly was the small (at least, by my standards, but not necessarily theirs) sum of money they would be receiving as "compensation" for their participation, as well as the full board throughout the program. I did not dare share this thought with them during the first sessions so as "not to offend them" and repeatedly censored myself in this respect. When, at one point, I found the courage and the words to do so, they burst out laughing like children that had been caught red-handed. Therefore, for a period of time I, too, was hypocritical towards them, by acting as if I believed in their honesty. The executives who had designed the program also had their share in the lie that they genuinely desired to help this specific population to change their mind-set in order to lead a better life. This was blatantly contradicted by the actual manner in which it had been designed (for example, certain topics that had been included, the choice of venue, the catering, etc.).

It is a fact that the conflicts generally manifested within a group, the covert or open aggressiveness, the transition to action, cannot be explained solely in terms of interpersonal interaction, here and now. They are unavoidably registered to a certain historicity. In other words, they are, unconsciously, overly defined by the interplay between transference and countertransference. It is as though the members of the group involved in such situations, unwittingly become the protagonists in a scene of a play. A scene, which although in its entirety—in other words, a gestalt—may deeply affect each individual member of the group, at a purely personal level, in spite of expressing—in the sense of transposition and repetition—something very personal, the individuals themselves appear not to realize. They experience it as something completely new, something that was primordially caused by the presence and behavior of the "other/s".

On the other hand, that which is repeated unconsciously is dramatized and might be enacted in a present conflict within the group, especially in a group such as the aforementioned, is not only related to the participants' repressed early childhood. It bears the imprint of the social relationships to which the participants themselves ascribe, through the social groups to which they belong and which they represent through their presence in the immediate intersubjective group presence. In other words, the script of the present conflict appears to have been written in social and political terms, to be overly defined by an interplay of social transferences and social countertransferences, and as though participants somehow also inadvertently personalize here and now a conflict which, at its core, is social as well as political.

Notes

1. A contrivance of René Kaës, where chairs still form a circle, but are placed facing outwards with their backs to the center of the circle, so that the members and group analyst/s are unable to make eye contact.
2. The concepts of diffraction and diffracted transference (the term "diffraction" derives from physics) were introduced by René Kaës (1987) within the framework of his theory on the Group Psychic Organ (*Appareil Psychique Groupal*) (1976) and are connected to his theory on internal groups, that is, the unconscious representations of groupishness. In addition, they are also connected to the concept of the group as an external reality: as in a dream scene it is possible for different members of a group to represent for a given subject at a given moment different aspects of his internal group.
3. Paraphrasing the term Real of Jacques Lacan, which means "what resists symbolization".
4. In Greek, the word *gyftos*, an extremely derogatory form of the word "gypsy", is used as an insult, insinuating that the other person is the basest being on earth.
5. The trauma of growing up as a gypsy, experiencing social rejection in a number of situations and being seen as a *gyftos*.
6. The representatives of the group, its spokespersons, *porte-parole* (Kaës, 2007).

References

Barus-Michel, J., Enriquez, E., & Lévy, A. (2002). *Vocabulaire de Psycho-sociologie*. Paris: Editions Eres.

Bion, W. R. (1962). *Learning from Experience*. London: Maresfield,

Castel, R. (1973). *Le psychanalysme*. Paris: Editions François Maspero.

De Gaulejac, V., Bonetti, M., & Fraisse, J. (1996). *L'ingénierie sociale* Paris: Editions Syros.

De Gaulejac, V., Hanique, F., & Roche, P. (2007). *La sociologie clinique: Enjeux théoriques et méthodologiques*. Paris: Editions Eres.

Foulkes, S. H. (1964). *Therapeutic Group Analysis*. London: Allen and Unwin.

Giust-Desprairies, F. (2003). *La figure de l'autre dans l'école républicaine*. Paris: Editions PUF.

Giust-Desprairies, F., & de Gaulejac, V. (Eds.) (2009). *La subjectivité a l'épreuve du social: Hommage a Jacqueline Barus-Michel*. Paris: L'Harmattan.

Hopper, E. (2003). *Traumatic Experience in The Unconscious Life of Groups: The Fourth Basic Assumption: Incohesion: Aggregation/Massification or (ba) I: A/M*. London: Jessica Kingsley.

Hopper, E. (2007). Theoretical and conceptual notes concerning transference and counter-transference in groups and by groups, and the social unconscious. *Group Analysis, 40*: 29–42.

Kaës, R. (1976). *L'Appareil Psychique Groupal. Construction du Groupe*. Paris: Bordas.

Kaës, R. (1987). La diffraction des groupes internes, *Revista italiana di Gruppoanalisi, II*(I): 39–57.

Kaës, R. (2007). *Un singulier pluriel*. Paris: Dunod.

Navridi, E., Navridis, K., & Midgley N. (2012). Separation and relating in a parent–toddler group setting. *Early Child Development and Care, 182*(2): 221–232.

Navridis, K. (2006). Between matrix and subjects: transitivity and the "use of objects" in group- psychotherapy. *Group Analysis*, 3(3): 316–174.

Ofer, G., & Hadar, B. (2001). The social unconscious reflected in politics, organizations and groups. *Group Analysis, 34*(3): 375–385.

Vacheret, C. (Ed.) (2002). *Pratiquer les médiations en groupes thérapeutiques*. Paris: Dunod.

CHAPTER SEVEN

"Untouchable infant gangs" in group and social matrices as obstacles to reconciliation

Marina Mojović

> I've built walls, a fortress deep and mighty, that none may penetrate.
> I have no need of friendship; friendship causes pain.
> It's laughter and it's loving I disdain.
> I am a rock, I am an island. I touch no one and no one touches me.
> (Paul Simon, 1965)

At the Untouchable International Conference (IIGA, 2013, Gonen, Golan Heights) the lecture "Untouchable 'infant gangs' in the group-analytic matrix" began with Simon and Garfunkel's song about coldness and withdrawal from love and friendship. Despite its content, it warmed people's hearts and many from the audience joined in the singing. Was the music slowly dissolving the untouchable, or were the memories of the Swinging Sixties' pop–rock movement and its enthusiastic ganging activating the youthful spirit?

In search of the rhythms of safety for conflict reconciliation

When the phenomenon of "frozen hearts" or selves "turned into rocks and islands" caused by relational traumas is symbolized by artists through their songs or fairy tales, through dream-telling (Friedman, 2011) and dialogues in families, friendships, or in our analytic groups, which are in turn mentalized (Fonagy, 2001) into images, narratives, and melodies, as precursors of further change, indeed a bit of warming up may begin. Sensitive tuning in with the areas of the untouchable through fine pulsations in the relational field, while searching for the optimal distance from one moment to the other, might create a safe enough space for some resonance and sharing within these strange paradigms. The ultra-vulnerabilities are often so extreme that the "sparks of being" might fly away from contact due to the smallest errors in tone, timing, or internal desire to touch the untouchable—perhaps somewhat resembling beautiful migrating birds that meet at the Golan Heights near the conference venue to come together to keep warm in their habitat while they prepare for their far journeys. We can get in touch with their beauty if we approach them with appreciation and honesty, trying to attune to "rhythms of safety" (Tustin, 1986) and the natural fluxes of attraction and distancing, earning a bit of trust to take one step closer to the heart of the matter.

Traumas disrupt rhythms of life with cracks and disarray. To prevent annihilation, self-defensive maneuvers such as dissociation, encapsulating defences, and others enclose the trauma zone to protect whole persons, groups, or societies from "flooding"; "shrinking the tsunami" in the words of Bromberg (2008). However, along with this enclosing against injuries and pain, there is also a freezing or deadening of the "vital sparks", and of "dying a partial death," as Winnicott has stated (1964). When we engage in reparation and conflict reconciliation, and try to reconnect with the entombed "hearts of being" with the "essence of aliveness and forgiveness", our endeavors inevitably clash with the defensive "fortresses" and their "safeguards".

We need to approach the complexity of change carefully: establishing a warm and stable setting is certainly one of the major requisites for developing a sufficiently solid foundation of trust for the relational matrix—a crucial aspect of the reconciliation space. It supports both positive mobilization from trauma-free zones and re-creation of transitional spaces, which had been foreclosed in the trauma zones, or the "non-traumatized" parts containing the "traumatized", as was recently emphasized by Lopez-Corvo (2014). However, if the change is too rough and fast, instead of helping, we might provoke further disarray and destruction. In searching for the right balance, it is noteworthy that precursors of containment and soothing may appear by intuition, aesthetic forms, rhythms, and other nonverbal communications that are able to resonate, crossing the walls as incipient mentalizations of the other side (Fonagy, 2009). Recent data from neuroscience inform us that traumatic memories are more easily available via implicit mythopoetic image communication (right brain) than via explicit interpretative language of insights (left brain) (Bromberg, 2008; Schore, 2011; Stern, 2004).

Conflict reconciliation processes always challenge defensive systems of persons and groups regardless of their circumstances, objectives, or settings; this is true no matter what their aim: peace processes applied to ethnic, religious, or political conflicts in communities, conflict management in organizations or families, psychotherapies, and others. Psychoanalytically or group analytically informed work tends to understand unconscious dynamics as being under the surface. Apart from the "soft skills" mentioned above, we also need to be prepared for destructive attacks from the defensive systems of "gangs" of organized objects or part-objects in relational matrices, both internal and external. Before transformative challenges begin, such gangs are usually invisibly lodged in the untouchable areas. With the shattering of defensive systems, gangs emerge to the scene more visibly, intruding into the matrices. They often become major obstacles to the task at hand. To contain and tame their wilderness, brutality, or manipulative perversity, additional skills are required. Prejudices frequently exist with regard to the internal images of infants and their groupings; it is often thought that these images always represent naïve or innocent aspects of a person's internal worlds. However, through my work over three decades with traumatized persons, groups, and communities, they often proved to be among the leading internal powers that sabotaged change. It is these gangs that are the focus of this chapter.

Shedding light on relational dynamics between them is important if we wish to discern this complexity. This is especially true when we wish to engage in reconciliation based on relational ethics involving acknowledgment, witnessing, and responsibility for damages and the dehumanization done to them and to us as sides in conflict, and to connect with otherness across fractures of hurt and suffering (Frosh, 2011). Coexistence of opposites within "thirdness" (Benjamin, 2009; Ogden, 1994), as a shared relational process of witnessing, attuning to, and recognizing psychic pain, potentially leads towards genuine concern, forgiveness, and mutual healing as an "area of faith", in terms of Eigen (2004).

Thus, among the major challenges in this regard is how these very contrasting paradigms can be held simultaneously—not only regarding opposite sides in conflicts, but also regarding the contrast between extreme vulnerability and aggressiveness that exist within each side. It initiates feelings of absurdity, confusion, fragmentation, and meaninglessness by all involved. This leads to the paradoxical situation in which it is easier to bear the "clarity" of opposing sides in conflict than to cope with the confusing mixtures. We are dealing with uncertain endeavors that move within shifting vagueness. Fonagy (2009) emphasizes that "genuine forgiveness is an elusive experience and that the label is more often used in relation to pseudo-manifestations than a genuine experience" (p. 450).

Labyrinth of professional texts about infant gangs

The untouchable psycho-social areas are defensive systems, which serve to isolate and protect us from touching the unbearable pain of the core aspects of the self—variously called the "true self" (Winnicott, 1971), "private self" (Modell, 1993), or "soul" (Eigen, 2004; Grotstein, 2000). The vulnerable core is frequently represented in fantasies, dreams, and stories as an innocent child figure (Grotstein, 2009; Kalsched, 2013). Either it was never exposed to outside contact, like an "unborn self" (foetus or baby images), or it was exposed at a certain point in the past; however, due to traumatic dissociation, it retreated from the human family in the form of an orphaned self at the age when child-images linked to the time of traumas appear (Mojović et al., 2004). For both types of self, exposing them to outside contact is unbearable, similar to an existential threat; it is the fear of a "catastrophic change" (Bion, 1970). It might be to such an extent that recognizing the existence of oneself in the mirror of the other, even for a moment, could mean being destroyed in an immediate, violent death (Symington, 2000).

Maneuvers that protect the self from "soul murder" (Modell, 1993, p. 76), in the forms of benign or malignant saviors, gather around trauma wounds starting in early childhood. Over the years, they develop into defensive systems appearing in fantasy as inanimate fortresses, caves, or islands with guardians in the form of friendly "toddler or youth gangs", "business organizations", "Mafia-like gangs", or "tyrannical sects" (Rosenfeld, 1987), etc. They keep *in* the trauma, that is, unsuffered pain of the traumatized/terrorized parts of the vulnerable self and keep *out* the annihilating persecutor/traumatizer/terrorizer. Any incipient relations are under ongoing perfidious "attacks on linking" (Bion, 1967) from those systems, similar to an autoimmune disease attack on the body's healthy tissues.

Interestingly enough, a clear picture of these phenomena quickly disappears even from our professional texts. Although illuminating traces can be found at the roots of psychoanalysis and group analysis, and certainly a vast literature on the subject matter exists, yet one can still feel trapped as if in a labyrinth. Similar to a subterranean river that disappears beneath the ground and then suddenly reappears, they are known as "internal saboteurs" (Fairbairn, 1952), "fantasizing" (Winnicott, 1971), "mafia gang" (Rosenfeld, 1971), "inner cocoon" (Modell, 1984), "claustrum" (Meltzer, 1992), "encapsulations" (Hopper, 1991; Tustin, 1981), "psychic retreats" (Grotstein, 2009; Steiner, 1993), "imprisoning sanctuary" (Eigen, 2004), "social-psychic retreats" (Mojović, 2011), etc. Each of us, of course, has his or her own favorite papers and authors, who have touched our professional selves, perhaps due to some specific style that helped us recognize his or her experiences while rediscovering them in a fresh and renewed manner (Ogden, 2009). However, when you think you see a big picture beginning to emerge at one moment, it is quickly obscured in the next, as if some special veils were operating at the heart of the matter. Recently, there are a growing number of authors (Bromberg, 2008; Hopper, 1991, 2003; Mojović, 2014; Schore, 2011) who hope to "rescue dissociation from obscurity" (Goldman, 2013, p. 338).

Do we dare to disturb the infant gangs?

Do we really dare to knock on these doors? "Do I dare disturb the universe?" Grotstein (2000) asked his teacher, Bion. Are we dealing with imagined dangers or with the real ones? In my experience, it is not only a fantasy of danger; many self-destructive, suicidal, or other destructive acts occur within "negative therapeutic reactions" (Hinshelwood, 1989). Many often forget that when you succeed in making contact with the hidden universe of persons, groups, or societies and "touch the untouchable", it is only one part of the endeavor. The other major part is coping with "emotional turbulence" (Bion, 1965) and crowds of shadow suites, which attack from underground. They are well represented in the persecutory landscape of Dante's Hell with bizarre images of demons, vivified creatures, phantom-like figures, archetypes of the Devil's servants, and fallen angels during the descending search for roots of suffering (Kalsched, 2013).

Omnipotent child figures, with their ghostly powers, are very much part of the whole drama. The true self is often surrounded by, and submits to, malevolent feral infant gangs as immediate guardians of the internal fortresses of psychic retreats. According to Grotstein, psychic retreats are a

> sabotaging cluster or organization of internal objects . . . that have all originated in Faustian bargain or a bargain with the devil in order to be safe—that is, the infant's "prophylactic" selective identification with the intolerable traits of his mother and/or father in order to "purify" them and keep them ideal, because they are needed. (2009, p. 191)

Those identifications, due to the internalization of bad, rejected aspects of parents, become aspects that further terrorize, traumatize, and are often lodged in the "cruel superego". Addiction to such internal arrangements, with fighting against injustice for the lost kingdom of the infant's omnipotence, increases with time. Special infancy addiction can be a kind of bitter martyrdom and grievance, with this "martyrdom" of the infant self becoming a sacred cause; abandoning this mission is experienced as unbearable disloyalty (Grotstein, 2009, p. 192).

The internal world of traumatized persons is populated by narcissistic infant gangs that hold decision-making power. While the adult parts might want to forgive and rebuild broken relationships, the angry internal child parts would rather hatefully and stubbornly maintain the position forever. Refusal to communicate with the adult world due to disappointment could characteristically be manifested in giving a privileged place to animals. During a quarrel in one group, a silent member recounted a recurring dream he had had since early childhood: "a child driving a car 'jaguar' with no humans in the car, but his close friends were sitting in the other seats in the car: a puma, a jaguar, and a leopard". There was a playful resonance with other examples of favoring animals, and coming into contact with fears of dreadful wild aggression if activated. Only after that was the member able to engage in a new way in the group, sharing and giving more authority to his own adulthood and that of others.

Poetry about feral children, abandoned by ordinary families, has existed since ancient times: in the myth of Gilgamesh, legends such as the one of Romulus and Remus, as well as in the stories about Mowgli, Tarzan, Pinocchio, Peter Pan and the lost boys in Neverland, and many of the *puer aeternus* archetypes (von Franz, 2000). Andersen's fairy tale *The Snow Queen* focuses on the struggle between good and evil as experienced by a little boy and girl, Kay and Gerda. An evil troll creates a magic mirror with the power to distort people's beautiful features, while magnifying all that is ugly. The mirror breaks and shatters into a million splinters, which become lodged in people's eyes and hearts, freezing their hearts and turning them into ice. One summer day, while Kay and Gerda are playing in their garden, small pieces of the smashed mirror fall into Kay's heart and eyes. Kay becomes ruthless. He marvels only at the perfection of the snowflakes that take him into the kingdom of the cruel Snow Queen. But how could they melt people's frozen hearts? Gerda, filled with childlike love and faith, succeeds through her devotion and courage in spite of all the dangers that challenge her on her journey to reach Kay.

Our analytic groups and conferences provide unique relational spaces for similar journeys. Like reaching the frozen self through contact with animals, so, too, might other similar child parts of other group members resonate easily when they come into contact with each other and take the initiative to communicate. It is similar to Gerda, who helped Kay reconnect with his soul. Only then was he able to forgive and let go of his trauma. Some changes are not possible without the warmth of sibling relationships: the malignant gangs can be transformed only through the embrace of positive sibling gangs.

The Swinging Sixties and rocky relationships

Let us now take a look at the rocky relationship of the duo, Simon and Garfunkel. They both grew up in the same, mainly Jewish, neighborhood. Over the years, their friendship swung back and forth, echoing the lines of their two hit songs "I Am a Rock", and "Bridge over Troubled Waters":

> I'll take your part, oh, when darkness comes,
> And pain is all around.
> Like a bridge over troubled water,
> I will lay me down,
>
> Sail on silver girl
> Sail on by,
> Your time has come to shine,
> All your dreams are on their way,
> See how they shine
> Oh, if you need a friend,
> I'm sailing right behind.
>
> (Paul Simon, 1969)

The latter lyric emerged just before their final break-up, as if it were one last appeal for reconciliation, not only between the two of them, but perhaps within the youth movement as a whole. It might have been an appeal to people's dreams to help them find their way to shine and sail on in spite of all the difficulties.

Indeed, "Bridge over Troubled Waters" appeared in 1969 in Songs of America, accompanying footage of John F. Kennedy, Robert Kennedy, and Martin Luther King Jr. It associates the assassinations of these three leaders with the huge disruption of the *Zeitgeist*, "when darkness comes, and pain is all around", betraying the pop–rock movement's faith in justice, turning its enthusiasm into despair and decadence with massive intrusions of drugs and other destructive agents. There are many illustrations of the movement's dominantly positive ganging being perverted into destructive ganging of various kinds. Instead of the peace protests being the counter-culture against the mainstream culture, which, in silence, conformed to the politics of Vietnam and other similar imperialistic wars, around the world we witnessed the emergence of violent demonstrations and destructive ganging of various terrorist groups such as the Red Brigade, Baader-Meinhof, ETA, IRA, and others. Over the years, they mutated into even more extreme forms of brutal guerrilla fighting groups, such as ISIS and other terrorist groups of today.

How the *Zeitgeist* and the forces of our social unconscious, in vast regions of the world, fluctuate between progressive and regressive directions over time is, in itself, a meaningful socio-historical theme (Penna, 2014). Let me remind that group and social traumas provoke regression with the collapse of boundaries between people and their groupings, when concepts of personal trauma are apposite for the study of group and social trauma (Hopper, 2014, p. xxxvi). Traumas of the Swinging Sixties are widely present in the social unconscious crossing many boundaries. Traumatic psychosocial disruptions of hope and faith fragment relational matrices, detaching people from their needs for friendship and love (Ofer, 2011), when the dehumanizing forces easily take the lead over forces engaged in bridging troubled waters. The basic assumption of incohesion: aggregation/massification (Hopper, 2003) expands with regression, massive splitting, and fragmentation. Capacities to contain and understand the "good" and the "evil" diminish. The power of archaic national and collective myths rises.

The twin dichotomy of the good and the evil child, which appears as the biblical theme of Cain and Abel, symbolizes the split occurring in the mind at birth. One twin is identified with the positive power of the sun. The other twin must bear the guilt of fallen light and travels as a mirror image through the shades of the underworld in identification with a sun that emits darkness. In our collective unconscious, we all have archetypes for twin dichotomies such as that of Cain and Abel, or of "evil-child gangs" and "good-child gangs", rooted in archaic histories of mankind. Versions of these myths exist in our social unconscious. These are specific to a particular society (Weinberg, 2007) influencing many generations. For example, Serbian epic-folk oral poetry is rich with motifs of the Serbian *hajduk*-gangs fighting the Turkish conqueror-gangs. In Serbian tradition, there are similar patterns in poetry about other guerrilla gangs such as the partisans who fought Nazis in the Second World War, dichotomies between communist partisans and *chetnik* gangs (associated to Serbian monarchy), and other civil war-related dichotomies. Lines of symbolization can be traced through to later fights during political protests or contemporary hooligan football violence. There is certainly a kaleidoscopic mix among such groupings, often making it difficult to distinguish between their types and roots.

Still, it is essential to understand the basic distinction between the different types of gangs: those protective positive gangs aimed at progress and those negative aimed at destruction, decadence, and extremism. Of course, one type can turn into the other, and *vice versa.*

To support the desired goal in reconciliation work with groups and societies, we need to learn to discern these differences. We need to be capable of recognizing the leading aspects in dialectic movements as well as having the skills needed to attune to, and offer, protection when destructive attacks intrude. How can we be equipped with such multiple skills with opposing styles of interaction?

Migrating bird habitats as transitional spaces

Another important question relates to the optimal quality and sustainability of a reconciliation space—symbolically, the *habitat*. In today's world, real human violence is everywhere, *ante portas*, ready to destroy various aspects of humanity. In this regard, I have often thought about the Golan birds, when, just a year after the Gonen Conference, the brutality of real war intruded into the region. Were their migrating rhythms disrupted? This brought to mind a similar habitat in my hometown of Belgrade, situated at the confluence of Danube and Sava rivers, co-creating a large, wild island in the heart of the city. Over the centuries of turbulent Serbian history, the island remained untouched by any human settlement, but embraced migrating birds. Why is it called the War Island? Is it because of its location at the edge of so many wars—similar to the Golan Heights? It might represent a transitional space for transforming hate into "sparks of hope", flying in their natural aesthetic rhythms of "going-on-being" (Winnicott, 1964), carrying potential meaning which is accessible only if sensitively approached. Group-analytic groups, workshops, and conferences remind us of those temporal habitats for warming up, the places where we can learn through experience the rhythms of safety, as well as the incipient skills needed to sail over troubled waters, for long journeys and going-on-being, skills and wisdom which can then be acquired and applied in faraway habitats.

Infant gangs in groups

Let me now share a few illustrative examples from my group-analytic groups and from the reflective citizens workshops held in Serbia.

The first is a description of the change in a woman of thirty-five, who is in therapy due to panic attacks with agoraphobia. At the time,

T had a daughter of five and was pregnant, expecting a baby boy. She often talked about her twin brother, who got most of their mother's attention during her whole childhood. She withdrew from many social situations, often feeling estranged from those around her.

A few weeks before the change she shared a dream with the group:

> "There was a huge wall clock, and suddenly a monkey jumped out of it, at first on my shoulder, then on Marina's lap, then on other group members. Maybe it was my wish that all of you see that I am not bad indeed!"

A few weeks later, there was an essential change:

> "I again felt that terrible dense cloud around my head pressuring me, making me anxious, almost to the point of leaving the group. However, during that session, while everybody was so empathic, something inside me, like a capsule, broke. I feel it will never return. The capsule broke, in which that little girl lived in the garden world full of narcissus flowers. They reminded me of those narcissi that grew in the garden of our family house. For all these years, the little girl refused to join the world due to its ugliness." She cried with deep sorrow. "I felt terrible, in total break-down, as if I were going to die of shock, being exposed to the new world. Even my skin was hurting. As if I was now growing a new skin and immunity. Not only that, I cannot go back to that garden refuge; I do not wish to do that anymore. However, it is so disturbing—I now see clearly—that the badness which I massively projected onto people and even to you here, is in fact part of myself. The dark cloud is a terrifying internal figure, selfish and cold, similar to an all-mighty God. But it is not somebody else—it is me! I see how I used to be indifferent, even cruel to many people. I behaved in a hysterical and confused manner, which I never wanted to admit. And at the same time, I see a weak baby with its eyes mainly closed, as if not wanting anything. It is lifeless." She cried again and talked about identification with the baby in her body and the worries she had for her baby boy. She wondered if she could have enough faith for him, since she had this feeling of the lifeless internal baby that paralyzed her.

We can see the transformation process of a zone which was for years "untouchable", when main components of the internal arrangement became vivid, in Grotstein's terms (2009, p. 213): "adult cooperative personality", the "stuck infant-self" (her lifeless baby-self), "sabotaging sub-personalities", who attack the relationship of the cooperative personality and the therapist/group (omnipotent garden-girl, teenage-refugee-girl, hysterical non-thinking woman), and the "ghost", the unconscious "wraith", threatening the change as part of the whole gang (the returning dark cloud).

* * *

To illustrate some aspects of a group process with the focus on infant gangs, I offer another vignette from a small weekly group-analytic group formed after the bombing of Serbia, gathering mixed disorders including borderline, phobia, depression, abused, and traumatized members with a few refugees.

One member of the group, a professional clown, D, came to the very first group session with his little dog and childishly sat on the floor. He shared his stories about being a "clown doctor", making children laugh in hospitals and orphanages. He was a nomadic person, living at times in caravans in the woods. It was surprising that he stayed with the group for the whole year. He succeeded in stopping much of his self-destructive behavior and apologized for having to leave. D personified the childish, manic, rebellious anti-group gang.

After D left, there was a silent, apathetic atmosphere with –K (Bion, 1962) dominating the matrix. A middle-aged, depressive man, who was a refugee from Sarajevo with a history of horrific family war losses, was forcing a deadly silence where all communication was blocked due to his massive projections of absurdity over any communication. Moreover, it was as if an invisible dreadful threat and wraith hovered over the group, allowing only horror images. An old artist talked about her sculpture: a lying body without a head, situated in a black metal cage. A mirror was placed below the body, and a huge black widow spider was placed on the cage. It was not easy to associate. Shudder and horror was felt in the air. A young man talked about his wish to poison the water system in a normal tone of voice, miming the actions—a story that completely stunned everybody. A student, who was putting off studying for exams so that he could gamble, stubbornly made comments that the group looked stupid and absurd, adding to –K. It was a group-phase in which perverse gangs dominated.

In dreams and fantasies, war dragons, water hydra-monsters, and gorgons seemed to be warning everybody to remain immobile. A dream appeared of a funeral procession marching in dark dense waters holding a baby, while the dreamer was sitting on a stone in the water with a grandmother telling old stories. Transgenerational transmission of trauma suffering was able to slowly emerge.

Generally, the setting was appreciated by the group members. Its containing function, with the stable presence of the therapist and the group, had to last long enough, without forcing the group to build safety and trust, encouraging growth in spite of turbulence. Personal psychic retreats of members were able to be disentangled step-by-step and join the various transient interpersonal group and subgroup social/psychic retreats as challenging transitional spaces (Mojović, 2011).

The stiff paralyzing atmosphere culminated in three sessions of practically total silence. A dream emerged of a group crouching for years in a submarine, stimulating rich reflections about whether the dream represented collective escape from personal problems, whether hiding from circumstances of war, or a sort of unconscious suicidal submarine journey. That session happened to be a turning point of the group process. Work group capacities increased.

Thus, in the matrix, there appeared to be feral haughty children: clown child, gambling child, spoiled arrogant child, funeral procession child, later a crusade child. From invisible territories of destructive narcissism, the hitherto invisible aspects of group matrix, the infant gangs in powerful mutual coalition, became increasingly open to thought.

In the last year, two female members joined, both divorced with children. The older one was sixty-four years of age, a refugee from Bosnia, and the other, a middle-aged consultant. There was welcoming behavior, but also a lot of anger towards them. Both were devoted to the problems of others and they shared that attitude often shown by strong women who are capable of enduring all suffering, which irritated a few members even more. They became group scapegoats. Group rebellion was enacted in relationship to them, as if symbolizing the cruel superego. The older one could not bear any more, saying that she was hurt. She told me, "I finally must not obey! You have to understand that I will not go to that group! It is my new freedom!"

That caused huge emotional turbulence in the group. There was a particularly strong reaction from a new painter, who was an orphan, and vulnerable to women's suffering. His few years spent with his mother, who became ill after delivering him, were a treasure for him. A few sessions of very emotional discussions, with fights among the members, resulted in very creative and fruitful group work.

The infant gangs, which were more or less hidden, finally came into the open—a lively desire to know each other better. A female refugee talked about a *hajduk*/guerrilla gang in herself, remembering how, at the age of twelve, when the war in Croatia (in the city of Vukovar) broke out, many Serbs were persecuted and massacred around her. At that point, she was compelled to take up arms to fight for the lives of her family. Terrible feelings of special loneliness cried out—pain she could share only with her refugee group: "What does any of you here know about the pain?!"

Splitting between refugees and others emerged. A student, who was a child in the mass exodus of the Serbs following the Croatian military operation, when over 200,000 Serbs were exiled from their homes in Croatia in only one day, opened up for the first time about that deeply rooted trauma. A dark internal girl came out, now visible to everybody in the group, totally submerged in murderousness, and shared her dream:

> "I rushed into the room in which that General was: 'Now, I shall torture you instead!'"

Other members' hatred became accessible for expression, too. It was a very difficult work group period, but it saw the beginnings of some deep healing. Terrible crying broke out and others joined in: "Why don't all these miserable children just hug each other for a while?! They should also hug Croat children!"

Immunity gradually increased. New themes came to the fore, such as rivalry, especially among infant parts. A new submarine group dream was shared:

> "This time the submarine was huge, with a lot of space inside and many colorful interesting rooms. It was on a journey towards the North Pole for the Eurovision Song Contest!"

There is certainly a lot of further work awaiting this group. Obviously, it still needs images of underwater environments and barriers of (untouchable) steel amor for their group-social-psychic retreats, but it now enjoys a wider space, in which it is easier to breathe and conduct dialogue.

* * *

Why a submarine headed towards the North Pole? Does the group feel brave enough now to encounter the Snow Queen jointly and directly? Her kingdom, as a metaphor for the "death narcissism" with the "dead mother complex" (Green, 2001) of people, in which selves are buried in her necropolis and all vitality for nourishing the tombs, might occur in our groups. This seems to be the case especially with traumatized people or in traumatized countries. However, when the anti-group is disarmed to some extent, and the deep hatred contained, then "group as an object of desire" (Nitsun, 2006) as an organizing principle may gain strength. Only then can some space emerge for the warm tears of love and faith, similar to Gerda's tears, to start melting frozen hearts and dislodge troll mirrors from human eyes. In this group, there are now tears in every session; the underlying sadness is oceanic. It is to be hoped that the mourning can last long enough before new traumas freeze it again.

Infant gangs in the group matrix, as coalitions of internal gangs of members, might, on the one hand, be the invisible cause of the group's resistance, rebellion, and refusal (Billow, 2010), but on the other hand, may also represent essential and vital assistance for positive transformation.

Appeal from the Reflective Citizens workshops: songs penetrating the ghetto walls

Let me share another illustrative event from the Gonen Conference which altered my internal walls: in connection to Serbia being, for decades, stuck and excluded from all families of countries, even from the Eurovision Song contest, but now slowly moving away from isolation, my Gonen lecture ended with a glimpse into Serbia's recent winning Eurovision song, called "Prayer", about love, but perhaps representing an appeal for hope for this country and its citizens. When the audience was touched, and began to sing and swing, I realized that my own internal ghetto with frozen parts of my social unconscious started to dissolve. These were meaningful emotions brought to life, which I was then able to take to my groups back home. So, this conference, like many others, which are co-created "by" and "for" our professional "tribes", can be an enriching temporal habitat for learning through experience, and also learning how to cope with untouchable matrices of our groups and societies, to earn a bit of additional trust and skills that can help us navigate through the whirlwinds and abysses originating in traumatic wounds and scars, to prepare us for further journeys and then to share this experience with matrices in our other faraway homes.

One such sibling, group-analytic learning space is the Serbian Reflective Citizens Project. The project consists of regular, seasonally held group-analytic workshops open for citizens interested in social dreaming, social drawing, and reflection in large and small groups on any freely emerging psychosocial content. We try to enable participants and groups to follow their own spontaneous rhythms of dissociating and integrating. In one of these groups in Kosovo, the topic of Rodriguez, a Mexican-American pop–rock star from the 1960s, portrayed in the Oscar-winning documentary *Sugarman*, emerged: while Rodriguez lived and worked as a construction worker in the USA in relative poverty and obscurity, he was an enormously popular and important figure in South Africa for years. His anti-establishment rock songs very much influenced citizens under apartheid, in times when this country was bound by conservative restrictions and cut off from the rest of the world by sanctions. The musician did not know anything about it, and neither did his fans know that he was alive and had not died during a concert, according to a widely circulating legend. One day, the reconnection of those two parts of Rodriguez's life happened, with a few very touching live concerts in Cape Town. In the Reflective Citizens' group, this story symbolized hope for the future reconnection of forgotten psychosocial aspects, which, for a long time, can be dissociated and frozen in some social/psychic retreats. Is it possible for those valuable, vibrant aspects of people, groups, and communities to be preserved, even if isolated in ghetto cities such as Kosovska Mitrovica, or countries such as Serbia, keeping them safe for some future time to come? Can unhealthy dissociative cracks be replaced by a healthier, creative use of dissociation—replacing frozen hearts with the sharing of imaginations and dreams (Goldman, 2013; Mojović, 2014; Winnicott, 1971) in the joint endeavor of uncovering their hidden meanings? Do we dare to let hope and love come in?

A beam of intense darkness: the pop–rock star as a forgotten peer

Splitting of peer relations is deeply rooted in the human mind, both ontogenetically and phylogenetically. It is represented in the myths of Cain and Abel, Apollo and Dionysus, and many others. Sibling rivalry in fighting for territory, possessions, power, and love shaped much of human history. Rejected or excluded peers hold at least some significant aspects for the others—processes which we always need to bear in mind when coping with reconciliation.

The troll servant of the Snow Queen distorted the beautiful aspects of people and magnified the ugly, similar to destructiveness that so massively occurs in human relations around us. Bion stressed that, in psychoanalytic work, "one must cast a beam of darkness so that something which has hitherto been obscured by the glare of the illumination can glitter all the more in that darkness" (1970, cited in Grotstein, 2006, p. 1).

Rodriguez had faith in his creativity, although his star was shining in a world far away, in an encapsulated apartheid country, where the splinters of his 1960's singing enthusiasm touched the people's hearts and caused them to start glittering in their social darkness. It is, perhaps, similar to the intensity of attachment and care for survival and creativity found among siblings who lose their family home (Hindle & Sherwin-White, 2014). Rodriguez had modestly to bear the burden of being a forgotten peer among his fellow American stars of the time, deprived of the joy of playing and swinging with his natural peer gang. He was left out from belonging, as was the country of his fans, and like many others who were destined for exclusion. Was it an enactment of America's social unconscious linked to his Mexican roots, or just the way the wheel of sibling destiny turned at the time—a fate attributable to the positions of the stars at that time?

When we carry the fallen light as mirror images through the shadows of the underworld journeys like splinters that emit darkness, either as individuals, families, or communities, we can easily lose our faith in justice, and in any meaning at all. How can we then be able to accept a friendly bridge over troubled water to be laid down for us, to trust that, indeed, the time has come for us to set sail and let our dreams shine and glitter in darkness? Or would we rather keep safe behind the shields in absence-of-being, with contempt for friendly laughter and love?

References

Benjamin, J. (2009). Beyond doer and done-to: an inter-subjective view of thirdness. *Psychoanalytic Quarterly, 73*: 5–46.

Billow, R. (2010). *Resistence, Rebellion, and Refusal in Groups*. London: Karnac.

Bion, W. R. (1962). *Learning from Experience*. London: Heineman.

Bion, W. R. (1965). *Transformations*. London: Karnac.

Bion, W. R. (1967). *Second Thoughts*. London: Heineman.

Bion, W. R. (1970). *Attention and Interpretation*. London: Heineman.

Bromberg, P. (2008). Shrinking the tsunami. *Contemporary Psychoanalysis, 44*(3): 329–350.

Eigen, M. (2004). *Psychic Deadness*. London: Karnac.

Fairbairn, W. R. D. (1952). *Psychoanalytic Studies of the Personality*. London: Routlege & Kegan Paul.

Fonagy, P. (2001). *Attachment Theory and Psychoanalysis*. New York: Other Press.

Fonagy, P. (2009). Commentary on "Forgiveness". In: S. Akhtar (Ed.), *Good Feelings* (pp. 441–452). London: Karnac.

Friedman, R. (2011). Dream-telling and beyond—in search for the trans-personal. Keynote lecture at GAS Symposium, London.

Frosh, S. (2011). The relational ethics of conflict and identity. *Psychoanalysis, Culture & Society, 16*: 225–243.

Goldman, D. (2013). Vital sparks and the form of things unknown. In: J. Abram (Ed.), *Donald Winnicott Today* (pp. 331–357). London: Karnac.

Green, A. (2001). *Life Narcissism, Death Narcissism*. London: Free Association.

Grotstein, J. (Ed.) (2000). *Do I Dare Disturb the Universe*? London: Karnac.

Grotstein, J. (Ed.) (2006). *A Beam of Intense Darkness: Wilfred Bion's Legacy to Psychoanalysis*. London: Karnac.

Grotstein, J. (2009). *. . . But At The Same Time and On Another Level . . . (Volume I)*. London: Karnac.

Hindle, D., & Sherwin-White, S. (Eds.) (2014). *Sibling Matters*. London: Karnac.

Hinshelwood, R. (1989). *The Dictionary of Kleinian Thought*. London: Free Associations.

Hopper, E. (1991). Encapsulation as a defense against the fear of annihilation. *International Journal of Psychoanalysis, 72*(4): 607–624.

Hopper, E. (2003). *Traumatic Experience in the Unconscious Life of Groups*. London: Jessica Kingsley.

Hopper, E. (Ed.) (2014). *Trauma and Organizations*. London: Karnac.

Kalsched, D. (2013). *Trauma and the Soul*. London: Routledge.

Lopez-Corvo, R. E. (2014). *Traumatised and Non-Traumatised States of the Personality*. London: Karnac.

Meltzer, D. (1992). *The Claustrum: An Investigation of Claustrophobic Phenomena*. Worcester: Ronald Harris Trust.

Modell, A. H. (1984). *Psychoanalysis in a New Context*. New York: International Universities Press.

Modell, A. H. (1993). *The Private Self*. Cambridge, MA: Harvard University Press.

Mojović, M. (2011). Manifestations of psychic retreats in social systems. In: E. Hopper & H. Weinberg (Eds.), *The Social Unconscious in Persons, Groups, and Societies* (pp. 209–232). London: Karnac.

Mojović, M. (2014). The matrix disrupted. Keynote address at the 16th GASI Symposium in Lisbon.

Mojović, M., Despotović, T., & Satarić, J. (2014). "Conception trauma" of group analysis in Serbia. *Group Analysis, 47*(2): 113–127.

Nitsun, M. (2006). *The Group as an Object of Desire*. London: Routledge.

Ofer, G. (2011). Enemies, love story: gender differences in the expression of love, hate and desire. In: L. Navaro, R. Friedman, & S. Schwartzberg (Eds.), *Desire, Passion & Gender* (pp. 139–148). New York: Nova Science.

Ogden, T. H. (1994). *Subjects of Analysis*. Northvale, NJ: Jason Aronson.

Ogden, T. H. (2009). *Rediscovering Psychoanalysis*. London: Routledge.

Penna, C. (2014). *Inconsciente Social* [Social Unconscious]. São Paulo: Casa do Psicólogo/Pearson.

Rosenfeld, H. (1987). *Impasse and Interpretation*. London: Routledge.

Schore, A. (2011). The right brain implicit self lies at the core of psychoanalysis. *Psychoanalytic Dialogues, 21*: 75–100.

Steiner, J. (1993). *Psychic Retreats*. London: Routledge.

Stern, D. (2004). *The Present Moment in Psychotherapy and Everyday Life*. New York: W. W. Norton.

Symington, J. (Ed.) (2000). *Imprisoned Pain and its Transformations*. London: Karnac.

Tustin, F. (1981). *Autistic States in Children*. London: Routledge & Kegan Paul.

Tustin, F. (1986). *Autistic Barriers in Neurotic Patients*. London: Karnac.

Von Franz, M. L. (2000). *The Problem of Puer Aeternus*. Toronto: Inner City.

Weinberg, H. (2007). So what is this social unconscious anyway? *Group Analysis, 40*(3): 307–322.

Winnicott, D. W. (1964). *The Child, the Family, and the Outside World*. Harmondsworth: Penguin.

Winnicott, D. W. (1971). *Playing and Reality*. London: Tavistock.

CHAPTER EIGHT

The social unconscious and issues of conflict and reconciliation in therapy*

Haim Weinberg

Definitions and questions

The social unconscious (Hopper, 2003; Hopper & Weinberg, 2011, 2016, 2017; Weinberg, 2007) refers to the existence of the restraints and constraints of social, cultural, and communication arrangements of which people are "unaware" to varying degrees. It includes anxieties, fantasies, myths, defenses, and object relations, as well as various aspects of socio-cultural–economic–political factors and forces, many of which are also co-constructed unconsciously by the members of particular groupings.

Many people understand this concept to mean that society has an unconscious. However, this interpretation is problematic, since society is not an organism, does not have a brain, and if we attribute some unconscious properties to the social system, it is unclear where it resides. Therefore, there are two ways to understand this concept. The first interpretation is to see the social unconscious as part of the individual unconscious. It can be understood as the internalization of social facts and norms, cultural aspects that we are unaware of, including the

* A version of part of this chapter is included in Weinberg (2015).

representation of social forces and power relations in our psyche (Dalal, 2001). In fact, when we look at the social unconscious this way, it is unclear whether we should separate the social unconscious from the individual unconscious, and, indeed, Knauss (2006, p. 163) claims that "There is no such thing as 'the group unconscious', the 'social unconscious or a collective, cultural unconscious'. Instead, each individual's unconscious is groupal."

Another way to understand the social unconscious is through the relational/intersubjective perspective (Mitchell, 1993).

> Relational theory is based on the shift from the classical idea that it is the patient's mind that is being studied (where mind is thought as independently and autonomously within the boundaries of the individual) to the relational notion that mind is inherently dyadic, social, interactional, and interpersonal. (Aron, 1996, p. x)

The relational/intersubjective conceptualization suggests a different reading of the unconscious and the way we understand it, in addition to the regular Freudian one. We are not talking about specific contents located in a certain area that exists *a priori* and that we help to illuminate in therapy. We are talking about creating the unconscious and acquiring "knowledge" about it, with the help of the other, through conversation. This co-created unconscious is an infinite, conversational, open system (Mitchell, 1993), or, as Tubert-Oklander (2006) termed it, a "free-floating conversation."

Looking at the social unconscious from this frame of reference, we can say that it resides in the potential space between people. The intersubjective field is a co-creation of the psyche of the people involved in the interaction, meaning that it is not the simple result of the people's unconscious but is a new co-unconscious (Moreno, 1978) belonging to neither of the participants. Extrapolating from two people to a group, or even society, this is the space of the social unconscious.

At any rate, however we define and understand the social unconscious (SU), it is still an evasive and abstract concept, and many clinicians argue that it is irrelevant to their practice. They do not know what to do with it in treatment and they seem to be unaware of its usefulness in clinical settings. Even those who fully understand the concept are sometimes convinced that it can be analyzed and applied only in large groups. It is true that it is easier to identify manifestations of the social unconscious in an unstructured psychodynamic large group, but there are clearly implications of the SU for individual and group therapy.

Groups in times of conflict

In times of group conflict, the safe space of the group is shaken. If not resolved satisfactorily, an intense conflict between two or more group members, many times breaking out unexpectedly and escalating very quickly, might lead to the emotional withdrawal of some members and sometimes even to premature group termination of one of the people involved. It can create more caution in group members in terms of self-disclosure or giving feedback, and can have a long-standing negative impact on the group. Sometimes, even months after the event seems to be forgotten, the group is still conflict-avoidant, tiptoeing around any disagreement or difference of opinion.

Usually, the emotional outburst of the conflict involves hurt, and is not only a matter of simple disagreement or difference of opinion that can regularly be resolved by discussion and negotiation. If differences play a role, it is more about the narcissism of small differences (Freud, 1930a). The development of a conflict in a group usually involves mechanisms of splitting, projection, and projective identification. These mechanisms can easily be identified in large groups, but they occur in small therapy groups as well.

The development of such a conflict might follow this pattern: One group member feels deeply hurt by the other, whether due to justified "objective" reasons or as a result of a narcissistic vulnerable self, or (most of the time) a combination of both. As a result, this member retaliates and attacks the other person, believing that this attack is justified, attempting to hurt the other in return. The result is that both parties are deeply hurt. As the conflict evolves, it does not matter anymore who started the fire. As we will see later, the group becomes involved as well, as it is difficult not to take sides. Each party sees the other as the "enemy" and projects on them the characteristics of a bad object. The "other" is perceived as mean, full of negative intentions, untrustworthy, and threatening. The same process and the same mechanisms work in social conflicts. Perceiving the "other" this way means that we focus on how different they are and how much better we are, leading to depersonalizing and even dehumanizing the person or subgroup with whom we have a fight.

When this process develops in the group, the fact that other members observe the scene exerts more pressure on the parties in conflict. Both feel that they are totally right and the other is totally wrong. They feel that injustice is done to them and they demand justice. Because this struggle takes place with witnesses, an element of shame is added to the fight. Each of the parties silently counts how many people support them and how many do not. Both parties try hard to convince the group that they are right and to recruit more group members to support them. They can become righteous and fight viciously to prove their righteousness. Group members who seem neutral and do not support them are considered to be against them. When someone gives negative feedback to one of the partners in conflict, they are seen as "enemies". Thus, splitting becomes prevalent and an atmosphere of "us and them" governs the scene (Berman et al., 2000). Similar processes are observed in social conflicts, and can easily be analyzed in large groups (Weinberg & Schneider, 2003; Weinberg & Weishut, 2011). These processes are strongly personified in a small group.

Many times, it is difficult to resolve these conflicts, whether in a small group, a large group, or in society at large, because some unconscious aspects are involved, especially social unconscious ones. Remember that the SU includes aspects of socio-cultural–economic–political factors and forces that people are unaware of, often relating to historical events that were unelaborated and undiscussed in the public sphere, which leads to what Volkan named "chosen trauma" (1997). We will see such an example later in a vignette taken from a large group.

Reconciliation and the role of the group conductor

Ghent (1999) distinguished between submission and surrender. Surrender is

> a path toward the discovery of one's identity, one's sense of self, one's sense of wholeness, even one's sense of unity with other living beings. This is quite unlike submission in which the reverse happens: one feels one's self as a puppet in the power of another; one's sense of identity atrophies. (p. 216)

Using these terms, we can say that in times of conflict, each party is stuck in a submissive position. In this situation, there is no ability to move and the participants are locked into, and submit to, their subjective experiences. Therefore, the therapist should help the participants move from submission to surrender. The task of the group and its leader is to restore the safe space as a place of reflection and processing. The main difficulty in pulling out of conflicts is that the participating parties lose their ability to see one another's subjectivity (Benjamin, 1998). Unless this ability is restored, they both continue to be convinced that only they are holding the "objective" truth, while only the other is inflicting pain and creating injustice. Hurt and pain make people very self-centered and disable their potential for seeing the suffering of the other. In order to start a reconciliation process, people or subgroups in conflict should develop the ability to recognize that their point of view is subjective.

People in conflict (and sometimes all the others actively or passively involved in the conflict) are trapped in the belief that injustice has been done only to them and that they themselves are not involved in inflicting any injustice. It is almost impossible to keep in mind the relativity and subjectivity of the experience, and, moreover, it is very difficult to remember that the other's subjectivity is legitimate. This is where the group leader is called upon to intervene. The concrete task of the leader is to help both parties see the other's subjective experience, acknowledge the legitimacy of the different points of view, confirm the fact that all parties involved are hurt, and gently help them to take responsibility for the pain they inflicted upon the other. Mutual recognition of the other's suffering and hurt is the best outcome of such a conflict and can lead to reconciliation.

One of the obstacles to recognizing the other's subjectivity and to moving from submission to surrender is the existence of the social unconscious, which increases the sense of hurt and injustice of a person or a group, against the background of earlier unelaborated social traumas. In order to help group members move towards reconciliation, the group therapist should be aware of possible social unconscious aspects involved in the conflict and actively intervene to point these out, bringing them to the participants' awareness. This is also the time for a very active effort to help both parties express their feelings, as irrational as they seem (and when they stem from unconscious motivations they *are* irrational). Usually, when group members feel injured, the last thing they want to do is to express the hurt, as they feel so vulnerable. The group therapist should stay attuned to the sounds of pain beyond the expression of anger or rage, and bring those sounds to the forefront. These sounds of pain echo not only in the present situation, but also from long forgotten painful events, not necessarily belonging to the individual history of the person involved. The difficult and delicate task is to help people who suffer to open their mouths to express their hurt, to open their ears to listen to the suffering of the other, to open their eyes to see the subjective experience of the other, and, especially, to open their hearts to acknowledge and recognize the other's pain. It is no less difficult to open a channel to reflect on vulnerabilities that are embedded in the social unconscious.

In order to help the reader understand how we can identify and use the concept of the SU in treatment, especially when conflict is involved, I bring several vignettes from therapy in which I applied the SU idea. The vignettes are taken from individual therapy, a small, median, and large group, and identifying details have been changed to protect confidentiality.

Individual therapy: the case of the Jew who ran out of church (transgenerational transmission)—marital conflict

As an Israeli Jew living in California, I get many referrals of Jews and Israelis in my private practice. A forty-five-year-old male, ex-Israeli living in the USA for twenty-two years and married for eighteen years to a non-Jewish North American woman, came to therapy due to difficulties in his relationship with his wife. He attributed these difficulties to his impatience, intolerance, and to cultural differences. There seemed to be a continuous underlying conflict in their relationship, although they never had an open fight. Throughout his marriage, he became more distant and estranged from his wife. They cooperated well in daily routine, but lived without real intimacy. The man observed the Shabbat and other Jewish religious commands, and his wife agreed to accept it. The woman was not religious and, although she grew up as a Catholic, she did not practice Christianity, and did not visit church regularly, so during their marriage they did not have to deal with differences of religious rituals and traditions.

However, while he was still in therapy, they were invited to participate in the confirmation ceremony of the wife's niece. Confirmation is a rite of initiation in Christian churches where an adolescent makes a commitment to belong to the church (reminiscent of the Jewish Bar Mitzvah ceremony at age thirteen). The ceremony took place in a church in another state where the wife's family lived, and my patient attended out of respect for his wife and her family. During the ceremony he felt inexplicable tension, but everything went fine until the priest started walking down the aisle, swinging the incense bowl, spreading its scent, and murmuring prayers. When the priest approached him, my patient felt intolerable anxiety, panicked, and ran out of church.

What happened there? I tried to establish some earlier or similar memories that could explain this event, but in vain. His associations took him to his family of origin and to his parents vaguely warning him to be careful of associating with Christians. He also remembered that when he studied in high school in Israel, they learned a certain poem describing how dangerous it was for the Rabbi's daughter to fall in love with a non-Jew. It became clear that deep inside there was a sense of danger when he got close to gentiles (non-Jews), but its source was unclear.

Based on my experience with other Jewish patients, I speculated that perhaps his parents survived the Holocaust, or other persecutions which might explain this deep irrational fear of gentiles. To my surprise, I found out that his parents grew up in Turkey, among Muslims, in a relatively peaceful environment, feeling no persecution. Only after a thorough exploration did we find out that his family originated from Spain, and that they were the descendants of the Jews who were expelled from Spain in 1492 (a very famous and traumatic event in Jewish history). It seems as if those events, which occurred at the end of the fifteenth century (at the same time that Columbus started his journey to discover America), took their toll hundreds of years later as they remained an unelaborated trauma in this man's social unconscious. The long-term unconscious social trauma contributed to his hidden conflict and distance from his wife.

Working through this event, exploring and understanding it, and especially the possibility of connecting it to the history of his forefathers and to the Jewish nation in general, became a turning point in therapy and in understanding the distance he created with his wife. In his unconscious fantasies, his wife represented the persecution of the Inquisition. Of course, there were other personal issues in his relationship with women, but without the significant part we discovered in the SU, exposed through the panic attack in church, we would have missed a very deep and meaningful part of therapy.

Group therapy: the woman who was angry with her father for being "weak" (mechanisms of disavowal, splitting, and projection)—generational conflict

A version of this case study appears in Nuttman-Shwartx & Weinberg (2012). In a group analytic session in Israel, triggered by one member's talking about her family of origin and her childhood, participants brought up memories and associations from their parents' homes and wondered how these memories shaped their personalities. One of the group members, a woman, started talking about her father, a Holocaust survivor. When she started telling her story, she became very emotional, her throat was clogged, she almost choked, and tears filled her eyes. The group was patient and waited until her emotional storm faded away. When she was able to talk, she recounted an event when her father came to visit her new house in the North of Israel a few years earlier. He came by bus. She met him on the main road and they had to walk through a peaceful Arab village in order to reach the Jewish village where she lived (in the Galilee). Her father became restless and asked her if it was safe to go through that village, suggesting that they bypass it. Suddenly and unexpectedly she felt a wave of rage towards him and shouted, "Why do you have to project your fears from the Diaspora onto me? I don't want to be influenced by this groveling attitude of yours."

This group vignette might seem to reflect this woman's relationship with her father and how angrily she tried to escape his traumatic past experiences unconsciously transmitted to her. At the same time, it reflects a central theme in the social unconscious of the Israelis (Weinberg, 2017). In contrast to the image of the weak Jew of the Diaspora, and in order to establish a new identity as an Israeli, Jews in Israel developed certain social-cultural myths and narratives, of which the most important was the image of the Sabra, the new generation, born in Israel. This heroic masculine figure should always be strong and show no weakness. The image of the strong Sabra appearing in the Israeli social unconscious can be explained as a counter-reaction to the weakness of the Jews in the Diaspora, who—in the social unconscious of the Israelis—went as sheep to the slaughter in the Holocaust and before. More than that, this image reflects a counter-reaction to the hundreds of years of Jews being helplessly dependent and living at the mercy of other nations.

Considering this woman's story as belonging to the Israeli social unconscious no less than to the person who brought it to the group, the group analyst decided not to focus only on the woman's family of origin and her father's traumatic past, but expanded it and invited the group members' resonance and associations. Not surprisingly, almost every group member had a story in which s/he rebelled against being "weak" or feeling helpless and instead behaved in a way that denied any vulnerability (often considered weakness in Israel). Without being aware of the Israeli SU and the possibility of using it to explore this conflict between generations and to focus on this theme in the small group, valuable information might have been ignored.

Median group: the group who refused translation to the dark stranger (symbolic enactment of historic events)—subgroup conflict

In an international group therapy conference in Granada, Spain, I led (in English) a median group of about twenty members for several days. At the beginning of the group, one of the members, who served as the translator as well, checked whether anyone needed translation from English to Spanish. Although the group members represented many nations, they all said that they spoke and understood English well. Fifteen minutes after the beginning of the group, the door opened and a tall, dark-skinned man entered the room. He was from North Africa, did not speak English, but was fluent in Spanish. A strange exchange of words took place in the group about translation, and the group members clarified that they preferred not to translate the communication in the group to him. They even criticized the translator for interrupting the flow of communication and, becoming angry, they neutralized him, saying that they would take responsibility for translation. This actually meant that the stranger would be left with no translation since they were already objecting to the translation.

It was so odd! What was happening? The irrational decision of a group of adult therapists to exclude a newcomer for no particular reason felt as if it stemmed from some unconscious motivation. My understanding was that it had nothing to do with language and communication. The man personified "the other" to the group, and they wanted to exclude him. I suggested exploring what he represented for different members. In response, I was told that probably he represented the Palestinian for me (the Israeli) and that the Israeli–Arab conflict was taking place in front of the group!

I told the group that they were ignoring the fact that there is a Muslim–Christian conflict taking place around the world nowadays. This denial was especially strong, I said, if we took into consideration the fact that the group was meeting in Granada, which was the last city conquered by the Spanish Christian kings during the Muslim–Christian struggle. And, I said, we were meeting under the shadow of the Alhambra, the famous palace of the Muslim kings, which could be seen out of the window. For me, this conflict, on the surface about language and translation, was actually between Muslims and Christians and about the world's current conflict. This dark North African man personified an Islamic extremist for the group members. It did not matter that he was far from a fanatical Muslim (later he spoke in the conference about stereotypes and pre-judgments. What an irony!)

During the group he sat quietly and contained all the group's projections, without fighting back or correcting these misperceptions. None of the interventions of the group leader seemed to help the group perceive him differently, and, after two days, although the language problem seemed to be resolved by people providing their own translation, he left the group. The group did not work through the projections, and the stranger definitely did not feel welcomed or included. After he left, the group seemed stuck, as if they could not go deeper. I assumed that this had to do with their ambivalence around his leaving, feeling both relieved and ashamed at the same time.

On the fourth day, he returned to the group. It was amazing how, with his return, the group was filled with hope and with messianic elation as if all the problems were going to be resolved. The group included him more in the conversation. The translator returned to his role and we found that some other members preferred translation into Spanish. We could talk more openly about other social conflicts, including gender, and address the anger of the group members towards the leader for his ineffective interventions.

On the last day, the North African participant told the group that before the conference he had met with an Italian who had been his friend long ago. They had parted ways because of differences in cultures and religions. When they met, he was touched by how warmly the friend still felt towards him. While relaying this to the group, he started crying. One of the Italian group members hugged him, while other group members simply cried with him.

In this example, it seems as if the social unconscious re-enacted in the median group a current conflict with historical roots. Apparently, only the resilience of the expelled member and his persistent attempts to be included, maintaining a position of surrender, according to Ghent (1999), resolved the conflict. The ultimate resolution only happened when the "stranger" expressed his subjective experience in his encounter with his old friend, allowing other group members to acknowledge his subjective experience and share theirs.

Large group: the Israelis whose help was rejected by the Palestinians—a conflict between two social unconsciousnesses

A version of this case study appears in Weinberg & Weishut (2011). This is an example from a large group that took place in an international conference in Israel (2008), shortly after Operation Cast Lead (the war on Gaza), which had highly controversial results both in Israel and abroad, leading to many protests against the government of Israel. During the large group, a Jewish Israeli woman, who identified with the suffering of the Palestinians, told the group that, in the middle of that war, when she heard about the life-threatening danger to children in Gaza, she and her daughter initiated a project trying to evacuate 500 children from the Gaza strip. They asked Israeli Jewish families from the southern parts of Israel to host these Palestinian children and were answered positively. They suggested this solution to the Palestinians and understood that they would never agree to come to Israel, so they approached Palestinian families in the West Bank to be hosts instead. The project had almost started when they received a response from the families in Gaza that they were not ready to send their children away. The Palestinians argued that this was an Israeli manipulation to get rid of their own guilt, and that after evacuating the children from Gaza there would be no reason for the Israelis not to bomb Gaza. The Palestinians said that this was a trick to take their land: First move the children, then force the adults out and make them refugees again.

Many emotions followed the woman's story in the large group: Israelis felt hurt that their good intentions were labeled "manipulative". Palestinians felt misunderstood as well. People from outside Israel felt excluded. The atmosphere changed when one Palestinian asked, "So, do you mean that Palestinian mothers care less about their children than Jewish mothers?" In addition, a British woman associated to the evacuation of children from London in the Second World War, and the research that showed that the children who were evacuated suffered more PTSD symptoms than those who stayed with their families in London. This helped the group become less reactive and more communicative.

This stormy event in a large group shows how difficult it is to really give up one's point of view and recognize the other's subjective experience, due to chosen trauma residing in the social unconscious. The amount of distrust between the parties in conflict (Israelis and Palestinians, in this case) was enormous. Although the arguments of the Palestinians were clearly stated, Israelis could not listen to them, drop their righteous attitude, and see the issue through the eyes of the Palestinians. What blocked their usual ability to listen was the memory of the Holocaust and the associations involved in the specific case. (Interestingly enough, a famous "children's transport" from Nazi Germany was mentioned in the large group. *Kindertransport* (Children's Transport) was the informal name of a series of rescue efforts which brought thousands of refugee Jewish children to Great Britain from Nazi Germany between 1938 and 1940.) The Palestinians were not able to listen to the well-intended Israeli's wish to do something positive during the war either, since they have their own trauma of the Nakba, which is the loss of their villages and houses following the Israeli War of Independence, resulting in their becoming refugees and feeling misled by Arab leaders (Tali, 2017). These historical events seemed to unconsciously creep into the discussion and influence its participants. Without acknowledging these traumas that are part of the Jewish-Israeli and Palestinian social unconscious, and without understanding the impact on members of both nations, dialogue would probably fail. It is also interesting that a historic memory of another nation, brought by a

British woman, could penetrate the parties' walls and help re-establish communication.

Summary

A conflict brought to therapy, whether to individual treatment, couples counseling, or a group meeting (where it is usually enacted in the group), should be understood not only as a manifestation of a current situation, but also against the background of unconscious aspects, especially issues associated to the social unconscious. One of the main difficulties in resolving conflicts is that people become deeply hurt and withdraw to righteous positions, feeling as if they are "objectively" right and the other is wrong. Unresolved unconscious issues, both from the individual background and, many times, from the social unconscious, can exacerbate the situation. In order to help with reconciliation, the therapist should help the client or the group shift from submission to surrender, and recognize and acknowledge the subjectivity and the pain of the "other". Keeping in mind the idea of the social unconscious and helping the people (or subgroups) in conflict to become aware of its impact can help with this transition.

References

Aron, L. (1996). *A Meeting of Minds*. Hillsdale, NJ: Analytic Press.

Benjamin, J. (1998). *Shadow of the Other: Intersubjectivity and Gender in Psychoanalysis*. New York: Routledge.

Berman, A., Berger, M., & Gutmann, D. (2000). The division into us and them as a universal social structure. *Mind and Human Interaction, 11*(1): 53–72.

Dalal, F. (2001). The social unconscious: a post-Foulkesian perspective. *Group Analysis, 34*(4): 539–555.

Freud, S. (1930a). *Civilization and Its Discontents. S. E., 21*: 59–145. London: Hogarth.

Ghent, E. (1999). Masochism, submission, surrender: masochism as a perversion of surrender. In: S. A. Mitchell & L. Aron (Eds.), *Relational Psychoanalysis: The Emergence of a Tradition* (pp. 211–243). Hillsdale, NJ: Analytic Press.

Hopper, E. (2003). *The Social Unconscious: Selected Papers*. London: Jessica Kingsley.

Hopper, E., & Weinberg, H. (Eds.) (2011). *The Social Unconscious in Persons, Groups, and Societies: Volume 1: Mainly Theory*. London: Karnac.

Hopper, E., & Weinberg, H. (2016). *The Social Unconscious in Persons, Groups, and Societies: Volume 2: Mainly Matrices*. London: Karnac.

Hopper, E., & Weinberg, H. (2017). *The Social Unconscious in Persons, Groups, and Societies: Volume 3: The Foundation Matrix Extended and Re-configured*. London: Karnac.

Knauss, W. (2006). The group in the unconscious—a bridge between the individual and the society. *Group Analysis, 39*(2): 159–170.

Mitchell, S. A. (1993). *Hope and Dread in Psychoanalysis*. New York: Basic Books.

Moreno, J. L. (1978). *Who Shall Survive? Foundations of Sociometry, Group Psychotherapy and Sociodrama*. New York: Beacon House.

Nuttman-Shwartz, O., & Weinberg, H. (2012). Organizations in traumatized societies: the Israeli case. In: E. Hopper (Ed.), *Trauma and Organizations* (pp. 215–231). London: Karnac.

Tali, S. (2017). The Palestinian social unconscious. In: E. Hopper & H. Weinberg (Eds.), *The Social Unconscious in Persons, Groups, and Societies: Volume 3: The Foundation Matrix Extended and Re-configured*. London: Karnac, in press.

Tubert-Oklander, J. (2006). I, thou, and us: relationality and the interpretive process. *Psychoanalytic Dialogues, 16*: 199–216.

Volkan, V. D. (1997). *Bloodlines from Ethnic Pride to Ethnic Terrorism*. New York: Farrar Straus & Giroux.

Weinberg, H. (2007). So what is this social unconscious anyway? *Group Analysis, 40*: 307–322.

Weinberg, H. (2015). The group as an inevitable relational field, especially in times of conflict. In: R. Grossmark & F. Wright (Eds.), *The One and the Many: Relational Approaches to Group Psychotherapy* (pp. 38–56). New York: Routledge.

Weinberg, H. (2017). The social unconscious of Israeli Jews—described and analysed by an Israeli living in North America. In: E. Hopper & H. Weinberg (Eds.), *The Social Unconscious in Persons, Groups, and Societies: Volume 3: The Foundation Matrix Extended and Re-configured*. London: Karnac, in press.

Weinberg, H., & Schneider, S. (2003). Introduction: Background, structure and dynamics of the large group. In: S. Schneider & H. Weinberg (Eds.), *The Large Group Revisited: The Herd, Primal Horde, Crowds and Masses* (pp. 13–26). London: Jessica Kingsley.

Weinberg, H., & Weishut, D. J. N. (2011). The large group: dynamics, social implications & therapeutic value. In: J. Kleinberg (Ed.), *The Wiley–Blackwell Handbook of Group Psychotherapy* (pp. 457–479). Chichester: Wiley Blackwell.

PART IV

PROCESSES OF RECONCILIATION IN INTER-GROUPS

CHAPTER NINE

Us and them: an object relations approach to understanding the dynamics of inter-groups conflicts

Uri Levin

> "Our current knowledge of human nature tells us that enemies are here to stay"
>
> (Volkan, 1986, 190)

On June 19, 1954, two groups of eleven-year-old boys stepped down from buses to begin summer camp in the Sans Bois Mountains in Oklahoma. The new arrivals were normative middle-class boys, none of them with a history of behavioral problems at home or at school. They had nothing on their minds other than high expectations for a fun-filled, three-week summer vacation, filled with fishing, swimming, canoeing, and hiking.

Nothing, however, was exactly as it seemed. The camp was actually about to become an arena for a seminal field study of intergroup conflicts designed and led by Muzaref Sherif—a study that came to be known as the Robber's Cave experiment (Sherif et al., 1961).

Unbeknown to the boys, however, and with their parents' agreement, the camp counselors and directors were replaced by social psychologists and research assistants. At first, none of the group members was aware of the fact that another group was sharing the campsite. During the first few days, as planned by Sherif, each group took part in activities designed to promote group cohesion, and develop leadership and norms. Group names were given—the Eagles and the Rattlers—and flags were designed and painted. Toward the end of the first week, the groups discovered each other's existence, and seeing the "other guys" using "our baseball field and hiking trails", sparked demands for a competition. The staff was happy to arrange a four-day tournament, including baseball, a treasure hunt, and other events. A fancy trophy, shiny badges, and pocket-knives were promised to the winners. Both groups practiced hard, cheered their teammates, and booed and insulted the competition. Hostilities escalated as the tournament progressed, culminating in a flag burning when the Eagles lost the tug-of-war.

The Eagles ultimately won the tournament, but, while they were taking a celebratory swim, the Rattlers raided the Eagle's cabins and stole the prizes they had collected. The rivalry had turned into a full-blown war, and the staff was kept busy silencing the name-calling, breaking up fights, and cleaning up after cabin raids. Twenty-two normal boys were transformed into two gangs of brawling trouble-makers, full of hostility and intent on exacting revenge for every real or imagined slight (Smith & Mackie, 1995).

Sherif's Robber's Cave study took place during an increasing trend among researchers from various fields, mainly social psychologists, to conceptualize the underlying sources that lead to inter-group conflicts. They were attempting to understand how conflicts could be mediated, and the manner in which solutions to those conflicts could be reached among social, cultural, political, economic, or religious groups. The realistic conflict theory (Levine & Campbell, 1972; Sherif, 1966) asserted that the main source for inter-group conflicts stems from competition over valuable material and natural resources; land, gas, oil, strategic sites, the labor force, and gems are merely a small portion of reasons that lead countries, economic societies, or groups of children—throughout human history—to engage in battle, in war, or ongoing struggles. The disturbing sense that there is a limited amount of material rewards for everyone (be it a real or imagined situation), creates competition for physical and economic survival and creates hostility between groups (Hepworth & West, 1988).

Groups, however, may enter states of conflict and competition not only over material resources, but over social assets as well—respect, honor, praise, and prestige being just a few examples. People's need to experience the group they belong to as being better than other groups is a powerful engine that feeds rivalry, prejudice, hatred, and intergroup struggles. Being part of the group can offer us a sense of belonging and value. It gives us the sense that we are part of "something greater than ourselves" and it provides us with moments of fame stemming from the achievements of other members of the group, allowing us to bask in the reflected glory.

Inter-group rivalry can occur even when material or social commodities are not scarce. The theory of relative deprivation asserts that social comparisons, the human tendency for people to relate to their own status by comparing it to that of others, is the main factor determining the extent of an individual's sense of satisfaction or discontent with his own situation, not necessarily by objective reality (Bernstein & Crosby, 1980; Crosby, 1976). An example would be if you were to buy a bright, new, shiny car, and were very pleased with it, right up until the moment that your neighbor purchases a newer, brighter, shinier car. The same is true concerning groups and belonging to a group. The fraternal deprivation theory asserts that people compare their own group to other groups and can experience a sense of inferiority and low self-esteem due to the fact that other groups are more successful (or seemingly more successful) (Runciman, 1966). This theory could well explain why a particular social group, while making progress, might feel frustrated if other social groups are perceived to be making more progress, or achieving it at a more rapid pace.

The psychoanalytic perspective

Psychoanalytic thinking has also dealt with social belongingness, group dynamics, and intergroup behavior. Freud (1921c) viewed the early form of human society as a tribe controlled by a dominant leader. The group's identity and the tribe members' sense of belonging to the group is achieved by the mutual identification of each individual with the leader, on whom they project their ego-ideal, making him an adored and beloved figure, creating a connection between them, and loving each of them equally. Simultaneously, the projection of responsibility on the almighty leader allows them to be released from moral limitations, setting in motion aggressive and paranoid processes toward other groups who are experienced as threatening to the libidinal connections between the leader and his followers.

Bion, whose theory deals greatly with the question of how an individual's ability to think develops (or is stalled), perceived the individual as a group creature in essence. In his seminal work, Bion (1961, p. 91) dealt with the attempt to understand the "inalienable inheritance as a group animal". Not only is the individual never outside the group, the group is a part of who we are, its impressions are imprinted upon us, or, in Bion's words, "There are characteristics in the individual whose real significance cannot be understood unless it is realized that they are part of his equipment as a herd animal" (p. 133).

Bion suggested that at any given moment, the group can act in one of two configurations, which he termed "group mentality". One of the ways in which the group acts is known as the "work group" mentality; the group acts rationally and is target-oriented while investing its utmost efforts in solving problems based on the reality principle. The group, however, can also act under the basic assumption mentality, a state in which defensive organization replaces the true objective of the group. The group's basic assumptions are its fearful orientations toward reality; they express their hatred in regards to "learning from experience". The group creates basic assumptions in order to avoid true thinking. In all basic assumptions, magical thinking replaces true thinking, leading the group to avoid dealing with the problems posed by reality.

A simulated division into "us" and "them"

One of the problems posed by reality is the fact that additional groups exist among us. Under the proper conditions of cooperation and challenge, these other groups could constitute a significant resource for growth and development (for instance, learning from another group how it goes about achieving success); however, similar to Sherif's depiction in his research, the natural tendency arising in the group during an encounter with a different group is to perceive the other group as an "enemy", which they should protect themselves against or attack.

Berman and colleagues (2000) ascertain that the division into "us" and "them" constitutes a basic social human organizational structure. This structure has an impulsive and unconscious character. In the opinion of these researchers, the purpose of this organization is to assist the evolving group (as a team, as an organization, and even as a nation) in the process of defining its identity; hence, a distinct and differentiated "me" group is formed, which is significantly different from anything that is "not me", meaning "not us". In this sense, the division into "us" and "them" functions as a psychological defense mechanism against the sense of chaos and loss of identity within the crowd. Furthermore, it incorporates a developmental role, allowing the individual to experience differentiation and individuation processes.

In their article, Berman and colleagues describe their observations as group leaders and consultants in experiential conferences held within the framework of the "Besod Siach" Voluntary Association, an Israeli association devoted to promoting dialogue between opposed segments of Israeli society.

The primary task of the simulation (based on an idea by Dr. David Gutmann) was to enhance dialogue between people from these opposed groups, by bringing them together. Each participant was randomly given a tag with the word "Right", "Left", or "Government". The room was divided into four areas defined by signs indicating Left, Right, Government, and "Town Square". This last area was set up so that representatives from different groups could meet. Participants were asked to explore the ways in which relationship between groups were developing. Staff acted as consultants, working to facilitate dialogue.

The primary dispute between right and left in Israel revolves around their respective differences in attitude toward the territories Israel conquered/liberated during the 1967 war, which are heavily populated by Palestinians. While right-wingers consider "the territories" a part of Israel, and are, therefore, against withdrawing from any of the territories, left-wingers are willing to withdraw from all, or at least most, of these territories, as part of a compromise for peace. Right-wingers are generally suspicious about the prospect of peace with the Arabs, and are sometimes considered by left-wingers to be paranoid. On the other hand, left-wingers hold strong beliefs in the chance for peace, and are seen by the right-wing followers as naïve.

One would find many religious Jews among the right-wing supporters, while left-wing supporters are basically secular. Right-wingers tend to be more nationalist and left-wingers tend to be more humanist. In Israel, as in many other societies, the political identification of a person is well grounded and considered to be part of one's personal identity, thus remaining constant with little change, regardless of political events.

The working assumption was that conflict would arise within the groups, and specifically between participants within the same group who held different political points of view. Bearing this in mind, the organizers hoped to enable better understanding among the participants. Here is a sumary of what actually occurred.

1. Participants divided submissively into groups according to the tag they received, with no signs of protest or discomfort. People who received a right-wing tag formed a circle, and so did the ones who had received a left-wing tag. Bear in mind that in each of these groups, half of the participants held a political agenda opposed to the tag they had received. All of the groups located themselves in the exact place assigned to them by the consultants.
2. From the very beginning, members in each group began making an effort to achieve an agreement based on a common denominator. An atmosphere of acceptance and warmth was observed within the groups. They were preoccupied with creating an ideology and rhetoric supporting and justifying the division. The language became binary and categorical.
3. As the groups representing left and right were quickly consolidated, the members of the Government group looked embarrassed and hesitant. After a period of time had passed, they preferred to individually join one or the other left/right group, finally leaving only two groups after a short time. The town square was left empty, and an inter-group meeting was not held in this area.
4. Little attention was paid by the participants to the primary task of exploring inter-group relations. When reminded of this by the consultants, members of the groups usually responded by saying, "First we have to know who we are."
5. When a participant from one group insisted on suggesting a meeting with the other group, he was met with hostility and

suspicion, and those attempts ended quickly, bringing an intensification of conflict and tension between the groups, and the idea of the "others" as enemies.

The division into "us" and "them" as an expression of psychological deep structure

This chapter offers a psychoanalytic observation, deriving mainly from the object relations school, through which the presented phenomenon can be understood. This observation perceives the quick division into "us" and "them" as a basic universal human structure. This supposition is based on concepts from the books of Thomas Ogden, primarily from *The Matrix of the Mind* (1986) and *Subjects of Analysis* (1994).

In his book *The Matrix of the Mind* (1986), Ogden asks the following question: If the infant is born without thoughts, how does he come by this "knowledge" of objects if not by experience? To answer this, Ogden introduced the concept of psychological deep structure, which can be understood by analogy to Noam Chomsky's concept of linguistic deep structure (1968).

According to Chomsky, infants are born not knowing English, French, Spanish, German, or any other language but, under certain basic conditions, each infant learns at least one of the languages spoken on this planet. It is simply not possible for a human being to deduce and operationalize the grammatical structure of language without an inherent system from which to select and organize the mass of sounds to which one is exposed. The individual does not have to create a grammatical structure. Chomsky tells us the infant is born with a code that determines the way he will organize auditory stimuli. Nothing is perceived absolutely freshly, free of preconceptions. A meaning cannot be generated absolutely *de novo*.

Examples are numerous. To begin with, our auditory organization of sound into phonemes is not a matter of passive reception. The distinction between the phonemes "ba" and "pa" is not the quality of the stimuli themselves, it is built into our system of organizing stimuli. The manner in which an infant organizes the shapes and shaded areas that compose the human face is another example. He or she will organize visual data into groupings (shapes and shaded areas) not of his or her own individual creation, but, rather, the product of a system for perceptual organization that is shared by all human beings. Yet another example: the chick, without prior experience of predatory danger, will scurry for cover upon sighting the wing pattern of a predator. It has an inherent code with which to organize and respond to stimuli, preceding any actual experience.

Ogden states that the Kleinian concept of inborn "knowledge inherent in bodily impulses" (Isaacs, 1952, p. 94) can be understood not as inherited thoughts, but as a biological code that is an integral part of our instincts. The infant is not born with the knowledge of tearing at the breast, but has a powerful predisposition to organize experience along some specific lines. For Klein (1952), those lines are the life and death instincts. Ogden writes that experience interpreted in accord with the death instinct will be attributed with aggressive and dangerous meanings, whereas experience organized in terms of the life instinct will be attributed with nurturing and loving meanings. Actual experience, at least in the beginning of life, is secondary to this inherent code. A sense of danger is not created by the real danger (aversive stimuli); real danger simply confirms the infant's anticipation that such danger exists (Klein, 1958). To put it in Bion's (1962) terms—preconception (which is not an idea, but the potential for an idea) meets a realization (a real experience) to create a conception (an idea, a thought). According to this theory, the infant is a prisoner of his own state of mind; that is, of his dichotomy of constructing meaning to what he experiences. In the very beginning, the infant sees in the external world only what he expects to see on the basis of his preconceptions. Imprisoned in his expectations, the infant is unable to learn from experience, because new experiences are interpreted only in terms of his expectations (as in paranoia or hypochondria).

How does the infant ever break free from the imprisonment of his own preconceptions, and become capable of learning from experience? Ogden answers this with the mechanisms of projective identification, of container–contained, and of alpha function. It is not before the mother allows herself to be used in these processes that the baby can move beyond himself.

How can we utilize these ideas to improve our understanding of the division into "us" *vs.* "them"? As seen earlier, the participants of each group quickly stepped into their assigned political roles. An ideology was suggested and developed in no time. Inter-group dialogue was blocked. The situation reflected a most regressive state, in which the binary psychological deep structure was automatically activated and could be seen as an example of the inability to learn from experience. When participants in the groups acted as they did, we could argue that they were in a regressive state of mind, one that was set into motion by the reactivation of a deep psychological structure. The presence of the "us" group, as an extended representation of "me", was perceived and interpreted by the life instinct. The presence of the other group, the object which is "not me", derived its meaning from the death instinct.

It can be suggested that this kind of division is adaptive to the initial phases of group formation, since it enables the groups to identify danger immediately, without the effort and resources that are involved in learning about an external reality. Group members, like the chick mentioned above, do not have to learn from experience in order to know that the delegate from the other group, who is looking for dialogue and exploration, is a dangerous enemy to be wary of. The presence of this delegate in their territory only confirms what the members of this group were predisposed to believe—that the world is a dangerous, persecutory place. The rejection of the delegate's efforts goes on to create the same situation in his or her own group, when he or she returns and reports the other group's rejection to his or her fellow members. The group's immediate interpretation of the "other" group is that they are dangerous. This seems clear to them, since the "others" do not want to talk, and we must prepare ourselves for a war. In Ogden's terms, it is not the delegate's rejection that created feelings of danger and threat; those were simply confirmed by what was already known.

These ideas will now be used as a means of deepening our understanding of the evolution of ideology and symbolism. Ideology and symbolism can be perceived as a form of internal organization for the group facing a complex reality. Kernberg (2003) perceives ideology as an integrative system of beliefs that provides the social group with a narrative, an explanation, and rationale for its mere existence, a sort of destiny. The ideology and the system of symbols and associated meanings that begin to be formed in each of the groups can be understood as a form of inner organization *vs.* the ambivalent and dual external environment.

It can be said that ideology is a narrative that reflects the psychological deep structure. In its nature, ideology is not only defensive, but it also expresses the state of mind of the closed system of this deep structure. In another simulation designed and led by Berman and colleagues (2000), the left and right tags were changed to blue and red. The participants assigned deep symbolic meanings to these colors. Participants in the red group saw the color blue as a symbol of nobility while identifying their own color, red, with humanism or the working class. In yet another simulation, some participants received a tag with a neutral word, and on other tags there was no word written. When this was discovered, one of the participants shouted, "They have something we're missing. They have—we don't. They are rich and we are the poor." An ideology of being exploited by the others became evident immediately.

It appears that the process of dividing into "us" *vs.* "them" is always ready to emerge within the context of a given reality. It appears as though we are dealing here with a basic universal structure of social organization that can be characterized as the impulsive unconscious process of division. The *raison d'être* of this form of organization is to assist the evolving group—a team, organization, or nation—in defining its own identity. Once a differentiated "us" has emerged, it helps to keep all that is *not us* at a safe distance. Hence, the division has both a defensive purpose—in that it helps the group to cope with feelings of chaos and loss of identity—and a developmental purpose, which enhances the process of separation–individuation.

Seen as an outcome from that, the fact that the Town Square remained empty is not then surprising. This territory, where representatives were asked to meet, represents the meeting point of instincts. During the initial phase, when the participants are still confined in the closed intrapsychic mentality of the psychological deep structure, the Town Square was experienced as dangerous, as it represented an external need, held by the consultants–parents. The consultants' invitation to meet only verifies the notion that the consultants cannot be seen as good objects. It is as if a mother bird, rather than protecting her baby chick, asks the chick to seek a dialogue and negotiate with its predator.

The Town Square is a kind of no-man's-land. Erlich (1997) emphasizes the significance of the term "on the boundary". This is a territory in which hostile parties can meet in order to maintain discussion with the other side, a type of transitional space (Winnicott, 1971), in which one can live and play, without straightaway leading to real results, hence its value. In this space, it is possible for one to experiment with dialogue and acquaintance, suggest creative ideas in order to bring the conflict to resolution, and attempt communication with the other party—verbally and symbolically. It is possible to face the existential fears and anxieties related to meeting and maintaining a dialogue with "them". However, in order for the Town Square to become a place in which a dialogue can be held with "the other", the foreigner, the enemy, he or she must be acknowledged as "the other" with whom it is necessary to speak. Erlich distinguishes between two categories of intrapsychic experience of an enemy. The earliest enemy, developmentally speaking, is the pre-oedipal enemy. The relationship with the pre-oedipal (inner) enemy is controlled by projection and projective identification mechanisms, and characterized by split, polarity, and demonization. This is an enemy that, according to Volkan (1986, 1988), is highly convenient for us to project all our bad traits on—the same traits that we do not wish to acknowledge as belonging to ourselves. There is no discussion with such an enemy. The exchange of words, once it occurs, is characterized by a "verbal spear cleaning" and is used for expressing and satisfying aggressive and destructive needs and wishes. The more mature enemy is the oedipal enemy, with whom we would be capable of maintaining a discussion. Trying to connect or relate to this type of an enemy is characterized by ambivalence and emotional complexity. Feelings such as hatred and rivalry exist alongside of emotions of love, respect, admiration, and identification. In order to fill the Town Square for an encounter of representatives from different groups, transformation from the inner enemy experience is required first, from the pre-oedipal enemy to the oedipal enemy.

The role of consultants and the potential for mental growth

Once two groups are trapped in a binary system, in which one of the groups is perceived as the enemy (or, at least, as a danger to be wary of), a perceptional deformation takes place, consisting of two central characteristics. The in-group is perceived as absolutely right, and, morally speaking, superior—making each action moral or giving it a moral justification. The out-group, on the other hand, is perceived as completely wrong; there is no point, therefore, in maintaining discussion with it. This perception often becomes radicalized and the out-group is then perceived as mean and even diabolical, which justifies the escalation of fighting it, or keeping extreme distance from it.

For this reason, the two groups are in need of external help, which can assist in opening a channel for thought, exploration, and reflection. Frequently, the role of the leader (or consultant) in small groups is to assist in reducing destructive splits and massive projections that lead to the collapse of the dialogue due to the "attack on the reflective space" (Hinshelwood, 1994). In international relations, the role of the "third" party is central in the transformation of pre-oedipal enemies who have not entered into a dialogue and discussion with one another into oedipal enemies who are capable of sitting and speaking together. This role is highly evident in the manner in which the USA acts as a mediating party in the conflict existing between Israel and its neighboring countries. In all peace ceremonies and signing of intermediate agreements (i.e., the peace treaty with Egypt, the peace treaty with Jordan, the Oslo treaty with the Palestinians), the photo always includes three parties, in which the President of the United States constitutes the significant "third" party in the triangle, allowing Israeli and Arab leaders to shake hands (Erlich, 1997).

Returning to the simulation described above, the role of the consultants is to facilitate the process in its main mission: to investigate the relationship between the groups (and, as such, also to investigate what takes place within the groups).

Ogden (1994) coined the term "the analytic third". It is a useful term that allows additional understanding of the described processes. Ogden writes (p. 4),

> The analytic process . . . is one in which the analysand is not simply the subject of analytic inquiry; the analysand at the same time must be the subject in that inquiry (that is, creating that inquiry) since his self-reflection is fundamental. . . . Similarly, the analyst cannot simply be the observing subject of this endeavor since his subjective experience in this endeavor is the only possible avenue through which he gains knowledge of the relationship he is attempting to understand.

In this way only, once the analyst and analysand allow the subjectivity of each to destroy, and be destroyed, by the otherness of the additional subject, the analyst and analysand are created. It is at this moment, once the analyst and analysand are created, that a third subject is also created—"the analytic third". According to Ogden (p. 5),

> . . . analyst and analysand come into being in the process of the creation of the analytic subject. The analytic third, although created jointly by (what is becoming) the analyst and the analysand, is not experienced identically by analyst and analysand since each remains a separate subject in dialectical tension with the other.

What is the role, then, of the consultants if we use this conceptual system? Berman and colleagues (2000) claimed that the consultant's central role is to mediate, interpret, and serve as a symbol. If we were to borrow Ogden's definition system, we could observe an additional aspect of the consultant's role, the actual experience and participation, being part of the situation occurring in the room. The consultants are a component of the processes taking place, and, in this sense, anything that takes place at any given moment in the room could be understood through the transference–countertransference relationship. The consultants' role in the room is to attempt to understand what is taking place while allowing it to occur, outside of and within themselves. The consultants should be occupied not only with questions such as "What does each group prevent from itself by limiting the dialogue with the other group", but also, "What arises within me once whatever takes place in the room occurs as it does, and once I am part of the creation of what takes place in the room at the moment". The consultants, similar to the participants, hide to a certain extent behind labels that were given to them, and they, too, seek a neutral place, in which they can be protected from experiences occurring in the room. They, too, are trapped, in a sense, in the same trap of "us" (the consultants) and "them" (the participants).

Dialogue can only exist when the subjectivity of each side is recognized through its acceptance by the "other", in a way that is related, but not necessarily identical, to the original experience. The groups had avoided engaging in dialogue because they had each been held back by the mechanism described above; that is, the psychological deep structure of "us" *vs.* "them". Consequently, each group was in a state of knowing, rather than one of experiencing. Since dialogue can only develop between two (or more) subjects, being in such a state inhibits the development of a true dialogue. In fact, it is possible to describe the consultant's main role as one of helping the groups to acknowledge the "otherness" which is part of our lives, and to be involved in a process of mutual recognition rather than ensnared in repeated projections, estrangement, and exclusion.

The consultants' willingness to join as subjects taking part in a mutual creation between themselves and the participants, and to allow the experience of the participants to subsist within themselves and be changed by it, is crucial for the success of transformation. The consultants' willingness and ability to be destroyed by the participants (as, for instance, by the participants' attacks on their interpretations) and survive the destruction from the participants, to ensure that the participants could use their interpretations, not only for the projection of their fantasies, are essential for successful change. In Winnicott's terms (1971), by successfully enduring the participants' attacks, the consultants allow transformation from object-relations to object usage; that is, the ability to use their interpretations in favor of growth and mental progress, expressed in an increasing ability to develop thinking that is not limited by the "psychological deep structure", which categorically divides the world into "them" and "us".

Summary

The division into "us" *vs.* "them" can be seen as inherent to the infrastructure of the social organization of human beings. Numerous parallels to this division can be found among the social organization of animals in nature. Often, animals tend to gather into herds, by assigning the herd they belong to as "friend" and the other herd as "enemy". A conflict develops when an intrusion into the territory of another herd occurs. This conflict might end with a fight, leading to the death of the intruder, sometimes also of the defending animal.

However, as human beings, we tend to perceive our belonging to a certain group as an expression of free will, moral values, ideological considerations, and a coherent point of view. In a similar way, we often portray our differences from other groups in terms of the different values and ideology held by these groups. But is it really only a matter of "free will" rather than "nature"? Is our social organization, in fact, so different to that of animals? Do concepts such as "instincts", "structure", and "human nature" not play a significant role in the process of dividing human beings into "us and them"?

The structural term "psychological deep structure" coined by Ogden, assists in understanding the universal tendency to divide into "us" and "them". Following Freud, Klein, and Bion, Ogden assumes that human beings interpret reality based on their inner world. This world is characterized by a basic predisposition to experience external stimulation in a binary manner, as belonging to one of two groups of experiences—good or bad. In ambivalent situations, such as once a person belongs to a new and unknown group, a regressive human tendency exists to experience the group to which one belongs as good and protective, and the other group as "foreign" and threatening. We need an ideology in order to justify our structural tendency to experience the world in a simplistic/literal manner. Volkan (1985) writes,

> After all, the main point of drawing lines between "Them" and "Us", however specious the justification for those lines may be, is to clarify and affirm the sense of "Us" in a way that strengthens positive self-representation. The self-portrait of any group is relative, depending in varying degrees on the kind of dark background that will bring its own light and strong qualities into relief. (p. 244)

The fact that this is human nature perhaps indicates that human beings cannot avoid the natural division of "us" and "them". All we can do is attempt to acknowledge this tendency, along with its implications, and strive to reduce its destructive results.

References

Berman, A., Berger, M., & Guttmann, D. (2000). "Us" and "them": a basic structure of human social organization. *Mekbaz, 5*(1): 7–27 (in Hebrew).

Bernstein, M., & Crosby, F. (1980). An experimental examination of relative deprivation theory. *Journal of Experimental Social Psychology, 16*: 442–456.

Bion, W. R. (1961). *Experiences in Groups*. New York: Basic Books.

Bion, W. R. (1962). A theory of thinking. In: *Second Thoughts: Selected Papers on Psycho-analysis* (pp. 110–119). New York: Karnac.

Chomsky, N. (1968). *Language and Mind*. New York: Harcourt, Brace and World.

Crosby, F. (1976). A model of egoistic relative deprivation. *Psychological Review, 83*: 85–113.

Erlich, H. S. (1997). On discourse with an enemy. In: E. R. Shapiro (Ed.), *The Inner World in the Outer World* (pp. 123–142). New Haven, CT: Yale University Press.

Freud, S. (1921c). *Group Psychology and the Analysis of the Ego. S. E., 18*: 65–143. London: Hogarth.

Hepworth, J. T., & West, S. G. (1988). Lynchings and the economy: a time-series reanalysis of Hovland and Sears (1940). *Journal of Personality and Social Psychology, 55*: 239–247.

Hinshelwood, R. D. (1994). Attacks on reflective space. In: V. L. Schremer & M. Pines (Eds.), *Ring of Fire—Primitive Affects and Object Relations in Group Psychotherapy* (pp. 86–106). London: Routledge.

Isaacs, S. (1952). The nature and function of phantasy. In: M. Klein, P. Heimann, S. Isaacs, & J. Riviere (Eds.), *Developments in Psycho-analysis* (pp. 67–121). London: Hogarth Press.

Kernberg, O. F. (2003). Socially sanctioned violence. In: S. Schneider & H. Weinberg (Eds.), *The Large Group Re-Visited* (pp. 125–149). London: Jessica Kingsley.

Klein, M. (1952). Some theoretical conclusions regarding the emotional life of the infant. In *Envy and Gratitude and Other Works, 1946–1963* (pp. 61–93). New York: Delacorte, 1975.

Klein, M. (1958). On the development of mental functioning. In: *Envy and Gratitude and Other Works, 1946–1963* (pp. 236–246). New York: Delacorte, 1975.

Levine, R. A., & Campbell, D. T. (1972). *Ethnocentrism: Theories of Conflict, Ethnic Attitudes and Group Behavior*. New York: Wiley.

Ogden, T. H. (1986). *The Matrix of the Mind*. London: Jason Aronson.

Ogden, T. H. (1994). *Subjects of Analysis*. London: Jason Aronson.

Runciman, W. G. (1966). *Relative Deprivation and Social Justice*. Berkeley, CA: University of California Press.

Sherif, M. (1966). *In Common Predicament: Social Psychology of Intergroup Conflict and Cooperation*. Boston: Houghton Mifflin.

Sherif, M., Harvey, O. J., White, B. J., Hood, W. E., & Sherif, C. W. (1961). *Intergroup Conflict and Cooperation: The Robber's Cave Experiment*. Norman, OK: University of Oklahoma Press/Book Exchange.

Smith, E. R., & Mackie, D. M. (1995). *Social Psychology*. New York: Worth.

Volkan, V. D. (1985). The need to have enemies and allies: a developmental approach. *Political Psychology*, *6*(2): 219–247.
Volkan, V. D. (1986). The narcissism of minor difference in the psychological gap between opposing nations. *Psychoanalytic Inquiry*, *6*: 175–191.
Winnicott, D. W. (1971). *Playing and Reality*. New York: Penguin.

CHAPTER TEN

Enemies' love story: reconciliation in the presence of foes

Hating and loving enemies in group analytic conflict dialogue

Robi Friedman

Introduction

How is it possible to talk to enemies? How do we move from talking to reconciliation? Is it possible at all? We know it is difficult to openly address the other in the face of the slightest personal differences: how do we achieve dialogue when the differences are vast?

This chapter is based on the unique behavior experienced during three sets of talks between professionals from the Palestinian Authority and Israel as part of ongoing, mixed Jewish–Arabic group-analytic dialogue groups.

Having been a participant or leader of several conflict dialogues, the real difficulty appears when the emotional involvement is intense: it is no surprise that when hate and existential fears emerge in deep relations, the entanglement is at its strongest. The two dialogues with Palestinians from the Palestinian Authority had the formal aim of professional exchange, together with a manifest wish to work towards reconciliation.

I want to include in this description the third set of talks with Palestinians, in which Jewish and Arab Israelis participated side by side in group-analytic (therapeutic) groups. Their aim did not include any direct wish to deal with political or social reconciliation, but to cope with personal suffering and disordered relations. They invested all their energy in changing personal intra- and interpersonal patterns, and working through ego-training-in-action (Foulkes, 1964, p. 82). However, perhaps unsurprisingly, it was a greater challenge for groups with mixed "personal" emotional and relational characteristics to engage in "political" discussions than for the conflict dialogue groups.

This difficulty seems to offer additional clinical evidence on the influence of the matrix: it is almost impossible to separate the individual from the society. This means that, in everyday life, individuals usually only momentarily and artificially separate themselves from their identification with social issues. Furthermore, one could say that social dynamics, which can latently influence a wide range of relationships (interpersonal, familiar, communal), are continuously—partly unconsciously—alive in the inner life of each person. They might reveal themselves more easily, almost categorically, when the person becomes a group member (either actually or virtually, for example through the media, or other forms of communication). The awareness and use of these processes could contribute to processes of reconciliation in the presence of enemies, and could also contribute to the understanding of pathological aspects of human relating.

Questions

The questions I ask myself during and after these group processes are:

- What are the requirements for a conductor who is willing to engage in reconciliation dialogue with the enemy?
- Are there settings that facilitate the meeting of enemies?
- How are reconciliation meetings different to "therapeutic" ones? And how do these differences impact on the requirements of a conductor?
- Is it possible for an involved "in-the-group" conductor to lead work on a conflict, or is external leadership preferential in these circumstances?
- Are multi-cultural groups consisting of "enemies" able to participate in therapy?

Although it seems politically correct to almost automatically answer all the questions with a modern "yes, we should", my experience is that we might easily be mistaken. Looking into it more carefully could help us to guide the conductor through an emotional maze, especially if he/she experiences existential dependency on the issues raised by these questions.

Example 1

Facing extremely uncomfortable feelings evoked by your enemy is much more difficult to contain than one assumes. In the second meeting of an ongoing dialogue group, a Jewish woman exclaimed in a highly emotional tone, "I hate those suicide bombers—how can they walk into the middle of a restaurant where families are having a meal together—elders and children—and self-detonate, after shouting 'Allah Akbar' [God is the greatest]?"

This member of a dialogue group voiced her community's emotions in the presence of her enemies, at a time when Israelis were suffering from the Palestinians' Intifada—the Palestinian attack on Israel, called "terrorism" by one side and "war" by the other. The resulting devastation caused by suicide bombings—sometimes twice a day, with hundreds of Israelis killed, and thousands physically and psychologically injured—infuriated and shocked the Israeli population, both Jews and Arabs.

Another participant in the group, a young Palestinian social worker from Ramallah, who was usually very softly spoken and friendly, reacted to this comment: "How can you believe that you cannot be blamed for these acts? Only you, the Jews, are the guilty ones!" The first woman and other Jewish members of the group were dismayed and overwhelmed by feelings of pain.

The Palestinian social worker had also voiced her community's position. The lack of regret or ambivalence in her identification with what was the large group atmosphere in her camp of the conflict influenced the dialogue.

Such a remark is an obstacle to reconciliation, because it negates any recognition of the suffering of the other. A lack of empathy has one meaning on an unconscious level: rejection. Maybe the worst kind of enmity is the one that does not feel any empathy for the other side. But who is able to choose his dialogue participants? Are there good and bad enemies? Who is right in this situation? Partners have to be able to contain the enemy's feelings of blame and hatred in order to encourage development. Therefore, one of the aims of the dialogue is to making communication less rejecting.

What is an enemy?

Dictionaries explain that an enemy is someone who feels hatred for, fosters harmful designs against, or engages in antagonistic activities against the other, an adversary or opponent. Psychologically, an enemy is an object of hate or fear that fulfills a role or acts as a persona, and who is not encountered as a person. This person is not a real subject, but an object. The subjectivity of the other is, at the very least, significantly diminished, if not entirely denied or eliminated, through a psychic mechanism. Identifications in small, median, or large groups promote the influence of psychological processes, which depersonalize the enemy—one of the main obstacles to reconciliation.

It might be depressing on the one hand, but it might also help the reconciliation process to understand that it is not only evil people who hate and foster animosity. Interestingly, "enemy making" seems such a universal interpersonal event that even very nice people, whom one has loved, cherished, and empathized with, can become the present "enemy". It is actually fascinating to see how people's emotional relationships are transformed by animosity.

Perhaps the main characteristic of feelings towards an enemy is the retraction of empathy. In our dialogue groups, we try to foster the opposite movement, transforming "enemies" into people. One major objective is to restore empathy. Events with the potential to restore humanity can be identified: suddenly, even after an antagonistic interaction like the one just described, relations change dramatically.

In our talks with Palestinians, sometimes a short encounter in the female toilets, surprisingly and naturally allowed for human feelings, empathy, and even sympathy to appear. The main advantage of personal encounters is that at times they might enable a break from the depersonalization processes, which often dominate conflict dialogues, and open some kind of communication.

Unfortunately, shortly afterwards, the distancing and depersonalization process usually returns, corresponding with the return to socially relevant groups. The empathic feelings that were previously felt as natural seem to vanish. Thus, in our experience, attempts at meeting the enemy in a more harmonious dyad are a double-edged sword because it sometimes opens an illusion of hope, which, if it cracks, could actually antagonize relations. The power of the group proves to completely overshadow individual positions. Is this evidence that a dominant social unconscious has a stronger influence than the personal unconscious?

Therefore, the task of reconciliation and the meeting of enemies should not only be conducted in groups, but in groups that deal with pathologies that are influenced by powerful and sometimes overwhelming emotions. Groups with borderline patients have to be structured in such a way that they can both hold and contain hate and dread. The group's setting is important, and the group's "task" should be defined as precisely as possible. In order to communicate their differences, a group requires the highest possible level of cohesion, together with a conductor who has significant experience with violent processes. All these factors can facilitate the building of a "working alliance" (Sandler et al., 1992) for a group seeking reconciliation with the enemy.

The power of the group: dynamics of destruction, change, and possible dialogue

Groups provide a necessary forum in which to address and contain conflicted emotions rooted in large social/political groups (Volkan, 2004). Perhaps this could also take place within median groups. If small groups are very small (in group-analytic therapy, it is usually up to eight participants and often fewer), they sometimes might not be able to represent the positions of the community and the society.

As de Maré (2002) stated, it is the median group and the large group that are driven more strongly by social and political issues, and, thus, represent the optimal setting for coping with conflict. The larger presence of social voices in median and large groups provide a chance to work through them more effectively than in dyads or very small groups.

If the underlying hate is covered by dyads, subgroups, or defended by small-group intimacy, it is very difficult to address and work through such hate, and could possibly provoke aggressive dynamics at a later time, some of which I call "rejecting" or "scapegoating" positions. This violent process uses splitting and projecting mechanisms that become instruments for the group's aggression. Scapegoating is a latent position, which can be present in any collective social and personal unconscious. Rejection from groups is probably the main result of societal anxieties from group survival and efficiency functions, or, from a parallel perspective, annihilation anxieties (Hopper & Weinberg, 2011). In order to use groups as a container of conflicts and as an instrument of reconciliation, we must make the effort to investigate the human tendency to hate and scapegoat, which are common in the "rejection relation disorder".

Identification processes with the group matrix are usually more influential in individual encounters than in personal ones. This powerful influence results in relation disorder in which group participants become dysfunctional due to inclusion and exclusion anxieties. Groups achieve change by the group participants' need to belong (Schlapobersky, 2016)—as well as by its flip side: coping with fears of annihilation (Hopper, 2001), a failure to link, and a fear of rejection from the group. This primal anxiety, which is a continuous aspect of the natural human foundation matrix (Foulkes, 1973), can be the product of early separation anxiety. Participating and working through the aggregation/massification continuum (Hopper, 2001) also has to do with the group leader's struggle to transform the group's attitudes, usually by a combination of his/her own maturity and his/her separation–individuation abilities. Such a change can only be maintained if the leader is supported by the group during the process. This means that leaders who are not left alone by opposing groups might be able to change societal approaches—for the best or the worst.

The setting: a working alliance in a dialogue space? The obstinacy of love

The stable relationship, which could be called a "working alliance" (Sandler et al., 1992), has a functional relationship with reconciliation, and is an emotional process which cannot be taken in an all-or-nothing way. Sometimes, a part of the work is achieved by including a good degree of reconciliation, for example, work on agreed water quality, or agreeing to cooperate on a health care project, as I witnessed myself in Amman, Jordan, in 2009. In this process meeting, for example, a "working alliance" occurred during, and as a result of, dialogue between representatives of the Palestinian Authority and Jordanian and Israeli administrations, some of which seem to continue until today.

In the beginning, a measure of good will is needed for most discussions, and may be taken as equivalent to the positive transference to a joint group's task. Usually, some assistance is needed to promote the relationship between two adverse opponents, sometimes by assigning two co-conductors.

Should the conductor be part of the dialogue group, or an outsider to the conflict?

The question of the conductor being the object and the subject of influence in a group leaves us with no clear-cut answer to the question: who should lead groups in great conflicts? Is it wiser to have representatives of the main enemies co-lead the groups? If a group chooses to have co-leaders, what seems central is the co-conductors' abilities to dialogue with one another. At any rate, the process aspect will probably always be part of a structural solution: one has to provide enough time and a convenient place to conduct an open dialogue. If a sole conductor does the job, he/she might be fixated on the same conflict solution approach. This usually means that the conductor is bound to former influences that have permeated the group's and his/her own psyche. He/she will conform to the usual setting orders and forms of elaborating identifications, projections and other conflicted feelings. Conflicts have epidemiological aspects and are contagious (Redl, 1942), and could, through projective identification, become part of the conductor's attitudes.

Group analysis, where the leader of the group is educated to be the "conductor in the group", provides one possible answer to this question. Not being necessarily enmeshed in the group emotionally and relationally, the conductor of the group could have potentially greater freedom to use the group's dynamic. Yet, in spite of all group leaders' psyches being permeable to the group's culture, one may find a group transformed into a partner to be a strong ally in a conflict dialogue. I have never seen a group that has been converted into a conflict dialogue solely by the leader. It is a reciprocal partnership, which moves the group into a space where emotional movements influence each other.

It seems important that the leaders have access to some kind of supervision, no matter how experienced they are. Conductors have to find elaborating partnerships for the containment of their own emotional difficulties. The path towards reconciliation is a difficult one, which requires a group process to support it, first by unpacking the emotional difficulties, then holding and containing them as if they are in psychic danger. In the first phase, the group might encounter quite frightening amounts of internal and external aggression while learning to give recognition to the pain of others. All participants have to cope with the competition of being a victim of the other, together with making an effort for mentalization (Fonagy et al., 2002) and more restraint. All agreed boundaries of meeting, communication, and behavior in the group are subject to scrutiny and are often chosen. If given the opportunity, the boundaries, and the structured communication and behavior, the group often does a lot of the elaboration work by itself, which adds to the conductor's interpretations. Hence, under some structuring conditions, not only can a local conductor lead a conflict dialogue in a group, but even a regular group member can be an efficient leader of the working-through process. The group-analytic approach of facilitating multiple containers is often a step-by-step process. Even if there is a more leader-centered first phase in the group's development (Agazarian, 1994), the group evolves from asking: "How does the leader contain this terrible emotion or relation?" to a more mature question: "Which of us will contain it?" The path towards reconciliation lies in the ability to be a working group that facilitates this.

What happens in group therapy that includes enemies?

Therapeutic transformational efforts usually start by building a secure space that provides an opportunity for free, communicative, and emotional movement. A conductor has to care for the wellbeing of all members and promote changing group processes by establishing and maintaining a stable setting with secure boundaries. For the leader of a therapeutic group, these frames of work are the equivalent of the maternal "primary concerns". They are conducive to building the "working alliance" in which participants come to "work" on reconciliation through their communication and their personal and interpersonal problems, tackling individual issues in a way that is different from the approach taken with social/political problems.

Therapy groups often "hate" social problems, especially because they antagonize group members, resulting in "hate to hate". Therapeutic groups often feel that dealing with a political conflict is a defense against working through personal problems. Nobody seems to come to therapy in order to solve social or political problems or for reconciliation. They will often feel their resources are "wasted" if not used towards the overt aim of therapy. Even in societies like ours, in Haifa and the North of Israel, where Arabs and Jews live closely together and might participate for years in the same therapy groups, dealing with political problems in a group-analytic group still seems a big obstacle to overcome. Thus, the question is, how can we work with this dissonance in individual, couple, family, and group problems if we also acknowledge that while we are individuals, we are also "nodal points in a matrix" (Foulkes, 1973). After some time, it becomes clear to most group members that the larger context influences their emotional lives. For example, it has been my experience that the more marginalized individuals and sub-groups feel, the more depression, immobility, and lack of development they will feel. In my take on pathology, such an "exclusion relations disorder" (Friedman, 2007, 2013) will have to be dealt with in order to achieve change in the individual's positioning within the group and its structural dynamics.

Example 2

Once, in a therapeutic group, I had to provide a space for an enemy subgroup to integrate. This could not happen if the group itself were not mature enough to take the challenge. But even in this relatively developed group, which used to feel like a "working-group" that could sometimes tackle difficult emotional issues, I understood that I could not become the only carrier of bridging and reconciliation. Two Arabic women attacked the group relentlessly, especially on highly emotional national holidays. I tried to help the process by providing a transparent example of my own position. I agreed to change the setting in order to accommodate Muslim holidays. Then I shared my own emotional response, trying to support the group members who resisted the difficulty of enduring the mental pain caused by cognitive and emotional divergences with enemies inside the group. I tried explaining and mentalizing (Fonagy et al., 2002) as an addition to transparent modeling of accepting adverse views. It helped but it took so much energy that many group participants asked if it was worth the effort. I do not have the answer.

In an ongoing group-analytic group that met during a Gaza war, a Jewish mother of a soldier who was in battle said that she was terrified about his fate and did not sleep at night. Finally, she said, "It's only a small comfort that our warriors fight the terrorists" and wept. A Palestinian woman responded, "I see how terrible you feel. But who is a warrior? Who is a Shahid? What do you think the Palestinians do if they are not warriors for their cause?" Later in this same session there was a discussion about democracy in Israel. Some of the Jewish group members were amazed to hear that the Palestinians thought the Jewish State was only partly democratic.

The different "beliefs", which include conscious and unconscious emotional attitudes that include hate and annihilation anxieties, were "contained" in the group by a working alliance which included a structural element—the fact that it offered the opportunity to talk once a week. As the conductor, I had to steer the group firmly, supporting some bouts of political and social moods. But it became increasingly clear that, paradoxically, the great difficulty of containing such a process in this group was due to the participants' closeness to each other. The established relations in the group were also responsible for the shared foundation matrix, which allowed for resonance, mirroring, exchange, and other reciprocal influences that were already established and in use by the group. The feeling of such a shared foundation matrix seemed to have provided a secure-enough feeling, which was supposed to hold against the threat to destroy the relationships established between enemies in the group. The evoked conflicted feelings were so powerful that the conductor had to hold the good and bad parts together in the group matrix.

Destructive difficulties

The two biggest threats to the matrix I experienced as conductor or participant in dialogue groups were: (a) the difficulty of coping with guilt, and (b) the handling of "over-identification". The difficulty of elaborating guilt was tremendous. The tendency to blame the enemy while installing oneself in the victim's position, and the avoidance of accepting neither guilt nor any responsibility for the violence, seem to be two sides of the same coin. These tendencies seemed to be as basic and tenacious as the "basic drives". The "war of guilt", as I later called it, appeared to be an unconscious necessity for those participants in the conflict who suffered from annihilation fears. People who perceive existential threats seem to consider the possibility of showing feelings of guilt towards their enemies as an impossible luxury. There seems to be a deep connection between the difficulty of feeling empathy towards an enemy and putting the blame on the other as a central position in war. It is a "war matrix" or what I now call a "soldiers matrix" (Friedman, 2014), which does not allow for shame, guilt or empathy.

The other salient difficulty had to do with the refusal to try to lower the high level of identification while in conflict. In dialogue groups, we coined these mental positions "over-identification", whose common ground was the difficulty in achieving separation from their own group, or, as Volkan (2010) calls it, shaking the large group identification. Over-identifying group participants could not "play" at adopting more flexible positions. They were often struck by remorse and strong feelings that they would betray family, friends, and communities.

Another related obstacle to reconciliation was intergenerational heritage (Volkan, 2010), which is partly unconscious and establishes identifications that seem almost innate to historic dynamics.

De-identification with one's former positions, which often appear to be a precondition to reconciliation, seems a rather complicated relational process, like de-idealization or any other primitive form of separation from a significant object. While it is important that the conductor and the group support such separation, this might be a formidable task, as one's own security in the face of annihilation anxiety is based on the closeness to family and friends and their support.

In these crucial moments for the group, it is important for the conductor to remain highly aware and in control of his/her own feelings. For example, in the first talks with Palestinians, we were somewhat aware of our feelings of guilt but, in fact, it was only much later that we discovered the extent of those feelings (Friedman, 2010).

I perceived the containment of our own guilt as happening in at least three steps: in the first step, we denied feelings of guilt almost completely, even though we, our parents, or our society had victimized Palestinians directly. In these talks, the entire Israeli sub-group had, in a direct or indirect way, participated in some belligerent activity targeting Palestinians (it was probably the same on the Palestinian side). Once we admitted to having feelings of guilt in a second step, they would strengthen, and sometimes we would find ourselves exaggerating our fantasized or real crimes. Only during a third stage, when we became able to differentiate between "feeling guilty" and "being guilty", could we improve our dialogue with our guilt, and, subsequently, with theirs. Interestingly, when we reached this stage, our Palestinian partners did not seem to particularly like it. In hindsight, I think that when the other side feels guilty, the enemy becomes a subject rather than an object: an "easy-to-hate enemy". The "war of guilt" is something that is quite complicated, and, interestingly, we thought that in this area our enemies felt like fish out of water.

Although containment does not necessarily have to be the conductor's sole responsibility, it is my experience that if he/she is not able to contain his/her own conflict, there is a good chance that the group will not be able to contain the difficulties either. It is our experience that he/she must reflect on the wish to avoid shame and guilt, but he/she also has other anxieties to consider. Sometimes, we referred to this effort as an act of love. We called it trying to establish a "place of love".

For example, when the reciprocal resonance between enemies is not communicated as hateful rejection, feelings of a developing love are experienced. The co-existence of these positive feelings, together with the aggression towards an enemy, changes the group's communication from malignant mirroring (Zinkin, 1983) to the possibility of introjecting and learning. Thus, the other is perceived as being "let in". Malignant mirroring is one of the most poisonous and destructive processes in groups, because it has to do with "taking in" poison and destruction and ejecting the best from the body. This process is also seen in rejecting and destructive scapegoating positions which are full of hate.

Sharing the conductor's thoughts and feelings might help to contain these processes. Like dream telling, he/she takes care to ensure that his/her inner world will not be shut out, but shared with others, including a potential supervisor and even the dialogue group. It is our experience that if the conductor closes his/her mind, he/she will be in trouble as a conflict dialogue facilitator. We found that openness to our difficult feelings influenced our capability to bear guilt—and in our case, we thought it extremely important for the Israeli and Palestinian "guilt phobia" to be elaborated and become less of a threat. The most demanding task is to remain in a "thinking" position when involved in the dynamics of rejection, hate, and splitting and the "scapegoating position". A reflected detachment from these positions can help to facilitate reconciliation.

References

Agazarian, Y. M. (1994). The phases of group development and the systems-centered group. In: V. L. Shermer & M. Pines (Eds.), *Ring of Fire* (pp. 36–86. London: Routledge.

De Maré, P. (2002). The millenium and the median group. *Group Analysis, 35*(2): 195–208.

Fonagy, P., Gergely, G., Jurist, E., & Target, M. (2002). *Affect Regulation, Mentalization, and the Development of the Self*. New York: Other Press.

Foulkes, S. H. (1964). *Therapeutic Group Analysis*. London: Allen and Unwin [reprinted London: Karnac, 1984].

Foulkes, S. H. (1973). The group as matrix of the individual's mental life. In: E. Foulkes (Ed.), *Selected Papers* (pp. 223–234). London: Karnac.

Friedman, R. (2007). Where to look? Supervising group analysis—a relations disorder perspective. *Group Analysis, 40*(2): 251–268.

Friedman, R. (2010). The group and the individual in conflict and war. *Group Analysis, 43*(3): 281–300.

Friedman, R. (2013). Individual or group therapy? Indications for optimal therapy. *Group Analysis, 46*: 164–170.

Friedman, R. (2014). *Die Soldatenmatrix*. Lecture at the annual DGPT conference in Lindau.

Hopper, E. (2001). The social unconscious: theoretical considerations. *Group Analysis, 43*(3): 281–300.

Hopper, E., & Weinberg, H. (2011). *The Social Unconscious in Persons, Groups, and Societies: Volume 1: Mainly Theory*. London: Karnac.

Redl, F. (1942). Group emotion and leadership. *Psychiatry, 5*: 573–596.

Sandler, J., Dare, C., & Holder, A. (1992). *The Patient and the Analyst* (2nd edn). London: Karnac.

Schlapobersky, J. (2016). *From The Couch To The Circle: Group Analytic Psychotherapy in Practice*. London: Routledge.

Volkan, V. (2010). *Pschoanalytic Technique Expanded: A Textbook on Psychoanalytic Treatment*. Istanbul: Oa.

Volkan, V. D. (2004). *Blind Trust: Large Groups and Their Leaders in Times of Crises and Terror*. Charlottesville, VA: Pitchstone.

Zinkin, L. (1983). Malignant mirroring. *Group Analysis, 16*: 113–126.

CHAPTER ELEVEN

Lines of conflict in psychoanalysis: reconciliation in the future?

Michael B. Buchholz

Introduction

Psychoanalytic discourse is nourished by the optimistic idea that conflicts can, and should, be resolved. But it is not always ensured that this goal can, and should, be achieved in every case. Too many conflicts cannot be resolved; often they cannot even be formulated or avoided. So, we must make a distinction between conflicts that can be resolved and those we have to endure. To bear unbearable conflicts in psychoanalysis often means to grow. Here, the word "conflict" acquires the special meaning of an unavoidable stimulus for change, growth, solving a paradox or a puzzle; somebody who has not experienced this conflict or gone through it could be identified as lacking in development. So, "solving" is not the counterword for "conflict"; it is growth. Growth potentially plays a very salient role in bearing unbearable conflicts. Thus, the task will be to answer the questions "What does growth mean?" "What kind of development are we thinking of here?" These are the questions I explore in this chapter, using examples from the history of psychoanalysis. The concept of growth has to be applied to psychoanalysis itself. I try to give an answer by distinguishing four levels of meaning within the concept of "growth": I begin with growth meaning successive use of perspectives, then follow with growth having the meaning of complementary, then simultaneous, use of perspectives, and I conclude with how growth can mean the development of an "excentric position". To say it clearly here: "excentric" does not mean "eccentricity" as a caricature of British lifestyle prototypically represented in figures such as, say, Lady Sitwell. "Excentric positionality" is a philosophical term, taken from the work of Hellmuth Plessner (1928), which is explained in the course of my contribution.

Growth meaning the successive use of different perspectives

Development in psychoanalysis has been seen as an irresolvable confrontation of different principles. The pleasure principle finds its limits in the reality principle. Primary narcissism cannot survive; it must accept the existence and needs of others. From Jean Piaget, the famous Genevan developmental psychologist, we have learned that children in their intellectual development have an egocentric (the starting point of excentricity) perspective in the beginning and only when they are three or four years old do they accept that others have other views of the same objects. Children start with morals where principles are set as absolute, only later do they accept heterogeneous principles in consideration of relevant circumstances. All those steps go forwards and backwards, from pleasure to reality, from narcissistic demands to partial acceptance of others, from egocentrism to altruistic perspectives, from morals set absolutely to free consideration of circumstances. The movement goes back and forth, many times.

This repetition of "many times" is important. It does not belong to "repetition compulsion". It is a creative process of producing a critical mass of events that then, suddenly, change and jump into another kind of dynamic process. The accumulation of such a critical mass is an important aspect of development in many areas. The child sucks mother's breasts and sucks and sucks—and suddenly the mother–child system jumps onto a higher level. The child loves his mother deeply and, suddenly, this love changes to the oedipal level and, then, oedipal conflicts; a new regime of experiencing is born which has to be overcome again and again.

Keeping this in mind, let us look at some events from the history of psychoanalysis, for example, the debates about the death instinct. The death instinct, as a concept, was first introduced by Wilhelm Stekel, who talked about Eros and Thanatos in 1910 (Makari, 2011). At that time the idea was rejected by Freud. Later, it appeared as an independent invention by Sabrina Spielrein and was more or less ignored. After the First World War, Freud (1920g) rediscovered the concept and introduced it to the audience as an original idea having recently come to his mind. The movement that followed inherited this pattern of going forwards and backwards, backwards and forwards, and it does not end in the present day. Many proponents argued for, and many argued against, the death instinct. After all these efforts to extinguish it, the death instinct is still alive. What kind of a problem is this? There seems to be no independent judgment possible; neither clinical debates nor comparisons with other fields such as ethology or ethnology have been able to advance the discussion on the topic. Whether the death instinct exists or not cannot be decided.

But consider the common experience that setting a problem in the right way is to solve the problem. Is the question posed in the right way? Do we want to know if the death instinct exists? Here, I do not want to touch on the problem directly; instead, I propose a detour.

This topic of "does it exist or not?" reminds one of another episode in the history of psychoanalysis. In 1910, the Vienna psychoanalysts had one of their energetic meetings. It was laden with conflicts, because Jung had denied the sexual unconscious! Binswanger declared that this was a crucial question. In natural science, it often happens that you conclude from observation that something not observed nevertheless exists. You observe something at the surface and conclude that, lying behind it, there must be something different. But this is always declared a conclusion, not a fact. What you have, then, is not proof of something existing, what you have is a concept for explaining something you can observe. This was a very modern observation by Binswanger. Freud answered: "The Unconscious is metapsychic, we simply set it as real!" (Makari, 2011, p. 351). Makari, reviewing this chapter in the history of psychoanalysis, admits that a postulation simply is not a fact! Today, we understand how important this is. There are authors who review what made Freud, for example, think of infantile sexuality and they conclude that other concepts can be applied in a useful way, for example, the concept of attachment theory (Busch, 2008; Dornes, 2002). It is not necessary here to take a position in this debate. For my purposes, it suffices to see that growth becomes possible when two perspectives, at least, can be adopted. Then the frame moves.

What is needed in this kind of debate is "frame reflection" (Schön & Rein, 1994): You no longer concentrate on what a problem is, but more on how it is conceptualized. What kind of frame is used unconsciously? Can we achieve by frame reflection a new frame used consciously? And what other frame is then used unconsciously (Carveth, 1984)? If some observable infantile phenomena become describable in the theoretical terms of attachment theory (or any other) then you can suddenly see that the frame changes: from ontological assertion ("it is infantile sexuality") to conceptualizing ("It can be considered as if it were . . ."). In the frame of ontological assertion, the conflict cannot be resolved, the debate must go on and on without end, thus repeating repetition compulsion.

This has relevance in how we think about "controversial discussions". Strachey, in a letter to Glover, termed the "attitudes on both sides [are] purely religious and the very antithesis of science" (quoted in Grosskurth, 1985, p. 257). Ontological debates have a tendency to take over religious formats. Controversies, then, have a strong tendency to be derailed and they take the form of a battle. Although scientific arguments often are very hard even on a personal level, historically they have been introduced as a measure to pacify these debates. Part of this scientific endeavor is to have an eye for one's own conceptualizing activity. In maintaining that something "is", this activity too often is made invisible.

In a conceptualizing frame, conflict resolution seems at least possible. You can debate which concepts best explain which. One criterion is the explanatory value of a concept. And you gain a new differentiation: between different concepts. Sometimes, two different concepts have a similar realm of explanatory power, sometimes not; sometimes they indicate a cultural style of thinking, as Fleck (1983) meant when he introduced the term of "thinking collectives". So, new debates open up and replace the old quarrels between factions of supporters who cannot but maintain what is or is not.

So, we may hope to find a solution for the question of the death instinct, too. We are now able to see that the mistake lies in the question itself. We cannot hope to find out about the existence of the death instinct. Thus, it makes more sense to give up the ontological frame. It would be better to ask, "What does this concept describe?" "What does it explain and what does it not?" On the topic of sexuality, this way of thinking brings considerable relief.

From time to time, psychoanalytic journals publish papers that lament the gradual loss of drive theory ever since narcissism has prevailed and even more after the re-emergence of attachment theory. Well, is it sexuality that is vanishing? No! This is ontological thinking. Sexuality cannot vanish. The discourse of sexuality might fade—and this is not beyond our influence. We can regain this territory and bring this discourse back in our theoretical debates and clinical conversations.

It is the topic of drive theory that vanishes from our discussions. We have learned to see that sexuality is more than drive-driven, that perhaps the most important thing in sex is not the biology of sexual chemistry, but words. Or hands, eyes, tongues, and bodies.

If you want to maintain the claim that sexuality is the most important and the most neglected thing in one's life, start talking about it. Talk about sex with your patients. Only in this way will you find out if drive theory is the best way to describe, or, what's more, to explain, what appears in conversation. It might be that the expansion of our concepts is urgently needed. The ontological frame hardly allows for growth; it tends to exclude the successive use of different views.

Growth means the complementary use of different perspectives

Meanwhile, this is not news for psychoanalysts. We do not have one psychoanalysis, we have many (Stepansky, 2009). Others (Giesers & Pohlmann, 2010; Pine, 1990) describe the four or more psychologies in the history of psychoanalysis: Starting with drive theory, then Kleinian psychology, then ego psychology, the object relation theories, and then, self psychology. Today, one could add intersubjectivist or relational concepts.

Of each of these we have to speak in the plural. There is more than one drive theory, more than one ego psychology, there are many versions of the object relations theory, and, of course, the number of self psychological theories and relational theories nearly equals the number of theorists writing them down. But here I shall simply put aside these differences and have a look at the central formulas and metaphors of disorder in each version of psychoanalytic theory. My aim is to gain a feeling for how each of these developments in theorizing clinical experience evolved the other. This is growth as the solution of theoretical conflicts—and this does not exclude the possibility that we are confronted with new and unexpected conflicts. Perhaps, we have to grow further, steadily going on.

In drive theory, there is a developmental pressure towards unifying the fragments of infantile polymorph-perverted sexuality. The variability of the resulting psychic *gestalt* is large but, in any case, there is pressure towards unification. Conflict is pervasive and will never end. It is not only a conflict between pleasure and abstinence; it is a conflict between diversification and unification, too. Out of these endless combinatorial patterns of development emerges the individual biography. One of these patterns, which Freud described as the Oedipus complex, is a central and powerful metaphor (Merl, 1986; Wilshire, 1982) for organizing sexual strivings and cultural integration. The Oedipus complex cannot be solved, it has to be overcome, as Freud so often emphasized. Drive theory in this respect has an air of tragedy, oedipal commands mean for the son "to be like father" and, at the same time, "not to be like father". Escape from this oedipal "double bind" (Bateson et al., 1956) goes in one direction only: upwards, through growth. Oedipal conflicts cannot be "won", they demand growth of personal structure. Thus, it seems that in the evolution of our theory would naturally develop, focusing more and more on ego and its relation to the new structure formation, the superego.

Ego psychology described an ego that is different from popular understandings. The ego is part of psychic structure and, as such, it opposes the id and the superego. The ego, at the same time, is seen as encompassing the whole psychic structure and then, ego equals self. It was Freud (1933a) who observed that the ego can split itself into different states. This splitting can be used as a defense when anxiety arises. Anxiety is more than a signal, it is a symbolic form of repressed memory. Let us consider the ego's growth in a few sentences.

The ego's central developmental origin is identification. In the beginning, there is no difference between object cathexis and identification. The ego comes into being when object cathexes are given up; it is their condensation. So, the central formula when considering disorder in terms of ego psychology is the pressure towards unification.

The central conflict is between this unification and the adaptation to environmental conditions. Hartmann postulated independent energies for this task and a conflict-free sphere for the ego, because the ego's coherence is not only threatened by early environmental circumstances, but also by the drives (Schafer, 1970). In ego psychology, the status of drives has changed. Drives are no longer the "energy" for development; they now have become a risk for the ego's coherence. They have to be "neutralized". The most important task for the ego becomes self-regulation. Thus, psychic disorder here centers conceptually on the level of independence the ego has achieved from the drives, from the superego, and from the environment. There is some fuzziness as to the role of identification here. Identification is seen as the process resulting in ego formation. But identification is also the central mechanism of melancholia (Freud, 1917e). So, the whole conception of ego psychology has a melancholy flair, in my view. Theodor Reik once remarked in the Vienna seminar that before, one was trained by Freud in sexual theory, and now, with ego psychology, one is trained in renunciation and defense.

Object relations theory expands the conceptual frame. This kind of theoretical reasoning does not start from drives or from ego coherence, but from the role of the object. Primary objects are seen to take up the task of emotional regulation for an ego that does not yet exist. Whereas, in drive theory, the object was seen as the most exchangeable part, now the object receives a central role. It is the object from which drives are constituted. It is not drive which is primary, but love, as Michael Balint formulated. The central metaphor is the inner stage where the internalized object relationships take place. We learned from Kernberg (1975, 1979, 1993a,b) that these are composed of three components: the imagined conception of an object, of a subject, and a related affect. Due to this basic idea, ego states are now promoted to the central topic of clinical consideration. The vicissitudes of altering ego states are described as a new form of defense. The ego is now seen as constituting itself through incorporation, which, at the same time, means annihilation of the object. Another kind of "double bind"-like conflict shows up here. The incorporated object disappears and is, thus, annihilated and, at the same time, is the founder of the ego. Anxiety arises from this process; the strength of anxious arousal indicates the fragility of the total state. Thus, disorder is no longer seen as a pathological conflict solution. In strict consequence, the "personality disorder" is set as central. It can be identified by its potential for the re-enactment of pathological object relationships. The therapeutic aim here becomes the integration of different states of personality. This integration can be achieved only from a superior point of view that requires growth by further integration: this outlines the direction from the ego as a psychic element among others to self as an encompassing psychic conception.

Self psychology directs our attention to a special form of object relationships which Kohut (Basch, 1995) termed "self-objects". Self-objects are not a special kind of objects, such as a teddy bear or another pet. Self-object is a name for any kind of object fulfilling a special function for the subject (Kohut, 1980, 1982). They inherit the baby's lost imagination of grandiosity that is either projected to idealized parental figures, or they are given the task of admiring and applauding the exhibitionistic grandiose self of the subject. Between these two poles, Kohut posed the conception of a twin, the desire for someone who is "like me" or, at least, similar. The central metaphor in this theory is mirroring, approval, or, at higher levels, acknowledgment by a self-object which helps to stabilize the self on its path to authenticity. While Kernberg's object-relation conception seems to incorporate an adultomorphic orientation which favors becoming independent of regulation by objects, Kohut sees a deeper need for the "mirroring" function of approving and acknowledging others. Kernberg favors the autonomous individual, whereas Kohut sees a person seeking connectedness in a state of being understood.

Self-objects thus fulfill important functions throughout life for the self and it is these functions, not a special kind of object, that Kohut stresses. Kohut points to traumatic disorders of the self's relationships with self-objects: Parents who were traumatically de-idealized (Gedo, 1975) or who cannot provide the subject with the necessary degree of admiration and acknowledgment. These disregulations of self-object relationships threaten self-coherence, as there is a danger of regression to grandiose delusions or feelings of emptiness when integrating ideals are lost. The paradox inherent in this conception is that what could give coherence to such personalities—grandiosity of the self or grandiosity of the self-object—is, at the same time, threatening this coherence by devaluation. While Kernberg postulated an independent drive for aggression, Kohut sees aggression as a result of non-optimal frustration in self-object relationships (Glassman, 1988). Kohut's theory can be considered tragic as well because he sees a human need for acknowledgment, for finding meaning in one's life and for the final acceptance that life is not grandiose, but finite.

I have sketched here a very rough outline of four of the psychoanalytic theories. Through wisdom and far-reaching experience, they all stress different dimensions of humanity and if I could include the work of Melanie Klein or Jacques Lacan here, one would see other dimensions of conceptualizing humanity. I want to restrict myself to these four psychologies; the picture in psychoanalysis is complicated enough and far from integration.

We can see the conflicts that can arise between the different psychoanalytic conceptions in a very clear fashion. I hope I can give an impression of the divergent views and how they result from these psychologies. When we consider treatment techniques, we can easily imagine how different procedures follow from each of these basic conceptions. I will not touch on that here. There are prominent authors such as Wallerstein (1990) who did not think of unifying theory in his search for "common ground", but who proposed seeking common ground in treatment technique: every analyst equally using equally hovering attention, transference, and countertransference, and so on. There are also others who said that Freud himself was the first self psychologist, when he took into account reports made from memory by some of his former patients on how he conducted his treatments.

Generally, it is not an easy task to dive deeply into another line of thinking, into the depths of diverging clinical conceptions that arise from a divergent psychoanalytic tradition. Stepansky (2009) muses if there is anyone who ever managed this at all, to really understand what another's psychoanalytic thinking actually is. With this serious difficulty in mind, we can appreciate what a challenge it is to use the four or five or six psychoanalytic psychologies in a complementary manner, from time to time and from case to case, without falling into the trap of arbitrariness. We somehow manage this difficulty in our clinical practice, but often, I suppose, we could not really justify how and why.

Growth means the simultaneous use of different perspectives

We are now proceeding from complementary to simultaneous use of different perspectives, and I am afraid you might lose your patience.

Besides, you probably will not expect any solutions from this new section. What is simultaneous use of different perspectives? You know that, you do it every moment, but normally one does not think about it. If you have two well-functioning eyes, you look at everything using different perspectives at the same time in a mode of operative unconsciousness. It just works. It was the biologist, epistemologist, communicative researcher, and anthropologist Gregory Bateson (Bateson, 1981, 1982) who raised the question of why nature endowed us with such a gift. If we use a very simple analogy, we might say that creating an upside-down copy of the world on the retina should suffice. The copy image is sharp, exact, and precise; it is so small that we can carry the whole world within us. Why do we have two eyes?

Of course, one reason is that the blind spot of each eye is corrected by the other. This operates in a way that normally allows us to see our world without realizing that there is a blind spot. Both blind spots correct each other, or, shall I say, two failures bring a gain. Of what kind? This is the second reason, Bateson declares. It is the gain of deepening one's view, a gain of depth. Using two eyes, we can estimate the distance between ourselves and an object in our world in a reliable way. Bateson adds that this creation of depth should interest psychology. Did not Freud speak of "depth psychology" as a synonym for psychoanalysis?

Here lies the solution to many of the conceptual conflicts I outlined above. With five or six or more psychologies in our minds, we can try to use them for the complementary process of different perspectives, but, as I said, this is such a difficult task in practice that there are serious doubts about who has ever managed it. How can we bring in the idea of simultaneity of views into the clinical situation? By viewing the psychoanalytic situation as composed of two participants with their respective perspectives. This means, in essence, seeing that we have a very special social situation of two persons trying to combine their different views—as in the analogy of the right and the left eye—in such a way that deep feelings and insights can be created. From Bateson's analysis of binocularity, one learns that depth is not a copy of the world, it is construed in a very complicated and useful way and includes error correction. Psychoanalytic practice can now be viewed as the depth that is produced by the two participants in a common endeavor. The results of this are immediately shared by using the tools of symbolic communication again, which deepens the process.

Ferro (2003) has a lovely metaphor for what is meant here. He talks of preparing for every patient a different meal in the analytic kitchen, estimating the amount of food that can be digested, proposing a suitable wine to accompany dinner, cleaning the table, and washing up the dishes and, let's not forget, handing over the invoice. In my view, this is a very convincing metaphor, describing in an amiable way the important operations that psychoanalysts carry out. But it leaves out one important thing. How come the analyst knows what is to a patient's taste? What dishes will he or she like? And what quantities will they be able to digest?

Resonating alignment

Following this consideration, one can see that there is something left out of the kitchen metaphor. Something operates before symbolic tools and operations can be applied usefully. Before propositions of our theories can guide us through a complicated process, we have to study the "pre-positions": how someone is perceived and should be addressed. Something always happens that cannot be described in a better way than by the metaphor of resonance and, of course, by the ruptures of this resonance. With such a musical metaphor in mind, we can see that creating vertical depth in the analytic situation demands the horizontal cooperation of the two participants, which one could perhaps describe as "resonating alignment". I would like to introduce this here as a concept following on from Aron's idea of framing the analytic conversation as a "meeting of minds" (Aron, 1996), similar to seeing it as a "healing conversation" (Symington, 2006). Meanwhile, these ideas are supported by many researchers who do not directly refer to the analytic origins, but their research does support the general idea. Mergenthaler (2008) talked of "resonating minds" and others (Jurist et al., 2008) integrate infant research and neuroscience through an enriching dialogue between researchers and experienced practitioners. Resonating alignment in my view (Buchholz, 2012; Buchholz & Gödde, 2013) includes several dimensions, some of which I mention here:

- mutual sympathy;
- the ever-evolving chances for empathy in both directions;

- fine-grained attention for each other, which we call attunement;
- a recognition of how different the other is;
- a growing understanding of this difference, which, paradoxically, results in a deepening of contact;
- a developing sense of how words and gestures are used by the other in different ways, and, of course, the interruptions of these process components which have to be made into a special object of shared interest.

When such an interruption becomes an object of shared consideration, one can see how the tools of symbolic communication gain a slightly different use. They are no longer simply propositions used for conveying information; they have a function in regulating the mutual relationship and they become "words that touch" (Quinodoz, 2003). Much depends on how the "pre-positions" are formulated. This acts in the horizontal dimension through resonating alignment, which is always a precondition before stepping down into the depths of early experience and biography.

When considering resonating alignment, we can see that the simultaneous use of different perspectives means just that. "Simultaneous" does not mean applying a multitude of concepts in one mind, but to develop a sense for the cooperation of different minds. It could be that in Freud's time this cooperation was such a natural matter of course that it escaped theoretical attention. But, as we all know, Freud had an eye for it. His central statement for a correct psychoanalytic adjustment was that the analyst should listen to the patient with equally hovering attention, including the idea that the unconscious would understand the unconscious. This is a statement so often quoted that it is hardly recognized as standing alone in the whole body of psychoanalytic theorizing. It does not easily fit with the dominant vertical direction of delving into depth.

Today, we can see what an important thing resonating alignment is. It opens up several opportunities. The first is that we can begin to study it when we mutually encourage each other to tape-record our sessions. I have been doing this for many years, and have an exchange with colleagues in supervision groups where we discuss psychoanalytic treatments by presenting each other twenty minutes of a tape-recorded session and then reading the precise transcript of the session. We work only with this small excerpt from the whole treatment, and

I can say we are very content with it. It is as the poet William Blake once formulated: a grain of sand and there is a whole world in it.

The second opportunity is the chance to come closer to solving the problem of defining what clinical facts are. Tuckett (1994) once showed us that, in presenting case materials, we always have such an amount of theoretically contaminated viewing that we have Winnicottian, Bionian, Kleinian, classical, and a lot of other facts. When we begin to study in detail the how and what of our clinical conversations, there is a chance that we might realize how different our clinical practices are and find out whether this difference might have to do with a common competence like practicing resonating alignment with very different personalities. I am sure there is more that can be found out in this regard.

Growth means the creation of an excentric point of view

Now I come to my final point. I want to direct attention to the ruptures of resonating alignment that we have learned to term enactments. These enactments contain histories, stories that can be told after overcoming many serious pains and resistances—in the case that they become an object of common interest. Here, the views of analyst and patient look at a common object, which creates a triangle consisting of two persons (analyst, patient) and a common imaginative object (the story or memory). We can call this a triangle of shared attentiveness (Buchholz, 1990). If this structure of cooperation happens often enough, the patient gains a stable experience that enables him or her to look into horrifying aspects of his or her life—because he or she has someone else in resonating alignment. And the analyst can become a (late) witness of events he can only view with his inner eye.

When this experience happens often enough in a psychoanalytic process, it has a tendency to transcend itself. In the triangle of shared attentiveness, one begins to view not only the other participant and the common object of imagination, but one begins to view the triangle itself as a very interesting structure of analysis. Analyzing from this moment on evolves into to a joyful experience that integrates intellectual interest and emotional needs because what is built up is best given a name as an "excentric point of view". Of course, excentricity is not meant here as a lifestyle.

The term "excentric position" is attributed to philosopher Hellmuth Plessner (Plessner, 1928, 1970, 1982), who used it to describe that we, as human beings, can be our body and can have our body at the same time. He thought this was a special human attribute. Plessner, who trained as a biologist before he became a philosopher, thought, in short, that plants do not have a "center" but animals have. They "look" into the world in which they live, but they cannot transcend this "centric" position. This is the human step, Plessner argues, preshaped by upright walking. Humans can direct their views into the world from their "center", which is their body, but, what is more, they can view this directedness from an imagined point outside their body. Not only do they have a relationship to the world, they have a relationship to this relationship. Humans can overcome their centricity. I feel that modern "mentalization theory" directly joins this line of thinking.

The integration of these two points of view (to be and to have a body) he called "excentric". It means the ability to stay inside and outside at the same time. Excentric positionality means to grow, to develop a higher point of view—paradoxically in order to delve deeper. Depth is generated by the cooperation of the two participants while musing about memories, imagination, fantasies, and other communicated psychic events. The development of such an excentric position is a central target in every minute of the analytic session. It can be achieved at any moment and, when this path opens, pleasure happens. Because you very soon realize that there are many other excentric points of view possible, and, further, excentric views of excentricity, and so a cascade of new possibilities of meaning production opens. There is not one definite meaning; there is a rich and enriching universe of meanings. A paradox is created and solved: In order to gain deep insight, you must achieve this higher point of view.

Conclusion

To integrate higher points of view by delving deeper (and *vice versa*) in the early years, we need the help of mothers and fathers, and where they failed, we sometimes have the fortune to find the help of analysis; an analysis growing in a world that, on its own, develops very many acceptable excentric positions. To integrate them becomes easier when we have learned that this is an unavoidable step in the process of growth, enabling us to deepen our own experiences and in resonating alignment with others. Integration and growth could actually represent helpful psychoanalytic contributions to some aspects of crisis in the world. To gain excentric positionality is necessary, not only in the eyes of different countries looking at and meeting each other in Europe, but in the world as a whole.

References

Aron, L. (1996). *A Meeting of Minds: Mutuality in Psychoanalysis*. Hillsdale, NJ: Analytic Press.

Basch, M. F. (1995). Kohut's contribution. *Psychoanalytic Dialogues, 5*: 367–373.

Bateson, G. (1981). *Ökologie des Geistes*. Frankfurt: Suhrkamp.

Bateson, G. (1982). *Geist und Natur. Eine notwendige Einheit*. Frankfurt: Suhrkamp.

Bateson, G., Jackson, D. D., Haley, J., & Weakland, J. H. (1956). Toward a theory of schizophrenia. *Behavioral Science, 1*:, 251–264.

Buchholz, M. B. (1990). Die Rotation der Triade. *Forum der Psychoanalyse, 6*: 116–134.

Buchholz, M. B. (2012). Die horizontale Dimension des Unbewussten. *Gruppenpsychother. Gruppendynamik, 48*: 6–25.

Buchholz, M. B., & Gödde, G. (2013). Balance, Rhythmus, Resonanz: Auf dem Weg zu einer Komplementarität zwischen "vertikaler" und "resonanter" Dimension des Unbewussten. *Psyche—Z Psychoanal, 67*(9–10): 844–880.

Busch, F. N. (Ed.) (2008). *Mentalization. Theoretical Considerations, Research Findings, and Clinical Implications*. London: Analytic Press.

Carveth, D. L. (1984). The analyst's metaphors. A deconstructionist perspective. *Psychoanalysis and Contemporary Thought, 7*: 491–560.

Dornes, M. (2002). Ist die Kleinkindforschung irrelevant für die Psychoanalyse? Anmerkungen zu einer Kontroverse und zur psychoanalytischen Epistemologie. *Psyche—Z Psychoanal, 56*: 888.

Ferro, A. (2003). *Das Bipersonale Feld. Konstruktivismus und Feldtheorie in der Kinderanalyse*. Giessen: Psychosozial.

Fleck, L. (1983). Erfahrung und Tatsache. Gesammelte Aufsätze. Mit einer Einleitung hg.v. Lothar Schäfer und Thomas Schnelle. *Gesammelte Aufsätze*. Frankfurt: Suhrkamp.

Freud, S. (1917e). Mourning and melancholia. *S. E., 14*: 239–258. London: Hogarth.

Freud, S. (1920g). *Beyond the Pleasure Principle. S. E., 18*: 7–64. London: Hogarth.

Freud, S. (1933a). *New Introdutory Lectures on Psycho-analysis. S. E., 22*: 3–182. London: Hogarth.

Gedo, J. E. (1975). Forms of idealization in the analytic transference. *Journal of the American Psychoanalytic Association, 23*: 485–506.

Giesers, P., & Pohlmann, W. (2010). Die Entwicklung der Neurosenformel in den vier Psychologien der Psychoanalyse. Vom Denken in "affektiven Zuständen" zur Logik des "Kräftespiels" und zurück. *Psyche—Z Psychoanal, 64*: 643–667.

Glassman, M. (1988). Kernberg and Kohut: a test of competing psychoanalytic models of narcissism. *Journal of the American Psychoanalytic Association, 36*: 597–615.

Grosskurth, P. (1985). *Melanie Klein: Her World and Her Work*. London: Hodder & Stoughton.

Jurist, E. E., Slade, A., & Bergner, S. (Eds.). (2008). *Mind to Mind. Infant Research, Neuroscience and Psychoanalysis*. New York: Other Press.

Kernberg, O. F. (1975). Further contributions to the treatment of narcissistic personalities: a reply to the discussion by Paul H. Ornstein. *International Journal of Psychoanalysis, 56*: 245–248.

Kernberg, O. F. (1979). Some implications of object relations theory for psychoanalytic technique. *Journal of the American Psychoanalytic Association, 27*[Suppl]: 207–239.

Kernberg, O. F. (1993a). Convergences and divergences in contemporary psychoanalytic technique. *International Journal of Psychoanalysis, 74*: 659–673.

Kernberg, O. F. (1993b). The current status of psychoanalysis. *Journal of the American Psychoanalytic Association, 41*: 45–62.

Kohut, H. (1980). Reflections on advances in self psychology. In: A. Goldberg (Ed.), *Advances in Self Psychology* (pp. 473–554). Madison, CT: International Universities Press.

Kohut, H. (1982). Introspection, empathy and the semi-circle of mental health. *International Journal of Psychoanalysis, 63*: 395–408.

Makari, G. J. (2011). *Revolution der Seele: Die Geburt der Psychoanalyse*. Gießen: Psychosozial, Bücherdienst.

Mergenthaler, E. (2008). Resonating minds: a school-independent theoretical conception and its empirical application to psychotherapeutic processes. *Psychotherapy Research, 18*: 109–127.

Merl, H. (1986). Der Ödipuskomplex als therapeutische Metapher in der Familientherapie der Ablösungsstörung. In: L. Reiter (Ed.), *Theorie und*

Praxis der systemischen Familientherapie (pp. 191–209). Wien: Facultas Universitätsverlag.

Pine, F. (1990). Die vier Psychologien der Psychoanalyse und ihre Bedeutung für die Praxis. *Forum der Psychoanalyse, 6*: 232–249.

Plessner, H. (1928). *Die Stufen des Organischen und der Mensch (3. Auflage 1975)*. Berlin: de Gruyter.

Plessner, H. (1970). Anthropologie der Sinne. In: G. Dux (Ed.), *Philosophische Anthropologie* (pp. 212–249). Frankfurt: S. Fischer.

Plessner, H. (1982). *Mit anderen Augen. Aspekte einer philosophischen Anthropologie*. Stuttgart: Reclam.

Quinodoz, D. (2003). Words that touch. *International Journal of Psychoanalysis, 84*: 1469–1485.

Schafer, R. (1970). An overview of Heinz Hartmann's contributions to psychoanalysis. *International Journal of Psychoanalysis, 51*: 425–446.

Schön, D. A., & Rein, M. (1994). *Frame Reflection. Toward the Resolution of Intractable Policy Controversies*. New York: Basic Books.

Stepansky, P. E. (2009). *Psychoanalysis at the Margins*. New York: Other Press. Accessed at: www.worldcat.org/oclc/320186696.

Symington, N. (2006). *A Healing Conversation: How Healing Happens*. London: Karnac.

Tuckett, D. (1994). The conceptualisation and communication of clinical facts in psychoanalysis. Foreword. *International Journal of Psychoanalysis, 75*: 865–870.

Wallerstein, R. S. (1990). Psychoanalysis: the common ground. *International Journal of Psychoanalysis, 71*: 3–20.

Wilshire, B. (1982). *Role-playing and Identity: the Limits of Theatre as Metaphor*. Bloomington, IN: Indiana University Press.

CHAPTER TWELVE

Psychoanalytic approaches to conflict resolution: the limits of intersubjective engagement

Shlomit Yadlin-Gadot

From its very beginnings, psychoanalysis has dealt with the issue of conflict between subject and other. Freud's sad legacy, as articulated in *Civilization and its Discontents* (Freud 1930a), was softened in Klein's translation of instinct into emotion and in her articulation of depressive capacities for concern and reparation. Winnicott and self psychology contested the innate status Freud granted to aggression, construing it as a reaction to failure in nurture. Thus, some optimism was instilled into the construal of the relations between subject and other.

Yet, as Benjamin argued, these attempts could not sustain hope for satisfying relations with an "other", as long as that other is conceived as an object, defined in relation to the subject's needs. Citing infant research and emphasizing the ability to perceive the subjectivity of the other very early in life, Benjamin reoriented the conception of the psychic world: from the subject's relation to its object toward a subject meeting another subject as an autonomous center of experience and agency.

Benjamin posits the ability to recognize otherness as innate, but she stresses that this ability needs to be cultivated if its psychological potential is to be realized. When this potential fails, due to developmental failures, conflict, or injury, the relation of subject-to-subject collapses into object relations:

> When recognition breaks down . . . the complementary structure takes over . . . parties are drawn into . . . escalating reactivity . . . Based on internal splitting . . . a structure of mutual accusation takes hold where neither party can truly recognize the pain or the struggles of the other . . . complementary relations are characterized by loss of agency and responsibility. (Benjamin, 2006, p. 7)

For Benjamin, communication is both the vehicle and prime example of recognition. It is simultaneously an ideal, an aspired norm, and a principle of therapeutic transformative practice. Benjamin clearly acknowledges that recognition processes often fall into destruction, but she believes this may be overcome by sticking creatively and tenaciously with communicative practices. Through instituting a mediating third, and in the best case scenario, having this third evolve from within a conflicted dyad, Benjamin believes that recognition and communication practices will triumph.

The main catch here has to do with the partial success of this model's implementations. In the light of this, I wish to present here a bit of Lacanian thought, which may add to, and perhaps complement, the directives gleaned from Benjamin's model. Lacan portrays intersubjectivity as a near-impossible feat. Yet, a close look at his pessimistic model could lead to surprising insights that might enhance our psychoanalytic conceptions of dealing with conflict.

For Lacan, subjectivity is formed only in relation to the pre-existing other. As he sees it, the human infant is born prematurely. This prematurity renders the infant totally helpless and determines his total and protracted reliance on others. Lacan describes the newborn's experience of himself as a dismembered limb, torn and exiled from the mother's body. In this terrifying realm of disintegration and pending death, the infant is offered the irresistible lure of his mirror image. This image presents the terrified infant with a unified whole, an integrated, coordinated totality. In a jubilant moment of "Aha!", the infant identifies himself with this promising imago, thus creating the imaginary nucleus of his ego (Lacan, 1997a).

Clearly, Lacan notes, this recognition in the mirror image is nothing but an absurd "misrecognition" that involves deep alienation. This alienation is, first, the consequence of the huge gulf that lies between the unified imago and the infant's fragmentary authentic experience. Second, this imago is steeped in the "discourse of the Other", suffused with momentous implications and connotations coming from the desire and narrative of others as they encourage the child to recognize him/herself in the mirror ("What a strong boy!" "You're going to be beautiful, just like Mommy," etc.). Thus, from the start, the child's ego and body image are overwritten by signifiers flowing from the libidinal economies of speaking others. These signifiers are branded in the infant's flesh and form the contingent basis of his being. Lacan calls these first imprints—"unary traits".[1]

Now, making matters worse, the infant quickly enters into an intense and ambivalent relation with his imago. This perfect, coherent image of himself arouses envy in the child, and he seeks to own it and put himself in its place. Simultaneously, the child feels that the image is there to usurp him, to further alienate and deplete his experience of self. This pattern of what Lacan terms narcissistic aggressivity is the basic trademark of imaginary relations, the relations of the ego with others. In cycles of introjection and projection, a basic paranoid positioning is created, boiling down to the binary choice: "It's me or you".

The entry into the symbolic order, via the oedipal complex and the transformation of the dyadic mother–child space into a triadic one eases the aggressivity of imaginary relations. Creating a third point of reference dissipates the immediacy of experience, and allows mediation and thought. This transformative third is not necessarily a flesh-and-blood imaginary father. It is, rather, the Name-of-the-Father that forbids endless *jouissance* with the mother and constitutes the child as a desiring subject within the confines of language and the law. The Name-of-the-Father is, effectively, any symbolic object in the mother's discourse that causes the child to realize that he is not the one-and-only object of his mother's desire.

This realization may be construed as an emancipatory tragedy of sorts. On the one hand, the child is no longer the mother's "all" and his primordial lack is brought back to him as a narcissistic injury that renews threats of disintegration. On the other hand, the child is freed from being the object of the mother's desire and is free to institute himself as a desiring subject.

Two themes can be gleaned from this account: The first is that alienation is inevitably involved in the constitution of subjectivity. The subject is born into the other: into her hopes, desires, and forms. He may slowly and laboriously constitute his subjectivity from this enmeshment in otherness, but it will be slow and hard going, with the ever-present threat of being *for* the other, *of* the other, *like* the other and in the grasp of her desires.

The second theme involves lack. For Lacan, birth marks the subject as a lack-in-being, one that he tries to escape when merging with the mirror image offered by the other. This lack resurfaces in its oedipal guise of castration anxiety when the child discovers he is not the sole object of mother's desire. For Lacan, this castration has little to do with gender or imaginary organs. It is all about lending meaning to the originary lack inherent in the subject's birth, a lack congealed in the imaginary, multiplied in the symbolic.

Alienation in otherness is the subject's solution to this lack that he is. The subject is on the run, hiding within the other, accepting the terror involved in being subjugated to the other's desire, because this terror mitigates a terror more intense: the recognition of the lack, the existential nothing which the subject *is*, a nothing in affinity to death.

From this perspective, the Hegelian dialectic of master–slave (Hegel, 1977), me–you, is not primary. It already serves a defensive function. Even as I battle with the other, I face *three* possibilities: I might master the other, I might serve him, or I might allow myself to be terrified and confront my lack. The possibility of intersubjective conflict here is a *choice*; a choice that avoids facing the primordial lack inherent in birth as a *fact* of the non-negotiable, traumatic Real.

Viewed thus, the Lacanian ethic of psychoanalysis becomes clear: it involves the recognition of lack, of failure in being, that the other might not supply, neither in his recognition nor in his death. This might seem a sad impasse, a tragic end to the promise of intersubjectivity, but it seems to carry some relief, as it allows setting the limits to intersubjectivity and its promising mirages, the failures of which lead to rage, hatred, and fear. The acknowledgment of this limit may send the subject into the realm of a solitary, existential mourning, a mourning that faces his lack, owns it, and subjectifies it.

For Lacan, the search for subjectivity, at a certain point, traverses the field of the other. As stated before, the subject is constituted by signifiers. The signifier is the vehicle of the subject's message and the message of the other, but its most far-reaching effects are in the material dimension. Because, apart from the communicative dimension, the signifier's materiality has effects in the Real, is imprinted in the subject's body as a "unary trait", contingent, senseless, irrevocable. For Lacan, the materiality of the signifier is the senseless music of the mother's vocal coos to her child, a music that will mark forever the nucleus of the child's *jouissance*. This nucleus will reveal itself as the uninterpretable nucleus of dreams and symptoms. Uninterpretable, carrying no message to be deciphered, only knowledge to be known, this nucleus is out of the realm of the "other" and the subject's advent into the Real.

For Lacan, the ability to identify this unary trait, and to position oneself in relation to it, is the farthest one can get in subjectifying one's self. Here, Lacan offers what seems to be an ethical decision—the subject is free to choose his positioning in relation to this contingent mark branded in his flesh. Following this logic, though, leads to an ethic of self-reflection and self-determination that dictates the release of the (intersubjective) other. She is no longer the problem, nor the solution. Lacan makes it clear: If you want to make progress, some self-recognition must replace the addiction to the recognition of others; subjectify yourself, grant meaning to contingencies, and stop denying lack. In Kleinian terms, the imperative is: Mourn. Mourn your lack, your imperfection.

How does all this translate into a psychoanalytic approach to conflict? I come from a country that experiences chronic threat. Perpetually bracing itself for attack, this country's "other" can be little more than an enemy. Intersubjective engagements, talks, negotiation, often prove futile, fueling fear and hatred rather than healing. The lowest point comes when the partner of intersubjective engagement is eventually proclaimed as a "non-partner". The cessation of talks leads to rounds of violence that reiterate the "me or you" logic of imaginary relations. The end of intersubjective, communicative engagement signals the end of initiative and reparative action. This is the limit I wish to question.

Last summer, I visited Hiroshima, the A-bomb site and museum. What struck me among the horrendous images of injury and destruction was the complete absence of any referral to the perpetrator. The USA is hardly mentioned. The Hiroshima monument reads: "we ... offer ... a pledge on behalf of all humanity, never to repeat the evil of war. It expresses the spirit of Hiroshima—enduring grief ...

transcending hatred, pursuing harmony and prosperity for all, and yearning for genuine, lasting world peace".

This inscription expresses the essence of post-war Japanese positioning in the face of the country's destruction. I cannot detail here the political and legal discussions carried out at the time. I will only mention a young and charismatic lawyer named Ocamoto, who tried to lead legal action that instates the atomic bombing of Hiroshima as a war crime. The government opposed this act and any externalization of blame. It formulated and implemented a policy called "Ichioku-So-Zange" (Wakabayashi, 1998, p. 274), a collective, nationwide repentance that focused on Japan's inner moral failure, construing this failure as the cause of Japan's defeat. Energies were channeled to recovery and achieving inner unity; defeat was approached and accepted with a dignity both pragmatic and philosophic. The Americans were not addressed in this process. In Lacanian terms, Hiroshima was immediately acknowledged as a unary trait, a contingent, opaque Real branding around which Japanese subjectivity chose to mobilize itself.

A prominent Jewish philosopher, David Hartman, emphasizes the juncture of choice that modern Jewish subjectivity must face. He marks both Auschwitz and Mount Sinai as pivotal collective events around which this subjectivity may evolve (Hartman, 1982). Auschwitz justifies and interprets Jewish national rebirth in terms of Jewish suffering and persecution. The model of Sinai interprets this same rebirth in terms of the awesome responsibility of becoming a holy people within a symbolic order. Creating humility, it is the antithesis of the moral narcissism that can result from viewing oneself as a suffering victim. This choice involves no "others", it is predicated on self-reflection. Both Auschwitz and Sinai function as unary traits, demanding the positioning of Jewish subjectivity in relation to them. The same moral quandary faces the Palestinian people: their national identity may be forged in terms of the "naqba", creating a moral narcissism that justifies the infliction of violence, justifies the victim's retaliation. Of course, different themes—unary traits—may be chosen as nuclei for the constitution of Palestinian national identity and subjectivity.

This positioning in relation to the unary trait is a solitary action. In therapy, it is prompted by the analyst playing dead, "cadaverizing his position" (Lacan, 1997b, p. 140), not agreeing to be the one who knows, fading out of existence as the one who desires, who supplies the demand to which the analysand will respond. Lacanian logic entreats the analyst to disappear, leaving the subject to acknowledge lack, to bow to the contingent, to position himself in relation to it. It begs the analyst to release the subject from the imaginary relation, from symbolic domination, from intersubjective engagement, to instill in him gradually the courage to subjectify the contingencies that formed him, to acknowledge the hollow in the center of his being.

In conflicted regions, this form of subjectification could have enormous effects. I believe it is often neglected under the noisy clamor of communicative practices. As relational psychoanalysts advocating intersubjective practices, we might be pushing intersubjectivity beyond the extreme of what can be expected from it, in it, by it. In our stance regarding conflict, we could be sending off a signal that is unidimensional, illusorily optimistic. We might be triggering movement into the abyss of dyadic murderous engagement.

We might also be party to the neglect of resources that lie *outside* the realm of intersubjectivity, that definitely lie alongside it—resources that draw on our ideals, our pragmatism, our coherence, our self-determination, our subject positioning in relation to the contingencies of geography and politics. Conflict-resolving actions can arise from within, without the other. The passage into the realm of self-determined positioning carries the additional value of leaning in the direction of action, independently initiated action.

I end with a quote from Frosh that describes an approach to conflict management that aligns with Lacanian insight:

> A certain kind of withdrawal is necessary; an acknowledgement that the place in which subjects meets may not be one of human encounter at all, but rather of an apparent emptiness ... This place is fought against but drawn upon, feared and exulted in. It is neither silence or speech, but the source of both. (Frosh, 2010, p. 145)

Note

1. In the context of subjectivity and its constitution, Lacan refers to this imprint as "ein einziger Zug" (Lacan, 1961) or a "one" (Lacan, 1981, p. 141).

References

Benjamin, J. (2006). Mutual injury and mutual acknowledgement: Lecture in honor of Andrew Samuels. World in Transition Conference, London, October.

Freud, S. (1930a). *Civilization and Its Discontents. S. E., 21*: 64–108. London: Hogarth.

Frosh, S. (2010). *Psychoanalysis Outside the Clinic: Interventions in Psychosocial Studies.* Basingstoke: Palgrave Macmillan.

Hartman, D. (1982). New Jewish religious voices II: Auschwitz or Sinai. *The Ecumenist, 21*(1): 6–8.

Hegel, G. W. F. (1977). Independence and dependence of self-consciousness. In: *Phenomenology of Spirit,* A. V. Miller (Trans.). Oxford: Oxford University Press.

Lacan, J. (1961). *The Seminar of Jacques Lacan: Identification (Book IX),* C. Gallagher (Trans.) from unedited French typescripts.

Lacan, J. (1981). *The Seminar of Jacques Lacan: The Four Fundamental Concepts of Psychoanalysis (Vol. XI),* A. Sheridan (Trans.). New York: Norton.

Lacan, J. (1997a). The mirror stage as formative of the function of the I as revealed in psychoanalytic experience. In: *Ecrits: A Selection,* A. Sheridan (Trans.). London: Tavistock.

Lacan, J. (1997b). The Freudian thing. In: *Ecrits: A Selection,* A. Sheridan (Trans.). London: Tavistock.

Wakabayashi, B. T. (Ed.) (1998). *Modern Japanese Thought.* Cambridge: Cambridge University Press

INDEX

For Product Safety Concerns and Information please contact our EU representative GPSR@taylorandfrancis.com
Taylor & Francis Verlag GmbH, Kaufingerstraße 24, 80331 München, Germany

www.ingramcontent.com/pod-product-compliance
Lightning Source LLC
LaVergne TN
LVHW021124300926
849160LV00010B/856
9781782205777